THE ETHICS OF TRAVEL

'Manzu Islam says that he wrote *The ethics of travel* in the spirit of Kafka, Fanon, Deleuze and Guattari, and Wilson Harris. This wonderfully engaging meditation on the philosophy of travel does full justice to such a splendid set of mentors.'

Peter Hulme, University of Essex

This book has two main objectives. On the one hand, Islam explores how travel narrative works as a form of cross-cultural representation and proposes a critical method for its study. On the other, he sets out the ethical imperatives of travel as a mode of encounter with difference that leads to the performative enactment of 'becoming other'.

Besides the works of Deleuze and Guattari, the ethical exploration of the first half of the book is carried out through close engagements with the philosophical works of Heidegger, Spinoza, Levinas, Lyotard and Fanon and the literary works of writers such as Daniel Defoe, Michel Tournier, Paul Auster, E. M. Forster, Wilson Harris and Franz Kafka. The second part of the book traces a genealogy of the Western non-travelling travel narrative through a reading of Marco Polo's *Travels*, but it also discusses the works of Aristotle, Dante, Machiavelli, Hobbes, François Bernier and Montesquieu.

SYED MANZURUL ISLAM
is Lecturer in English Studies
at Cheltenham and Gloucester
College of Higher Education

SYED MANZURUL ISLAM

THE ETHICS OF TRAVEL

From Marco Polo to Kafka

MANCHESTER UNIVERSITY PRESS

Manchester and New York

distributed exclusively in the USA and Canada
by ST. MARTIN'S PRESS

Published by Manchester University Press
Oxford Road, Manchester M13 9NR, UK
and Room 400, 175 Fifth Avenue, New York, NY 10010, USA

Distributed exclusively in the USA and Canada
by St. Martin's Press Inc., 175 Fifth Avenue, New York, NY 10010, USA

British Library Cataloguing-in-Publication Data
A catalogue record is available from the British Library

Library of Congress cataloging-in-publication data applied for

ISBN 0 7190 4119 8 *hardback*

First published in 1996

00 99 98 97 96   10 9 8 7 6 5 4 3 2 1

Typeset in 10/12 Scala
by Koinonia Ltd, Manchester
Printed in Great Britain
by Bookcraft (Bath) Ltd

CONTENTS

Preface   *page* vii
Acknowledgements   xi

PART I Travel and the ethics of the other

1 Marking boundaries/crossing lines   2

2 Othering and the other   78

PART II Marco Polo: travelogue as a machine of othering

3 Marco Polo and his travels   118

4 Exorbitant others and transgressive topoi   138

5 The political technology of order   167

Postscript   209
Notes   213
Index   235

PREFACE

This book arose out of a quest and a gradual realisation. Being an involuntary traveller in the Western metropolis, I have often asked myself what does it mean to travel? How is it possible to travel? What is travel, anyway? Am I really a traveller? This was the quest. Then when I began to read Western travel books a certain sense of unease, amidst the seductions of some searing narrative, haunted me. At first I thought what bothered me was the narcissism and the racist paranoia so effortlessly strewn across the pages of the books I was reading. Of course, these things bothered me. But I had a suspicion that they were a part of a larger phenomenon. Then it dawned on me that all these intrepid travellers, despite moving so much and so far in space, did not seem to have travelled at all. The elation of the quest and this brutal realisation – and the tension of the paradox between them – led me to write this double-focused book.

The quest into the labyrinthine mystery of travel inexorably leads one to an ethical exploration. Hence, the first part of the book is given to the ethics of travel as encounter with otherness and difference. But since the second part deals with Marco Polo's narrative as a machine of othering that captures difference in representation, the response to it has taken a critical form – one that demands the tracing of a genealogy. It goes without saying, then, that the two parts are orientated by two very different modes of travel: the sedentary and the nomadic, with their corresponding rigidity and suppleness. Nomadic travel is to do with encounters with otherness that fracture both a boundary and an apparatus of representation: it is a performative enactment of becoming-other. In the ethical sense, only nomadic travel deserves the name 'travel'. Furthermore, nomadic travel offers a non-essentialist and a non-sedentary vision of living where dwelling and travelling merge into one another. And on the cross-cultural plane, nomadic travel also impels one to come face to face with the other, without the paranoia of othering that represents the other in relation to oneself.

From an ethical perspective, sedentary travel hardly deserves to be called 'travel' at all. Of course, it involves a movement across geo-graphical and textual space, but it settles for a representational prac-tice that scarcely registers an encounter with the other. Conse-quently, it seems that the movement of sedentary travel is driven by the need to secure a vantage point from which to carry out a repre-sentation of difference. Inevitably, then, sedentary travellers, bur-dened as they are by the need to establish essential difference on a binary frame and to capture otherness in knowledge, obsessively bring into existence a rigid boundary which separates them from the other.

Although this is a book of two parts – and the first part is not written as a theoretical exposition for the work carried out in the second part, which has a different orientation – the two parts are not wholly unrelated. In the process of puzzling over the nature of travel in the first part, some attempts have been made to define how travel works as a genre of representation, in which the sedentary mode of travel establishes itself as a machine of othering. Since the second part is to do with sedentary travel, this aspect of the first part pro-vides an obvious point of contact with it. However, apart from this, the two parts of the book are separate from one another; they are self-contained, with their own unities, and their composition re-quired two very different methods of working. Although the first part contains a good deal of philosophical exploration of the ques-tion of space and the nature of boundary, its orientation is in the main, as I have already indicated, ethical: it is written, albeit with unavoidable contradictions, in the spirit of nomadic travel itself, and with the aim of overcoming the fixity of boundary and the paranoia of othering, so that an opening can be created for the ethics of differ-ence. Furthermore, this exploration yields a number of practical imperatives as to how one can conduct oneself justly in a cross-cultural relationship, and how can one become the other.

Given the orientation of a critical study of one representation of a sedentary traveller, the second part is driven by the need to trace the genealogy of its discursive production. Here the task is to offer diagrammatically a discourse of cross-cultural mapping, so that its internal economies are disclosed and its authority questioned. Hence the study of Marco Polo's travel narrative, taken as an exem-plary case of sedentary travel, is done from the critical perspective of tracing a genealogy of its textual production. Marco Polo's text is taken as exemplary, not because it has perfected the representa-tional apparatus of sedentary travel, but because as an inceptional

text of the transitional process it registers all the contradictory moments through which the modern discourse of othering emerged in
the West. Therefore, the tracing of the genealogy of Marco Polo's
text will give us the very anatomy of Western discourses of othering.
In the process we shall see how Marco Polo charts the paradoxical
passage of a sedentary traveller, strives to establish empirical taxonomy as the mode of cross-cultural representation, invents a functional logic of politics, and mediates the old despot who has long
been a Western preoccupation, but always displaced into the East.

Since the ethical and the critical modes of thought do not sit
comfortably together, there remains a tension between the two parts
of the book. Yet an ethical undertaking should not lead to a surren-
dering of the critical discourse. Both these modes of engagement,
despite all the risks inherent in them, are needed. Kafka understood
this very well. His profoundly engaged ethical writings, orientated
by the need to find a way out of rational-bureaucratic power and the
nightmares of the pogrom, are given over, in a large measure, to the
meticulous tracing of how those powers work. I have written this
book in the spirit of his example, but also that of Deleuze and
Guattari, Fanon, and Wilson Harris.

ACKNOWLEDGEMENTS

I have carried the ideas contained in this book for a number of years. Bringing them to fruition though has only been possible thanks to the help and support I have received from a whole host of people. I cannot begin to attempt to list the names of all those to whom I'm indebted, but I will say that I remember with gratitude David Musselwhite and Ian Craib for introducing me, while still a student, to various ideas that shaped my thinking on the subject of this book. I would like also to thank Philip Martin, the head of Humanities at Cheltenham and Gloucester College of Higher Education, for sorting out the practicalities that effectively allowed me the time to dedicate myself to writing this book. I want to thank all my colleagues in Cheltenham as I fondly remember discussions I had with Lynette Turner and John Hughes which provided me with much intellectual stimulus; the supportive presence of Shelly Rogers and Martin Aske; and the meticulous reading and judicious advice on great chunks of the manuscript received from Professor Peter Widdowson. Professor Roger Bromley has always been supportive of this project and beyond. Professor Paul Gilroy has encouraged and supported me variously over the years. I am specially grateful for his careful reading of the manuscript and his incisive comments. I would like to thank Professor Peter Hulme for reading the manuscript. Thanks to Anita Roy for keeping faith both in this project and in me. Finally, my special thanks to Ines Aguirre, who has patiently listened to my ideas, helped me to clarify my thoughts, and given me her loving companionship.

Now what's going to happen to us without barbarians?
C. P. Cavafy

PART I

Travel and the ethics of the other

I

MARKING BOUNDARIES/
CROSSING LINES

Robinson Crusoe, lost on a desert island yet haunted by the footprints of the other, is driven to a singular obsession: he draws circles, constructs fences, erects walls in an endless pursuance of boundaries. Yet his boundaries are more than lines of defence against the imaginary horror of being devoured alive, dreamt up by a lost soul in a spasm of delusion. On the anonymous plain of the island, made intolerable by the absence of the other, Robinson creates a citadel of his selfhood by enclosing himself within a boundary. He begins, in accordance with the mythology of his self-fashioning genius, by fashioning 'piles in the woods ... and driv [ing] them into the earth.'[1] The violence of this thrust on the blank face of the earth, cuts Robinson off in an island within an island, bringing the castaway back into the castle of his selfhood. Otherwise, on a desert island without the other, Robinson would have been destined for an anonymous existence, where the distinction between the self and the other would have dissolved into the intensive flow of pre-formed matter. This is precisely what happens in Michel Tournier's recasting of the figure of Robinson in *The Other Island*.[2]

The fences and the walls, erected on the marks of incision on the body of the island, provide Robinson with more than an enclosure for what he himself calls 'habitation'. The bounded space enables Robinson to reproduce a self in the uncanny likeness of his 'eternal' Englishness, and pretend that the series of searing dislocations haven't made the slightest impression on him. The otherness of the island is miraculously domesticated in the tracing of a boundary line; and Robinson, circulating within, never goes anywhere except from home to home. For Robinson, despite covering so many tracts of ocean and landmass, never manages to travel anywhere, like Don Quixote, who endlessly trails the same old traces on the monotonous plain of La Mancha. This paradox is perhaps best expressed by the primary narrator of Conrad's *Heart of Darkness*. He contrasts Marlow, the 'wanderer', with other seamen who, paradoxically, remain 'sedentary' and carry their 'home' in the enclosure of their ship, like the house of the tortoise, while perhaps crossing a tempestuous sea.[3] This is a scenario so familiar in the Manichaean tales of two cities on the colonial landscape.

The boundary Robinson traces has all the rigidity of an 'iron curtain' which effects a number of consequences: the ushering in of total immobility – a space without movement; the forming of a binary divide; the constructing of a petrified subject who not only possesses the island by obstinately digging his heels in but, predictably enough, installs himself as a master with a slave of his own.

Robinson, petrified within his rigid boundary, has a specular precursor in the forlorn figure of Narcissus. Fleeing the call of the other, the solicitation of lovelorn Echo, Narcissus creates his own rigid boundary in the smooth, specular surface of water.[4] There is no way that Narcissus could hear the call of the other or traverse the line, let alone make himself a wanderer, because he has enclosed himself within the most rigid of all boundaries – the deceptively benign surface of the *speculum*. It is more rigid than the 'mighty ocean ... highways or mountains, or the city walls with close-barred gates'.[5] It only returns the self to the self and most obstinately prevents any possible crossing of the line. Paradoxically, the luminous surface of the mirror that returns a transparent face, in the same event, reveals the absolute rigidity of its cast: rigid surface begets a rigid body: 'Spellbound by his own self, he remained there motionless, with fixed gaze, like a statue carved from Parian marble'.[6] Here we have the archetypal scenario of the coming into being of a subject, who remains motionless in the shadow of its own reflection. The egocentric subject and the rigid boundary always go hand in hand; they are the identical twins born on the same moment from the same womb. Jacques Lacan, following both Freud and Heidegger, claims that the specular subject, despite its obsessive claim to plenitude, is not at home in its protective enclosure. There are fissures in the opaque body of the mirror, and the subject, along with the impenetrable boundary, breaks down every time it proclaims its self-sufficiency. In Gabriel García Márquez's novel *One Hundred Years of Solitude*, José Arcadio Buendía's originary act of founding a pre-lapsarian city – Macondo, the city of mirror – to provide the European colonial voyages of discovery a place for undertaking the self-fashioning of a purified subject of history proves more than illusory: it is an apocalypse prefigured in the very foundational act, because the city of mirror is the double of the city of mirage.[7] If on the other hand, the mirror is met without the mirage of the ego, and its surface is sensed as a pure surface of duplication without the promise of return, then we have an image of the labyrinth in the mirror as imaged by Borges.[8] The mirror then opens its surface up, forming innumerable passages through which one can slide into a thousand journeys.

Alice, playing with Kitty the black kitten, stumbles right in front of the 'passage'. There, facing her beguilingly, is the mirror which turns 'soft like gauze'[9] as soon as Alice playfully turns her eyes on it. It cannot bounce back to Alice an alluring image of herself, so that, enfolded in its spectral light, she can enclose herself in a self-possessed subject. Instead, the rigidity of the surface comes under the corrosive process of evaporation that leads to the melting away of the boundary. The passage is now clear. The opaque face of the mirror, as Gilles Deleuze suggests, becomes 'a pure surface, a continuity of the outside and the inside'.[10] Alice passes through it without the slightest effort and lands on the other side. Here, against the rigidity that immobilises both Robinson Crusoe and Narcissus, we have the smooth passage and the supple boundary.

But between these two forms of boundary a good deal more is at stake than the mere question of self-possessing subjectivity. We have already, in passing, witnessed Robinson's mastery and Narcissus's deafness to the call of the other. However, the question of the boundary looms large in cross-cultural discourse, and the implications are enormous. Perhaps we are moving a bit too fast, for hasn't the apparent innocence of the adjective 'cross-cultural' belied its origin? Doesn't it presuppose the naturalness of cultural boundaries, as if the cut that divides and establishes polarities is somehow given? These questions must be addressed before the possible effects of various boundaries can be understood.

Perhaps we should begin with an ontology of space. While there is no absolute reason for according this privilege to space, a number of strategic considerations suggest that we take the question of space seriously. First of all, it concerns the genre itself: the present study has as its main focus the narratives of travel. Taken at its simplest, the narrative of travel unfolds the events of trekking space. The events we call travel can be said to be composed of movement between spatial locations: leaving one spatial marker and arriving at another. The presumed departure and arrival, in the very process of their movement, paradoxically stages the threshold to be crossed, and enacts 'the between' that divides and joins spatial locations. If we were to explicate further the anatomy of a traveller, we could say that it is precisely in the very process of negotiating 'the between', traversing threshold and crossing boundary, that s/he makes her/himself a traveller. However, there are as many travellers as there are travels, each taking shape along the marks of the boundaries and thresholds they trace; and some, on account of the rigidity of their boundaries and the trap of their petrified thresholds, never manage to travel at all. They are the inhabitants of the black hole.

Since travel is immanent in space, its form can only be envisioned from within an ontology of space. Moreover, the relation between the *same* and the other, more often than not, is grounded in spatial locations, as if space has the natural propensity to entwine individual bodies inhabiting it, shaping them in its very image. This is the immobile locating of the sons and daughters of the soil, who, possessed by an organic resonance, offer themselves to the sacrificial altar of father- or motherland. Whenever one asks why the communities of earthly bodies are segmented into bounded enclosures, the finger is often pointed at the allegedly natural fissures on the body of the earth itself. The image of space as a plenitude, as the organic sculptor of social bodies, harbours the most intractable trope of essential belonging. Once communal self-identity is fashioned in the image of the segmented body of the earth, the relationship with others invariably takes shape in terms of an essential and binary difference: the fixity of location. There are, of course, other ways of forging binary difference: time, physiognomy, knowledge, and so on. However, these markers often find their way to reside in the solid distribution of space.

Saleem Sinai, the autobiographical narrator of Salman Rushdie's *Midnight's Children,* observes the singular drift of linguistic nationalism: 'Language marchers demanded the partition of the state of Bombay along linguistic boundaries'.[11] Even if the logic of some binary difference – say, evolutionism or biologism – does not lead inexorably towards the founding of geographical homelands, their intelligibility rests upon their being placed in the segmented spaces of representation. Moreover, historically, space has been the most enduring trope of essential difference. Hippocrates ascribed to space the key to cultural difference.[12] Herodotus, at the end of his long narrative journey through the spaces of the known and the unknown world, records the eternal truth of spatial determination in the representation of Cyrus's alleged speech: 'Soft countries ... breed soft men'.[13] When Aristotle came to chart the master/slave relationship in a cross-cultural ambit (the relationship between the Greeks and the Asiatics) in his *Politics*, it was geographic location that provided him with the logic of difference.[14] And Hegel, despite all the temporalisation of space dramatised in the movement of *Geist*, remains caught in the old fable of the spatial determination of culture. In the introduction to the *Philosophy of History*, he writes:

> natural type of locality, as intimately connected with the type and character of the people which is the offspring of such soil. This character is nothing more nor less than the mode and form in which nations make their appearance in History, and take place and position in it.[15]

The deductive logic of this fable leads Hegel to draw its chilling corollary: 'In the Frigid and in the Torrid zone the locality of World-historical peoples cannot be found'.[16] The rest is the well-known story of the 'Negro' – the inhabitant of the torrid zone of Africa, whom Hegel called the inhabitant of 'Africa proper' – who 'is enveloped in the dark mantel of night'.[17] He is yet to be touched by self-consciousness, hence remains beyond the pale of history,[18] and is condemned to be oblivious to the movement of *Geist* in his 'completely wild and untamed state'.[19] The inhabitants of the new world, as a result of the immaturity of its geological formation, 'show a physical immaturity'.[20] And Asia, the space of *Geist*'s dawn, is a space from which *Geist* has already moved without having returned. This condemns Asia, as being in the space of the rising sun and, consequently, being too perfect too early, to eternal childhood; like Peter Pan, it never grows up. We must not forget the baron de Montesquieu (Charles de Secondat), who can be said to embody the burgeoning spirit of the Enlightenment in the early eighteenth century. For the baron, everything from the constitution of the human body to forms of governments spring forth from the depths of space. Naturally, the torrid zones of Asia and Africa only beget slaves and the most horrid despots.[21]

The history of the nation-state and colonial possession has had a long obsession, not free of paradox, with the space of 'We the people'.[22] Moreover, the binary difference between Europe and its others is often grounded in the 'truth' of the natural antipathy presumed to exist between geographical locations. The 'truth' of this position draws its validity from the ontological assumption that there exists an unalterable sympathy between the spaces of dwelling and the spaces of human bodies. Their mutual penetration, and their consequent unfolding, is taken as the matrix of culture.

Space as a trope of essential difference, upon which rests the rigid boundary, is pivoted on a conception that celebrates it as eternally given. Unless this conception is displaced in its turn, it will continue to provide legitimation for holding onto notions of fixed locations and rigid boundaries. This should be reason enough to take a detour through the ontological grounds of space.

Ontology and the poetics of space

From the baroque labyrinth of Immanuel Kant's first critique, a unique solution to the Cartesian duality of res cogitans and res extensa emerges. In the Kantian faculty of knowledge, the discursive meditation is not embarked upon its course, already floated in the unerring vision of a self-determined subject, to capture the passive exteriority of res extensa. Rather it begins with a rather arduous process of 'metaphysical exposition' which discloses the 'powers of understanding'.[23] The task these powers assign themselves involves a systematic legislation of the synthetic formation of knowledge. This they conduct by harnessing the resources of intuitive deduction, a set of 'transcendental principles'. Among these, along with time, space occupies a fundamental position. Space, in its position as an a priori form of intuition, is firmly located in the interior of the subject. However, Kant's 'transcendental idealism', as Gilles Deleuze rightly suggests, is orientated at the behest of an 'Empirical realism'.[24] Kant never makes light of the exteriority of the Cartesian res extensa: it remains both the object of knowledge and the occasion of its validation, to which he simply adds the dimension of interiority. And here lies his novelty: the synthesis of a priori/a posteriori, interior/exterior, active/passive. The commingling of these incongruent pairs, always perilously on the verge of paradox, inheres within it none of the violent antipathy characteristic of the coming together of opposites. In fact, Kant's aim has been to effect harmony between these conflicting principles.

At this stage an excerpt from Kant might help us understand

what role space plays in his philosophy. In the process of drawing conclusions from his 'Transcendental Exposition of the Conception of Space', and in a highly condensed passage, he captures nearly all the possible relations of his synthetic meditation on space:

> the proposition, 'All objects are beside each other in space,' is valid only under the limitation that these things are taken as objects of our sensuous intuition. But if I join the condition to the conception, and say, 'All things, as external phenomena, are beside each other in space,' then the rule is valid universally, and without any limitation. Our expositions, consequently, teach the *reality* (i.e. the objective validity) of space in regard of all which can be presented to us externally as object, and at the same time also the *ideality* of space in regard to objects when they are considered by means of reason as things in themselves, that is, without reference to the constitution of our sensibility. We maintain, therefore, the *empirical reality* of space in regard to all possible external experience, although we must admit its *transcendental ideality*; in other words, that it is nothing, so soon as we withdraw the condition upon which the possibility of all experience depends, and look upon space as something that belongs to things in themselves.[25]

Here, under the legislative protocol of understanding, Kant labours to harmonise empirical reality with the transcendental. In so far as empirical reality is concerned – which, as the object of knowledge, is taken by Kant to belong to phenomenal rather than noumenal reality – it is given to the subject in moments of passive reception. By exercising the active faculty of understanding the subject synthesises phenomenal perceptions, thus producing realist knowledge about reality. Kant's claim to synthetic *a priori* knowledge about space is grounded in accepting, as a matter of course, the axiomatics of Euclidean geometry, with its squares and circles and triangles, whose transcendental beings correspond to experience in the world. 'Geometry', writes Kant, 'is a science which determines the properties of space synthetically, and yet *a priori*'.[26] Under the protocol of geometry, Kant inaugurated the modern empirical science of space: geography, in which the Greek *ge* = earth and *graphe* = writing, comprise the notion of 'the writing of earth'. It is a descriptive science of spatial classification, measurement, location, distance, and so on.

To begin our excursions into the ontology of space by rehearsing the protocols of Kantian philosophy might seem rather misplaced. Two arguments can be advanced for this strategy. First, there is Kant's relationship with geography as an academic discipline, as it emerged in the nineteenth century. Most historians of geography often reserve for Kant the role of a precursor of the discipline. It is

generally held that Kant's meditations on the role of geographic location in the formation of human characters and customs helped
shape the object of inquiry around which academic geography
constituted itself as a discipline.[27] Second, Kant's transcendental
idealism represents the highest point in the epistemological tradition – the pursuit of the knowledge of *res extensa*. Kant's critical
project, as outlined in *Critique of Pure Reason*, despite its transcendental grounding and the phenomenal orientation, is preoccupied
with the certitude of spatial knowledge. This is the whole point of
Kant's distinction between the legitimate and the illegitimate
employment of the faculty of understanding, thereby distinguishing,
judged on empirical criteria, valid from invalid forms of knowledge.
The subject of apperception, to whom Kant assigns the task of judging the validity of knowledge, achieves its self- confirmation through
the recognition of the empirical.[28] The labyrinth of the first critique
seems curiously circular – we are back to where we began: the old
Cartesian duality of *res cogitans* and *res extensa* assumes once more
its rightful place in the pantheon of Western philosophy. Moreover,
Kant's employment of the axiomatics of Euclidean geometry, with its
abstraction and rigidity, lends itself to the drawing of linear boundary and homogenous space.

Deleuze and Guattari, rhizoming through the plateau of the
smooth and the striated, write: 'Geometry lies at the cross-roads of a
physics problem and the affair of the state'.[29] It is a technology of
space and a technique of power. Henri Lefebvre, in the course of
outlining his unitary theory of space, articulates their symbiosis in
much clearer terms: the 'Political territory', of European modernity,
he writes, is 'founded on classical perspective and Euclidean
space'.[30] Inevitably, the marking of space, with the collusion of
power and knowledge, produces only the fixed location and rigid
boundary. Now we know the problem, but the question is how to
overcome it? One thing is certain though: unless the epistemological
grip on space is loosened, it cannot be thought otherwise. Consequently, dwelling in space, without the stifling presence of rigid
parameters, and travelling along supple lines cannot come to pass.
Perhaps we have overstated the case: the undoing of epistemology
alone will not give us the non-essentialised existence of a wanderer
in a space where all boundaries melt like Alice's mirror. However,
the fissuring of epistemology is a necessary first move for opening
space to an ethics of dwelling and non-sedentary travel. For that, we
need to bring into play an alternative ontology of space.

Robinson of Michel Tournier's *The Other Island*, caught in the molecular process of becoming-other, learns to dwell at last. In a journal entry towards the end of the novel, Robinson muses on his 'moment of innocence':

> I seemed to glimpse *another island* hidden beneath the buildings and tilled fields I had created on Speranza. Now I have been transported to that other Speranza, I am fixed in a moment of innocence. Speranza is no longer a virgin land which I must make fruitful, nor Friday a savage whom I must teach to behave. Both call for my attention.[31]

Robinson learns to 'dwell' upon renouncing his mastery over land and the other man, by responding to their summons, and by becoming other than himself. Whoever dwells does so by escaping the dreary stability of location, by learning how to live a life without rigid boundary, by leaving the door open onto the outside, and by erasing the savage polarities of the *same* and the other with joyous affirmation. One dwells by moving and by possessing the attributes of Toynbee or Deleuze and Guattari's nomad, who moves without moving.[32] Or as Merleau-Ponty writes, 'I can be somewhere else ... while staying here'.[33] George Jackson, imprisoned in Soledad, knew the secret art of becoming a traveller: one does not need space so much as the overcoming of 'individualism'. And by overcoming individualism, George Jackson also overcomes the most formidable enclosure that the US penitentiary system has devised: he breaks himself free 'to see the indivisible thing cutting across the artificial barricades'.[34] He floats on other waters than Conrad's sedentary voyagers, who never move even when crossing boundless tracts of ocean. Perhaps Michel de Certeau has best described the predicament of the immobile traveller, firmly placed in the gridwork of a railway compartment, and caught in a 'Travelling Incarceration'.[35] It is, however, not an easy task to be a dweller; one has to walk a perilous tightrope, and along the way, much undoing, forgetting and becoming is needed.

One can only learn to dwell as a traveller by forgetting to ask the habitual cognitive question: what is 'it'? Otherwise, one would remain immobilised in an epistemological trap. 'It was something like the word "it" in the phrase "it is raining" or "it is night". What that "it" referred to Quinn had never known,' Paul Auster writes of Quinn, who has become a traveller in the *City of Glass*.[36] Whether Quinn has forgotten his knowledge of the referent by becoming a traveller, or has become a traveller because he has forgotten, is a puzzle we cannot untangle. Yet we can hardly doubt the link between Quinn's renunciation of epistemological mastery and his becoming a traveller. It is because a traveller who is not trapped in a 'travelling incarceration' is forever affected by the urgency of speed and dwells in shifting dwellings. Consequently, he cannot congeal his being into a castle of selfhood to set the machine of knowledge on its course to represent the world. At the beginning of *City of Glass*, we catch Quinn – a close cousin of the nomad – in his process of becoming a traveller:

> New York was an inexhaustible space, a labyrinth of endless steps, and no matter how far he walked, no matter how well he came to know its neighbourhoods and streets, it always left him with the feeling of being lost. Lost, not only in the city, but within himself as well. Each time he took a walk, he felt as though he were leaving himself behind, and by giving himself up to the movement of the streets ... The world was outside of him, around him, before him, and the speed with which it kept changing made it impossible for him to dwell on any one thing for very long. Motion was the essence.[37]

Quinn has risked the power of naming the referent by becoming a traveller. It is a risk all travellers carry, yet most travel accounts aspire to no more than the task of capturing other places in representation. In so doing they repress the speed their travels incur, and turn sedentary to represent the spectacle of the world. Thus they remain content to be mere theatrical impresarios. We will explore their plight later.

Dwelling has a philosophical moment too. A consideration of this moment takes us to the ontology of space, and we come face to face with the primordial condition of being in space. It is a moment, needless to stress, which lies before and beneath epistemological capture. Perhaps the best place to begin is the enigmatic existential ontology of Martin Heidegger. Heidegger's work represents, on the one hand, a relentless onslaught on the basic fabric of the epistemological tradition and, on the other, a summons to the *poesis* of dwelling. Unfortunately, the scope of this book does not allow a close critical engagement with Heidegger's work. Its exploration, therefore, will be limited to Heidegger's thinking on space and dwelling alone.

Despite the marked predilection for time announced in the title, Heidegger's *magnum opus*, *Being and Time*, devotes some fascinating pages to space, which also dominates his later works. The epistemological tradition – either under the transcendental protocols of the axiomatic of geometry or under the premise of the absolute givenness of objects which empiricists celebrate – always tried to master space by bringing it within its orbit of knowledge. One of the paradoxes of the Western epistemological tradition lies in its claim, on the one hand, that space is nothing more than what is passively given to the knowing vision and to the introspection of the subject; on the other, that space is made to function, not only as the ultimate port of call of its own validation as the proper object of knowledge, but also that it shapes men and their relationship with other men. Heidegger could not care less about resolving this paradox. His is the question that questions the epistemological tradition itself. To remain within the parameters set by epistemology is to forget the question of Being (*Das Sein des Seienden*). Hence Heidegger embarks on a different journey altogether, which involves a drift back to the primordial moment of being (*Das Sein des Seienden*). However, Heidegger's drift back, unlike that of Kant, does not impel him to search the grounds that knowledge must presuppose in order to appear as such, but to find a way to the primordial condition of existence itself. Emmanuel Levinas, perhaps with Kant in mind, and drawing on Heidegger, clearly sets out in *Totality and Infinity* the contrasting preoccupations of these two very different traditions of Western philosophy:

> Concretely speaking the dwelling is not situated in the objective world, but the objective world is situated by relation to my dwelling. The idealist subject which constitutes a priori its object and even the site at which it is found does not strictly speaking constitute them a priori but precisely *after the event*, after having dwelt in them as concrete being. The event of dwelling exceeds the knowing, the thought, and the idea in which, after the event, the subject will want to contain what is incommensurable with a knowing.[38]

Heidegger's thinking dwells on the dwelling of concrete beings in the world; and only to a dweller is the Being of being (*Das Sein des Seienden*) revealed. To conceive of the space of living either through the axiomatic of geometry or as the object of the knowing gaze of an indifferent subject is symptomatic of the forgetting of Being (*Das Sein des Seienden*). Heidegger's fundamental ontological odyssey, the drift back to the primordial question of the Being of being leads to the 'unconcealment' (*aletheia*) of originary nothingness (*Nichtung*). It must be remembered that this nothingness, despite any seeming resemblance, has nothing in common with negation or lack, or, for that matter, with the degree zero. Rather, nothingness reveals that

Being cannot be contained in a reductive entity or limited to an object of the knowing gaze – which Heidegger expressed in the curious phrase 'presentness-at-hand' (*Vorhandenheit*), which the ontic sciences take as their object. If Being cannot be known as an entity or an object, how does it reveal itself? As a way of approaching this almost unanswerable question, Heidegger sets about the task of 'clearing' (*Lichtung*), so that Being may find a place to dwell and unconceal (*aletheia*) itself. However, the task of clearing cannot be undertaken in a hurry. To arrive at the point of clearing one has to tread a rather circuitous route, on the way, engaging metaphysics in a deadly duel; and, upon its ruin, from its ontic resonance proceed by piecing together the fore-structures of *Dasein* (Being in the world). It is at the level of existential analytic – the elucidation of the fore-structure of being – that Heidegger first thinks space in *Being and Time*. It seems that the drift back of thinking, set in motion by the fundamental question of Being, is returned to face being once more. The sudden lapse, the track back from the seeming heights of transcendental revelation, from the promise of almost mystical apperception, comes as a rude awakening from the dreams of the absolute. Yet, there could not have been any other course open to Heidegger than to return. Otherwise, he would have been caught in the orbit of ontotheology – the most archaic and enduring of all the metaphysical quests for plenitude. Unavoidably then, the climb up the rungs of the ladder in quest for Being and finding none there, the thinking comes to realise the 'thrownness' (*Geworfenheit*) of existence. Hence the question of Being can only be asked in what is given in the 'thrownness'. In other words, in the thereness of being (*Dasein*). Being 'there' – the '*da*' of *Dasein* – tells us the always alreadyness of existence in the world. Having fallen, and having in the midst of always already, the question of Being can only properly be asked through being-in-the-world (*In-der-Welt-sein*). In other words, the proper site of questioning is the everydayness of what Heidegger's precursor, Edmund Husserl, called '*Lebenswelt*' (life world).

Once thinking has found its direction, the task of the unconcealing of Being can proceed towards the light by entering the play of the hermeneutic circle. Heidegger propels the circle on its ever inwardly spiralling movement by invoking a series of existentials (*Existenzialien*) which *Dasein* makes use of to experience the world. The thereness of *Dasein*, its being in the world, tells us that being is already in space. Hence, space is one of the existentials. As such, it can neither be equated with the category of knowledge, nor can it be reduced to the object of knowledge. Once space is brought into the hermeneutic circle, it becomes spatiality – the experience of space in the course of everyday experience.

Even though the worldhood of being is always already grounded in space, its presence is never present, nor is it pre-given in the way scientific introspection conceives it. Yet, or because of this, it is never encountered with indifference. Space is primordially distant, its opaqueness defying the indifference of the knowing subject; it is an other that never surrenders its eternal separation. Yet it is also so close. This astounding paradox is one of the noblest insights of Heideggerian thinking, whose ethical reverberations exceed Heidegger himself, especially in the way in which they are taken up in the prophetic sayings of Emmanuel Levinas. We will return to this line of thinking in the next chapter.

And yet the paradox reveals the primordial secret of our habitation in space: it is, literally, the most literal and mundane of all secrets. All it takes are our doings in the course of everyday life and a little bit of care. Here is Heidegger:

> The 'environment' does not arrange itself in a space which has been given in advance; but its specific worldhood in its significance, articulates the context of involvement which belongs to some current totality of circumspectively allotted places. The world at such a time always reveals the partiality of the space which belongs to it.[39]

The framing of the 'environment' within the parenthesis reveals the enigma of our dwelling: it is revealed to us in our caring relationship with it, and in the course of our day-to-day activities. In order to elucidate further the process through which we have our place in the world, Heidegger introduces a number of existentials. However, every time Heidegger introduces an ontic description of the fore-structure of *Dasein*, it is always to arrive at the 'unconcealment' of Being. Hence the move from the ontic towards ontology requires a new existential for the 'object': now we have readiness-to-hand (*Zuhandenheit*) instead of presentness-at-hand (*Vorhandenheit*). It is because 'readiness-to-hand, expresses the Being of equipment'.[40] It is in the course of our caring use that we derive our spatiality from space, which is described as 'to-hand' rather than the objectivist 'at hand'. 'Every entity that is, "to hand" has a different closeness, which is not to be ascertained by measuring distance.'[41] How does this closeness come to us? Apart from those things we have already mentioned, such as the acts of living, work, use, care or circumspective concern, Heidegger introduces the existential of 'de-severance' (*Ent-fernung*). Once we encounter space with circumspective concern it is de-severed from its primordial distance and brought closer. Space is never given, but the space of living – our spatiality – is severed from it in the contingent acts of dwelling. Hence, the absolute space and the fullness of its meaning eludes the being in the world. '*Dasein* is partial', writes Heidegger, 'in that it discovers space circumspectly, so that it constantly comports itself deseverantly towards the entities thus spatially encountered'.[42]

The spatiality of dwelling remains contingent and partial, appearing only transiently to each moment of call. Hence we not only have partial spaces but also multiple spaces. However, the partiality and multiplicity of spaces do not, by any means, mean that they lack direction. In fact, each act of 'de-severance ... gives directionality'.[43]

By de-severing space, by bringing it close through circumspective concern, we assign location; and, thereby, we have a place (*Platz*): 'Such a place and such a multiplicity of places are not to be interpreted "where" of some random Being-present-at-hand of things. In each case, the place is the definite "there" or "yonder" ("*Dort*" und "*Da*") of an item of equipment which belongs somewhere'.[44] It is, however, a pre-conceptual, pre-geometric, pre-natural, non-abstract, and non-juridical notion of location. It neither possesses the absolute of the objective space of scientific introspection, nor does it claim the eternal truth of the mimetic space of pictorial representation. It is the provisional location of everyday experience, and, as such, 'var [ies] in [its] length from day to day'.[45] It is because all 'wheres', writes Heidegger, 'are discovered and circumspectively interpreted as we go our ways in every day dealings; they are not ascertained and catalogued by the observational measurement of space'.[46] The place discovered in such a way is described by Heidegger as 'region' (*Gegend*).[47] It is the most immediate of existential locations, and it offers us the existential range and the direction to our places. Its mode of appearance, apart from being provisional and multiple, is microcosmic: we have as many regions as places, and their ensemble gives us the environment (*umwelt*) of our dwelling. 'The regional orientation of the multiplicity of places belonging to the ready-to-hand goes to make up the aroundness – the 'round-about-us (*das Um-uns-herum*) of those entities which we encounter as closest environmentally'.[48]

Simmering beneath, yet prior to the homogeneity of the epistemological and pictorial space, lie the provisional and multiple spaces of regions. They are brought close, or made into places of dwelling, by the ongoing acts of concernful engagements. Spaces come to us, despite their eternal distance, with our loving but ever-changing calls. Consequently, 'there are as many spaces as there are distinct spatial experiences,'[49] writes Merleau-Ponty in *Phenomenology of Perception*. From their trembling depth, from beneath the camouflage of eternal fixities of 'geographical space' and 'landscape space', the primordially multiple and moving spaces explode, argues Merleau-Ponty, in schizophrenic experience. As the solitary hero of the multiple, the schizophrenic experiences the zonal murmuring of locations as so many spectacles in the carnal depths of his body. In so doing, in the very paradox of his intensely private experience, the schizophrenic reveals the existential condition of space itself, 'which is ceaselessly composed by our way of projecting the world'.[50] The location of the 'subject' in this space is not grounded in the fixed perspective of isotropic space, whose dispersion annuls the function of the gaze as a 'knowledge machine'.[51] Eye is now 'a certain power of making contact with things'.[52] And space too has its 'direct power over my body'.[53] Perhaps Robinson of *The Other Island*, on the threshold of shedding rational mastery, expresses it in a rather dramatic image: 'My eye is the corpse of light and colour'.[54] The living 'spectacle' which defines the perceptual contour of the world is affected through the interpenetrations of the power of a virtual body and the power of a virtual space. It bespeaks the multiple and contingent nature of existence, where bodies and spaces are constantly made and remade in the flux of their encounters. However, body and space can only live through their virtuality in schizophrenic breakdown; or by people not yet imprisoned by the 'knowledge machine'.

In his later works, thinking beyond the existential analytic, and thinking as a poet, Heidegger asks the question of dwelling (*Bauen*) in response to the summons of Being. It illuminates, in particular, the threshold of locations, the contours of regions, the disjunctions where boundaries make their appearance. In the course of thinking 'building', Heidegger asks, 'In what way does building belong to dwelling?'[55] This question takes Heidegger to think the being of bridge. The bridge does more than simply connect the gulf between pre-given spaces. In fact, spatial disjunction emerges from the very connecting task undertaken by the bridge itself: 'One side is set off against the other by the bridge.'[56] The bridge not only creates difference by connecting spatial environments, it also brings into proximity the landscapes that lie beyond the threshold of difference: 'The bridge *gathers* the earth as landscape around the stream'.[57] Heidegger then goes on to announce the un-nameable bridgeness of the bridge as the site of existential encounter. In the ensuing epiphany, *Dasein* comes to experience the wholeness of its being – the fourfold of earth, sky, divinities and mortals – in the gathering fold of the bridge. The *Es gibt* of the bridge – the 'thereness' that gives (*Geben*) – offers an intimation of *Dasein*'s Being (*Das Sein des Seienden*), which remains nameless, a shadow in the flickering of light. Here Heidegger, especially when he dwells on the gathering of the fourfold, verges almost into mysticism. Moreover, in his preoc-cupation with the presence of the truth of Being he remains profoundly metaphysical. Jacques Derrida, in his characteristic interrogative mode, points precisely to this drift in Heideggerian thinking, which preoccupies Heidegger throughout his *oeuvre*.

> And yet, are not the thought of the *meaning* or *truth* of Being, the deter-mination of différance as the ontico-ontological difference, difference thought within the horizon of the question of Being, still intra-metaphysical effects of *différance*?[58]

We will leave Heidegger the poet with his epiphany of the fourfold. This is a troubling aspect of Heidegger's thought and it requires a deeper engagement than this book will allow (see long note).[59]

Yet, despite the metaphysical resonance of the fourfold, the exis-tential reverberation of the bridge that separates by bringing together, and that gathers the beyonds, is worth our attention. For the bridge, by standing in for *Dasein*'s environment (*Umwelt*), gives 'itself a location' and, 'make[s] space for a site'.[60] Thus it provides the space for dwelling – *Raum*.

> A space ... that has been made room for, something that is cleared and free, namely within a boundary, Greek *peras*. A boundary is not at which something stops but, as the Greeks recognised, the boundary from which something begins its presencing ... That for which room is made is always granted and hence is joined, that is, gathered by virtue of location ... *Accordingly, spaces receive their being from locations and not from 'space'.*[61]

Heidegger takes enormous care in letting the 'presencing' of the place of dwelling, and the boundary that gives it its location, emerge from the being of the bridge. This move denies boundary the rigidity of the rampart characteristics of the space conceived as '*extensio*'. It produces a notion of the boundary which not only separates and closes in, but also gathers the beyond and opens onto the outside. The space of dwelling as the bounded location, as it comes into being from the very presence of bridging, shows the inside to be a fold of the outside. Thereby, Heidegger produces an image of the boundary whose ontological suppleness militates against the binary fixation of essential separation. Moreover, it offers a space of dwelling whose very shifting existence places it at the threshold of travel.

Gaston Bachelard, who spent much of his time in the space of scientific rationality, also came to address the same questions in his *The Poetics of Space*. He embraces phenomenology, but he does so without the rigour of Heidegger or Merleau-Ponty. His is an intuitive poetic apprehension of phenomena as they suddenly impinge 'on the surface of the psyche'.[62] In his 'topophilic' imagination, he reinforces many of the ontological insights that Heidegger so painstakingly reveals. The imaginative space of poetic epiphany, just like Heidegger's spatiality of circumspective concern 'cannot remain indifferent space subject to the measures and estimates of the surveyor'.[63] The spaces apprehended in the flux of poetic encounter are not only prior to geometrism, they, also 'do not readily lend themselves to description'.[64] It is the space of elemental passion, where difference is experienced as attraction and repulsion, without the binary framing of rational language. Only by 'becoming of expression' in the poetic reverie does it reveal a fleeting glimpse of itself. Apart from disclosing the indescribable moments of poetic encounters with space, Bachelard also conducts 'topoanalysis' – an idiosyncratic brand of the psychoanalysis of space. Here, his poetics and his rationalism, which he so desperately wanted to forget, come into friction. Yet they produce some interesting insights. Against the Bergsonian notion of duration, Bachelard argues:

> At times we think we know ourselves in time, when all we know is a sequence of fixation in the space of the being's stability – a being who does not want to melt away, and who, even in the past, when he sets out in search of things past, wants time to 'suspend' its flight.[65]

These fixations in space, through the grounding of memories, provide Bachelard with the rationale for establishing the psychic relationship between spaces. Here, Bachelard's explanations, by virtue of their opposition to Bergsonian virtuality, come perilously close to the geometrical fixity that he so passionately opposes. However, Bachelard argues that these fixities are only an 'illusion of stability'; and, in fact, are subject to constant 're-imagining'.[66] The tension between these two positions is never resolved in Bachelard's work. Perhaps, given that he wants both to explain the psychical ground of spatial apprehension and register the poetic encounter with space, this is inevitable. However, the psychic fixations produced through the poetic memories do not necessarily lead to rigid boundaries. Only a rational epistemology and a dialectics of opposition congeal simple difference into barrier: 'the dialectics of outside and inside is supported by a reinforced geometrism, in which limits are barriers'.[67]

What, then, is the psychic process of the differentiation of space on which geometrism and an oppositional dialectics establish their rigid boundaries? A house enveloped in winter snow sparks off Bachelard's meditation; or rather, to be more precise, it is a fragment from Rimbaud's *Les Déserts de l'amour*:

> *C'était comme une nuit d'hiver, avec une neige pour étouffer le monde décidément.* (It was like a winter night, with snow to stifle the world for certain).[68]

Upon these lines Bachelard writes:

> In any case, outside the occupied house, the winter cosmos is a simplified cosmos. It is a non-house in the same way that metaphysicians speak of a non-I, and between the house and non-house it is easy to establish all sorts of contradictions. Inside the house, everything may be differentiated and multiplied. The house derives reserves and refinements of intimacy from winter; while in the outside world, snow covers all tracts, blurs the road, muffles every sound, conceals all colours. As a result of this universal whiteness, we feel a form of cosmic negation in action. The dreamer of houses knows and senses this, and because of the diminished entity of the outside world, experiences all qualities of intimacy with increased intensity.[69]

The process of attraction/repulsion that produces the elemental relationship of inside/outside is the very psychic basis of all difference. It already harbours the potential for being framed by the binary logic of the metaphysicians. Bachelard does not explain how and when the transition from the elemental psychic experience of simple inside/outside to the rigid boundary of geometrism takes place. However, an enigmatic comment points towards the course to be taken: 'formal opposition is incapable of remaining calm'.[70] Violence always lurks in the space of opposition; it is the haunt of power. I will shortly explore the savage inscription of space by power, but before that, one last visit to the dwelling of Heidegger is required.

A haunting verse from Georg Trakl's 'A Winter Evening', 'Pain

has turned the threshold to stone', provides Heidegger with the
perfect pretext to take the question of inside/outside to the heart of
difference.

> It is only in turning to stone that the threshold presences at all ... It
> sustains the middle in which the two, the outside and inside, penetrate
> each other. The threshold bears the between. What goes out and goes
> in, in the between, is joined in the between's dependability ... The
> threshold, as the settlement of the between, is hard because pain has
> petrified it. But the pain that became appropriated to stone did not
> harden into the threshold in order to congeal there. The pain presences
> unflagging in the threshold, as pain. But what is pain? Pain is rift ...
> Pain indeed tears asunder, it separates, yet so that at the same time it
> draws everything to itself, gathers it to itself. Its ending, as a separating
> that gathers, is at the same time that drawing which, like the
> pendrawing of a plan or sketch, draws and joins together what is held
> apart in separation. Pain is the joining agent in the rending that divides
> and gathers. Pain is the joining of the rift. The joining is the threshold.
> It settles the between, the middle of the two that are separated in it. Pain
> joins the rift of the difference. Pain is the difference itself.[71]

In this sumptuous passage, Heidegger both squares the circle by
showing the other side of the bridge, and shows the originary rupture that allows joining and separation. If the bridge separates by
joining, the threshold joins by separating. If the bridge gathers the
beyond, the threshold allows the interpenetration of inside and outside. But how can a petrified threshold enable this interpenetration?
How are we to take the paradox of that which hardens yet does not
congeal? A number of speculations can be advanced.

First of all, the inside/outside distinction that Heidegger articulates is very different from that which holds between geographical or
geometric locations. They are revealed to *Dasein* in his circumspective concern. Hence, their relation is never that of opposition or
fixity, but of the co-presence of difference. I dwell in my house which
has an outside; but the house brings in the outside, which is the
environment (*Umwelt*) of its location. Now the pain of the rift that
petrifies the threshold suggests something entirely different than
the inside/outside of locations. Perhaps it suggests the originary
force of difference that remains eternally separate and unnameable,
yet allowing the inside/outside to emerge. From the point of view of
Dasein, and in so far as language both speaks him and speaks
through him, 'The *Riss* forever remains to rend ... subject. The truth
"known" in the un-forgetting of *a-letheia* is a truth that always carries
a shadow in the midst of its lighting'.[72]

From our ontological and poetic explorations of space, a number of insights have been established. Beyond the homogeneity of geometric space and the givenness of geographical space, there emerges a primordial space, which is provisionary, multiple, and microcosmic. Moreover, the intimation of the process involved in the establishment of existential or poetic locations gives us a supple inside/outside relationship, where mutual interpenetration in division is always an open possibility. Crucially, though, it brings home the idea that once we lift the iron curtain of geometry and geography we find neither natural space nor natural boundary. Our relationship with space is a deferred relationship, its elusive presence only brought closer through the supplement[73] of projection. This is how we create places out of space.[74] Hence, the places (projected space) are no more than supplements. The contours, thresholds, and borders that allow the placeness of the places to emerge are supplements too. This is the way we want to read Heidegger's pain of dif-ference and the paradox of the threshold – which is as hard as stone yet does not congeal. It cannot congeal precisely because the originary difference denies the plenitude of present by allowing presence only through absence. Perhaps this is too strong a Derridean reading of Heidegger – some would say misreading – because the Heideggerian Dif-ference is given the task of revealing by way of the structural corruption of traces rather than by offering a glimpse of the authentic presence of Being. However, by deliberately reading in a Derridean way, I want to place Heidegger's insight into dwelling and boundary within the supplementary structure of the trace, so that the danger of authentic dif-ference does not endanger dif-ference itself. On the other hand, the Heideggerian insistence that it is through practical engagement and caring relationship that we assign places offers the openness for conceiving a pragmatic ethics of dwelling. Despite all the subtle variations of Derrida's thinking, at its heart pulsates the monotony of Saussurian 'difference', framed in a formal linguistic structure. Consequently, the Derridean difference (*Différance*), with its insistence that 'presentation of the being-present'[75] takes place entirely in the play of difference or through the structure of traces, leaves no room for a non-textual ethics of practice. Caught in this formal trap, Derrida introduces the ethics of practice through the invocation of Nietzsche's joyful affirmation almost as a supplementary afterthought. One could pick many instances of it from different phases of Derrida's work. At the end of '*Différance*', for instance, after having detailed the working of the general economy of meaning – the structure of traces with its delay and spacing – Derrida, in the process of countering Heidegger's 'nostalgia' for 'a lost native country of thought', suddenly invokes Nietzsche: 'On the contrary [to Heidegger's nostalgia], we must *affirm* this, in the sense in which Nietzsche puts affirmation into play, in a certain laughter and a certain step of the dance'.[76] Because of the supplementary nature of ethics in Derrida's work, the Nietzschean affirmation simply becomes saying 'yes' to the originary structure of difference (*Différance*) itself, which then becomes simply a cue to play the endless games of the general economy of meaning. However, my reading of Heidegger's world of concernful relationship in everyday life through Derridean traces both guards against a certain metaphysical tendency in Heidegger, and allows a conception of practice which can be other than the structural play of difference. Even so, to arrive at an adequate theory of practice, we need to make a number of moves. I will pursue these in the rest of this chapter and in the next.

If, as Heidegger so mournfully and so often repeats, we have forgotten Being, the question arises as to how this has happened? Before we pursue Heidegger's answer to this, we ought to ask another question: where does one receive an intimation of provisional, multiple, and the microcosmic space? Heidegger and Bachelard seem to answer by pointing to the residual moments of poetic epiphanies, which somehow escape the monstrous grasp of rational and empirical space, as a way of affirming existential space. However, they remain intensely private experiences and wilt like delicate flowers under the savage heat of intersubjective space. The multiple dance of the carnal spaces that Merleau-Ponty foregrounds does not seem to find many avenues for self-expression either: it can only be glimpsed in schizophrenic breakdowns or in the lost memories of disappearing tribes. Again we ask: if existential space is the originary mode of apprehending space, how come it reveals itself only in highly marginal instances? One answer, as we have repeated on a number of occasions – one that Heidegger, Merleau-Ponty and Bachelard share – would point at the preponderance of the rational space of geometry and the empirical space of geography. Yet the source of the problem seems to extend far beyond geography and geometry. Heidegger himself has located the problem by taking cognisance of *Dasein*'s actual predicament. However, before that, he extends *Dasein*'s existentials to place 'it' in the intersubjective world: now, 'the world of *Dasein* is a with-world (*Mitwelt*). Being-in is Being-with-others'.[77] *Dasein*'s condition invariably places him with others in an intersubjective space which Heidegger calls 'they' (*das man*). Now, the question is: how does *Dasein* live with the others or negotiate the world of 'they' ? It is in the process of answering this question that Heidegger observes *Dasein*'s actual predicament. It is in the intersubjective world of 'they' that *Dasein* relates to others with solicitude, which has two possible recourses: 'it can, as it were, take away "care" from the other and put itself in his position in concern; it can leap in for him'.[78] The mode of solicitude that dominates the intersubjective is that which robs *Dasein* of his 'care': it is a world where generalised alienation proliferates and 'everyone is the other, and no one is himself'.[79] Because 'The "they" which supplies the answer to the question of the "who" of everyday *Dasein*, is "nobody" to whom every *Dasein* has already surrendered itself in Being-among-one-other'.[80] It induces *Dasein* to distance 'itself' from 'itself', and drags 'it' to assume the averageness of conformity. These conditions 'constitute what we know as "publicness"'.[81] Heidegger's thinking here clearly parallels Lacan's demonstration of the subject's entry into the public realm through the specular loss and symbolic compensation. This is hardly surprising, since Lacan drew his insights from Heidegger. However, this is not the place to conduct that discussion.

The whole point of our return to Heidegger is to think why the primordial experience of space is lost to *Dasein*'s actual existence. Heidegger deals with this question in two different but interrelated ways: firstly, by taking stock of the process of *Dasein's* transition from the private to the public or social or cultural space; secondly, by observing the homogenisation and the objectification of space carried out by the ontic sciences, such as geometry and geography. Yet the rigid boundaries that these processes impose are not as intractable as it might appear. The possibilities of dwelling within non-rigid boundaries and becoming-traveller are immanent in the fundamental ontological condition of being: they loom like so many uncanny presences concealed in the placid uniformity of epistemological space. All it takes is a twinkle for them to surface. Thomas De Quincey, steeped in opium, goes on a *flâneur*-like saunter in London, he discovers the speed of motion, and becomes a traveller:

> Some of these rambles led me to great distances: for an opium-eater is too happy to observe the motion of time. And sometimes in my attempts to steer homewards, upon nautical principles, by fixing my eye on the pole-star, and seeking ambitiously for a north-west passage,

instead of circumnavigating all the capes and headlands I had doubled
in my outward voyage, I came suddenly upon such knotty problems of
alleys, such enigmatic entries, and such sphinx's riddles of streets without thoroughfares, as must, I conceive, baffle the audacity of porters,
and confound the intellects of hackney-coachmen. I could almost have
believed, at times, that I must be the first discoverer of some of these
terrae incognitae, and doubted, whether they had yet been laid down in
the modern charts of London.[82]

In the speed of movement, the geographic 'charts of London' evapo-
rate; and from its vapour emerges a new city – with De Quincey
becoming-traveller of an unknown topos of '*terrae incognitae*'. Yet,
despite all the imaginative power, De Quincey would not be able to
traverse the rigidity of cross-cultural boundary: the social space that
inscribes and imprisons him in the haunted castle of his Englishness, immobilising him before the congealed threshold: 'I have
often thought that if I were compelled to forego England, and to live
in China, and among Chinese manners and modes of life and
scenery, I should go mad'.[83]

The ominous presence of cultural space and its onerous boundary that swallows up the transitory, multiple and the microcosmic
space of primordial experience, impels us to pay attention to it. The
question we want to address here is: how does social space produce
rigid boundaries? Perhaps Bachelard has already pointed out the
next move that we must make: 'formal opposition is incapable of
remaining calm'. But why is the formal difference upon which the
order of the binary comes to rest incapable of remaining calm?
Bachelard does not answer this question. I want to read in it the
murderous passion of power, which resonates Robinson Crusoe's
originary violence, the act of cutting a boundary by driving piles of
wood into the earth. Now it is time to explore what happens when
power comes to space.

The inscription of power

Outside the law there stands a doorkeeper. A man from the country
comes up to the doorkeeper and asks to be admitted to the law. But the
doorkeeper says he cannot admit him at the moment ... The door of the
law standing open as always and the doorkeeper stepping aside, the
man bends down to look through into the interior. The doorkeeper
notices and says with a laugh, 'If you're that keen why don't you try to
get in despite my ban? But remember: I am powerful'.[84]

Kafka's parable of the law discloses the invisible force that pulsates behind the threshold that divides the inside from the outside. The door of the law never closes. There is no physical barrier blocking the passage of the man from the country. He can gain his entry inside if he so wishes. Yet the seemingly open passage is as closed as the transparent surface of the mirror (with its opaque underside). The paradox of the openness that cannot be opened reveals the inscription of power – the force that remains invisible yet marks the boundary between inside and outside. The line that gives body to both sides of the divide is bodiless in itself. Edmund Leach traces the phantomatic origin of boundary: 'a boundary has no dimension ... But if the boundary is to be marked on the ground the marker itself will take up the space'.[85]

The paradox of the open, yet closed, door owes its origin to the invisible force of power. The force of difference is spaceless – or, to put it in Derridean language, 'The re-mark of belonging does not belong'.[86] Yet the invisible lines that mark boundaries are often given corporeal solidity by fences and walls. When, at the end of Kafka's parable of the law, the door literally closes, we are hardly surprised. It merely actualises the forces of closure that pulsate in the open passage that cannot be passed. Furthermore, even the event of the closing of the door is unnecessary to realise the prohibitive effects of power. Who is the doorkeeper if not the very embodiment of power, the living rampart keeping the open door closed? Yet the embodiment of power in the rampart serves more than a merely symbolic function. For one thing, the boundary that affects the inside/outside distinction creates the binary of order/disorder to sustain the very fabric of the social and moral laws of society. Moreover, the embodied boundaries are the basic techniques of power which help fashion the subject in its own image. I will shortly explore this proposition.

By revealing its arbitrary nature, the functional insubstantiality of the boundary echoes its non-natural origin that the existential ontology endeavours to establish. Yet some boundaries, because they are framed by natural barriers, seem to embody natural divisions. Academic geography made much of it. From its very inception in the nineteenth century, the natural, topographic division served as the *raison d'être* of its discourse. The works of Carl Ritter and Fredric Ratzel, with their emphasis on *genus loci*, held that each segment of the earth was an organic unity where cultural and political forms of life resonate with the natural givenness of the earth itself.[87]

The prominent landscape features, such as oceans, rivers, forests and mountains, which often marked the physical limits of experience, were pressed into the roles of organic boundaries. To be fair to geographers, however, dissenting voices were raised from within the discipline as early as the 1920s, and none more eloquently than that of Lucien Febvre. In the process of drawing a genealogy of the concept *'frontière'*, he quotes Danton's celebrated speech of 31 January 1793:

> *Ses limites sont marquées par la Nature; nous les atteindrons toutes quatre de l'horizon, du côte du Rhin, du côte de l'Océan, du côte des Alpes.* (Its limits are marked out by Nature; we shall reach them all at the four corners of the horizon, at the Rhine, at the Ocean and at the Alps.)[88]

Febvre calls it a 'beautiful mirage' – the rhetoric of 'natural right' rather than that of nature;[89] and sets about unpacking the natural indices of boundaries (river, sea, mountain and the forest) by showing that 'nature only serves as a mask; it is the mask worn by long-standing historical and political facts'.[90] Natural boundaries are simply repeated masks of power adorned on the face of nature. Moreover, it is the abstract law of nature rather than nature as *Physis* as Nietzsche conceived it: the destructive and the affirmative forces of eternal repetition, 'an interior of the earth opposed to the laws of its surface'.[91] The locales of natural boundaries are not to be found in nature but in the inscription of nature, whose origin lies, argues Febvre, in 'the desire and belief, the human and psychological factors'.[92]

Perhaps it is the walled city, often celebrated in the history of civilisation, that reveals the panoply of operations that power enacts through walls and boundaries. Notwithstanding its protective and religious functions, the walled city not only symbolises power but also gives vent to its passion. The great historian of the city, Lewis Mumford, speaks of the walled city as the locus of the 'paranoid psychic structure of power'.[93] In its theatrical visibility, at the level of the symbolic, the walled difference of inside/outside accords solidity to the sense of order (against the disordered outside).

The rational internal order of the walled city has another face on the outside: Mumford evaluates it as being 'irrational and malign'.[94] It never fails to be predatory towards what lies beyond the pale – plundering the resources without the slightest sense of iniquity. Moreover, the ordered inside harbours, Mumford points out, a genocidal passion for 'extermination' every time it ventures into its 'chaotic' outside. However, it is in relation to what the walled order does on the inside that Mumford provides his most subtle insight. From the inside, the space within is a container. As such, it prevents those who are lodged inside from escaping, subjects them to round-the-clock surveillance, regiments their bodies to form regular habits, and extracts their labour power with the minimum of cost. Mumford calls the subjects inside 'a permanently captive farm population'.[95] The wall, then, among other things, is a technique for producing a disciplined and normalised subject. Here Mumford's work antici-pates an important line in Foucault's research.

Much of Michel Foucault's *oeuvre* is given to writing genealogies of divisions that structured the order of post-Enlightenment Europe. In the face of a series of penetrating questions from the editors of *Hérodote*, Foucault comes to see that the idea of spatial difference, which plays an important role throughout his work, is more than a metaphor. It is a technique of power with which to police and pro-duce normalised subjects. Just as in prison, the 'national man' of the state must accept his destiny as an 'inmate'.[96] The arrangement of space, as a technique of disciplinary power which possesses the utmost subtlety yet is murderous in its effects, appears in Foucault's thought in the image of Jeremy Bentham's 'Panopticon'. The exer-cise of power in post-Enlightenment, or what Foucault calls the 'carceral', society has none of the grand theatricality of the *ancien régime*. It is no longer a question of the equation of pain or of the sovereign's extravagant display of vengeance on the body of the con-demned. Nor is it a spectacle in the open air. The power of the 'carceral' works precisely the opposite way: it is a matter of erecting enclosures in the open air – a culture obsessed with divisions and boundaries *à la* Robinson Crusoe. Hence, it is of little surprise that in a carceral system 'The first principle was isolation':[97] it is a system of exclusion and confinement. In *Madness and Civilisation*, Foucault shows how the burgeoning culture of Enlightenment, of which the founding of the Hôpital Général in Paris in 1656 stands both as a symbolic and technical expression, produced a new kind of spatial boundary: the result is 'a new homeland for madness'.[98] The wall of the asylum, just as much as the wall of the prison, will create a rigid boundary between the world of the normals (reasonable, sane, non-criminals, non-delinquent, etc.) and the excluded (unreasonable, mad, criminal, delinquent, etc.). Thus the homelands of the *same* and the other will be cut off by unsurpassable boundaries. The jour-ney between the two, which the figure of the fool in Renaissance

culture so perilously undertook, would rarely be possible. The inhabitants of the homeland of the sane – the prison guards, doctors,
psychologists, social workers – would venture into the homeland of
madness without ever travelling. There would be hardly any encounter between them. The inhabitants of the world of the sane or the
same would frequent the other spaces of the insane or the criminal
only to reinforce the border between them, to congeal them as hard
as the stone of the wall of the asylum or prison. Cocooned in the law
of the normal, the figure of the *same* will frequent, like Conrad's
sedentary traveller, the spaces of the other only to return, after
having exercised the power of the *same*, to the *same*. His is the
pseudo-movement, where the doubling simply mimics the routine
of a tautologist, of a monologist, and of a Hegelian dialectician. This
scenario of internal difference within post-Enlightenment Europe,
through analogy and displacement, is duplicated in its cross-cultural
relationships with other spaces. The homeland of the others, beyond
the boundary of Europe, would come to mirror the 'homeland of
madness' within. Similarly, like the functionaries of the self-same
reason – doctors and prison guards – the 'travellers' from Europe
would frequent the homelands of the others, either on a mission to
represent, or to conquer or govern, and return to the fold of the *same*
without ever having risked travelling.

The panopticon, however, is more than a bounded space of
exclusion and confinement: it is the very *dispositif* of the carceral
society in microcosm. It is an arrangement of space and an architectural machine which is not content with simply erecting walls and
creating cellular slots; it brings into play the entire disciplinary order
by inventing a system of light. It produces a visibility trap which,
through the arrangement of 'spatial unities ... make[s] it possible to
see constantly and to recognise immediately'.[99] Nothing escapes the
eye of power; it sees and records in the automatic mode, while
remaining invisible. It articulates a mode of power through the logic
of light. Gilles Deleuze is right to see Panopticism 'as a system of
light before being a figure of stone',[100] because power here takes the
form of 'visual assemblage and a luminous environment'.[101] Moreover, the architectural arrangement of the panopticon shows in
micro-space the disciplinary arrangement of the entire society. However, the figure of stone, despite the reduction of its potency, does
not disappear.

Foucault, in the *Hérodote* interview, comes to see the frontier of
the nation-state, which produces the 'national man', as the spatial

confinement of the panopticonic order.[102] The system of visibility produces the disciplined bodies and the normal subjects, but the old spatial divisions and boundaries, no matter to what extent they are refined in Panopticism, continues to be used as an indispensable technique of power. In the panopticonic order, even the flimsy contact of the asylum – between the inhabitants of the inside and the outside – disappears. For the panopticonic order has no outside; the entire society has come under its regime of vision. Moreover, the inmate is subject to an anonymous and impersonal gaze: 'He is seen, but he does not see; he is the object of information, never a subject in communication'.[103]

The knowledge through anonymous vision, the diffusion of power through light, is the passion of the en-light-en-ment. The subjects of the panopticonic regime, grown normal in the saturation of light, become the very eye-machine themselves when they cross the frontier of the state into the spaces of other states, nations or cultures. Driven by a scopic mania, the cross-cultural 'travellers' of post-Enlightenment Europe simply frequent other places to shed light: to record, to represent, and to produce knowledge. It is hardly surprising, therefore, if we do not find many travellers among the many so-called travellers of post-Enlightenment Europe.

Renaissance culture, uncertain about the figure of the mad, found an equally ambivalent solution to its predicament. Between exclusion and passage, sailed the 'Stultifera Navis' with its 'liminal' cargo of madmen, whose strange power had not yet been completely tamed in the light of reason. And between embarkation and disembarkation, confined on the ship, the madman became the 'prisoner of the passage'.[104] This is a strange paradox: the prisoner of the inside (both driven out of the city and confined within the boat) is, at the same time, a prisoner of the outside (of the passage and sea). Although a prisoner of the same, the Renaissance madman, shrouded in liminality, does not return to the same: 'It is for the other world that the madman sets sail in his fools' boat; it is from the other world that he comes when he disembarks'.[105]

The liminal ambivalence with which Renaissance culture cast the madman threw him into the perpetual motion of the passage. Lacking conviction enough to lock him up once and for all, the madman was offered to the world of the other – to the strange space of 'the interior of the exterior'.[106] Gilles Deleuze explains it in the Heideggerian language of 'the folding' – the inside as the fold of the outside: the ship as the folding of the 'dark mass' of the sea.[107]

Condemned never to return and never to arrive, the madman, in 'the redoubling of the Other', is offered the perilous destiny of a traveller, whom Michel Foucault calls 'the passenger *par excellence*'. Although the Renaissance madman never chose to be a traveller, insofar as he was consigned to it, his predicament reveals the tremulous secret of travelling. The opening of a passage, and the possibilities of travel, are unthinkable without difference, without letting oneself be in the fold of the outside, without going to the other.

In the preface to *The Order of Things*, Foucault offers an image of space which is the opposite of the panopticon and the carceral, and which he calls *Heterotopia*.[108] Upon surfacing from a Borgesian labyrinth staged on a strange Chinese encyclopaedia, Foucault conceives the *Heterotopia* with a Dionysiac (or Zarathustrian) laughter. The spaces of this encyclopaedia, where taxonomic grids fold into each other, effectuate the annulment of the neat contiguous order upon which 'the distinction between the Same and the Other' is grounded.[109] The neat cellular structure of the panopticon, and the wall that encloses it, parallels the taxonomic grid of representation. In fact, they are more than parallels: they are doubles of each other. The panopticonic cell, which functions as a discrete unit of visibility, works as a taxonomic grid of knowledge, and the collusion of space and knowledge produces the docile soul of the normal subject. In this space of neat boundary and light, as we have argued, travelling does not take place easily, if it takes place at all. *Heterotopia*, being a fold of the outside, is the space of passage and travel. It is the 'dark mass' of the sea folded in the *Stultifera Navis*. If panopticon is the space of power, rigid boundary and non-travel, *Heterotopia* is the space that slips through the net of power: it is of supple boundary, and offers perilous voyages beyond threshold. It is the ethical counterpoint to the logic of panopticon.

This is the affirmative space of which Zarathustra spoke to himself on the way to the summit, where 'summit and abyss ... united in one!'[110] To climb this *Heterotopic* space – where the inside of the summit is folded in the outside of the abyss – one must know how to 'climb upward otherwise?' and 'in order to see *much* one must learn to *look away* from one self'.[111] Zarathustra's ethics of self-difference is the 'coming home' to the *Heterotopic* space, which is inseparable from becoming-traveller. Hence Zarathustra longs to travel: 'I want to sail across broad seas like a cry and a shout'.[112] He is also a friend of those who travel: 'Zarathustra, however, was a friend to all who take long journeys and do not want to live without danger'.[113] However, Zarathustra's ethics is an ethics of self-affirmation. So on the way to the summit – which is a passage to a *Heterotopic* space – Zarathustra affirms his being as a traveller: 'I am a wanderer and a mountain-climber (he said to his heart), I do not like the plains and it seems I cannot sit still for long'.[114]

Panopticon and *Heterotopia*: two kinds of spaces, two different positions in a power relation, to which correspond the sedentary, non-travelling immobility in the grid, and the speed of a traveller in the movement of self-difference.

Of these two kinds of spaces, the *Heterotopic*, as we have seen in the ontological and the poetic meditations, is primordial. Kafka knew it very well, and produced his own metastable ontology of being. Writing on the awesome barrier in *The Great Wall of China*, he says, 'Human nature, essentially changeable, unstable as the dust, can endure no restraint; if it binds itself it soon brings to tear at its bonds, until it rends everything asunder, the wall, the bonds and its very self'.[115] Yet multitudes flocked from the distant provinces to labour on the Great Wall: 'the desire once more to labour on the wall of the nation became irresistible'.[116] The wall is useless as a protection against the nomads of the north, as the piecemeal and discontinuous construction left innumerable gaps in it. Moreover, the broken wall only increased the restless mobility of the nomads. Why, then, did men who are as 'unstable as the dust' make their own enclosure? The imaginary horror of the menacing other is one possible reason, but the men from the distant provinces had never seen the menacing others of the north. The image of the other that inspires men to their fruitless labour is simply a 'representation of the artist'.[117]

For Kafka, it points to only one thing: power. Who else but the 'high command' would conceive of a wall like this; and the horror of the other, so conveniently held up in the 'representation of the artist', can only be a clever strategic move on their part. Yet, if the discontinuous wall is ineffectual as a protection, is it not also, and to the same extent, ineffectual as an enclosure? Kafka approaches this question from two very different angles. First, the unending labour on the wall keeps the imprisoning force of the wall in place in the labourer's mind. We are told that the wall was conceived as the foundation of a tower, but the structure does not lend itself for the construction of a tower. Kafka explains that the tower was 'meant only in a spiritual sense'. The imaginary tower then is the tower of power that creates a continuous wall through unending labour on the discontinuous wall. Second, and perhaps the more subtle of the two approaches, Kafka explains this apparently futile exercise as a deliberate act on the part of the high command itself – as if the 'high command', cognisant of the metastable origin of men, left enough gaps so that the very order the wall contrived would not explode like an over-heated cauldron. No doubt it is a crafty ploy on the part of the 'high command', and most of the time it bears fruit. Yet it confirms, even though obliquely, the ontological primacy of the *Heterotopic* space: walls have to have holes because the recalcitrant matters that throb in men are ever on the alert for a line of escape. Even though most of the time the cunning of the panopticonic power immobilises most of the men, it cannot wish away the ontological possibilities of travel. There are holes in the wall, and no lining can cover them up once and for all. Michel de Certeau calls it 'a sieve-order'.[118] One can always become, through a performative repetition of the sieve-order, a traveller. For that one just has to learn to climb to the summit with Zarathustra.

Apart from rare examples such as the Chinese wall or the Berlin wall, larger territorial unities such as empires or states are rarely walled (in a literal sense). Yet all territorial unities, irrespective of their size, are enclosed spaces. Of course – depending on the kind of power, the principle of sovereignty and the organisation of society – the nature of enclosure changes. However, what is constant among all forms of enclosures and boundaries is what Lewis Mumford calls the 'paranoid psychic structure of power'. Even the old myths confirm it: Henri Lefebvre retells the fable of the founding of Rome: 'the founder, Remus, described a circle with his plough, thus subtracting a space from nature and investing it with a political meaning'.[119]

When the cities were swallowed up by extended territorial unities, their walls provided the prototypes of new divisions. Mumford, therefore, concludes that in the nation-state 'the old city walls became the "national frontier"'.[120] Although, as we have observed, very few 'national frontiers' are literal walls, they continue to function as the enclosure of power. Now the 'paranoid psychic structure' is dispersed into the wide, luminous space of the panopticon. Just as the panopticonic space of prison clings to the function of the wall, so does the space of the nation in its pursuit of founding a new threshold of difference. The border of a nation is often barbedwired; watch-towers and armed patrols form one of its regular features; and all entries and exits through it are scrupulously monitored by the techniques of passport and visa controls. They keep away, just as much as they keep in. Moreover, the coming of the state, at least for Hegel, signals that 'space brought historical time to an end, and the master of space was the state'.[121] In the consequent rigidification of space, travelling would be that much more difficult.

The wall of the old city was an immediate barrier. The border of a nation, despite the 'beautiful mirage' of the natural parameter, is something more ghostly. The contour of the landmass that encloses the 'national man' and endows him with his soul could be as much as, or even more than, a thousand miles away. Moreover, the national border, unlike Kafka's Chinese wall, is not discontinuous. It is sapped by the geometrical fantasy of the sieveless order: a neat homogenous line rounding a circle. The art of map-making, ancient though its provenance has been, came into its own at the provocation of national boundaries. Its own abstract geometrical lines, and the neatly segmented spaces in contiguous relationships, mirror perfectly the borderline of a nation. Or perhaps it is the other way around: the abstract logic of the map, with its crystal-clear outlines that excise the slightest flutter of ambiguity, provides the national boundary with a mimetic model. In whatever order their relationship might stand, the effects of their mutual dependence force upon us the notion of clear identity and difference. It smoothes the jagged edges, glosses the gaps, so that a full body of space may emerge to take the burden of identity for its citizens. The consequence is a paradox: the space of the nation is homogenous and empty, yet it is made to function as the full sovereign body of the state. If the principle of sovereignty, in the old monarchical formation, is embodied in the body of the king/queen, in the national formation it is embodied in the geographical body. Hence the transformation of space into the role of an arch-subject: the father/mother land which is supposed to offer each of its bewildered citizens/offspring of modernity an identity with which to anchor themselves in the world. The result is the obsession with spatial identity and the paranoia of maps – often fostering genocidal passions.

The separation of Misra and Askar in the infernal war of the Ogaden, in Nuruddin Farah's *Maps*, tells the tale of the recurrent pathos of the spatial configurations of nation-states.[122] Askar, who lost his mother at birth, became so close to Misra – his foster mother – that their bodies become one. Askar even replaced Allah and became the 'space and time' in the maternal universe of Misra.[123] Yet the passion for maps and the national boundary made Askar – the

Somali – a nationalist warrior, and Misra – the non-Somali (Oromo) – a traitor. In fact, it is under the ghostly, yet binary, force of the map that their differences emerge in a process of othering which parallels their bodily, anatomical sense of separation. Askar, in an imaginary interlocution with Misra, tells himself that, 'the other, i.e. the maps which give me the distance in scales of kilometre – [are] the distance that is between you and me'.[124] The passion for the map, and its attendant passion for the space of the nation, is the articulation of the impossibility of the cohabitation of difference: it creates a rigid boundary between the 'we' and 'they' people.

Ernest Renan, one of the early genealogists of nation, points out that the obsession with the unitary space of a singular people is founded on forgetting the mixed economy of its origin.[125] The myth of the nation moves like a giant erasure, obliterating the traces of so many crossings of spatial and racial boundaries. Moreover, the desire to force the arbitrary and the abstract line of the map to coincide with the natural contours of space leads only to violence.[126] What is lacking in Renan's account is the failure to see that the 'rich legacy of memories', which he called the 'spiritual principle'[127] of the nation, is itself an effect of violence. It is a memory produced in the capillary circuits of power and in a space saturated with light, which can only be staged in the theatre of cruelty. Nietzsche, in the second essay on the *Genealogy of Morals*, traces the origin of mnemonics:

> Man could never do without blood, torture, and sacrifices when he felt the need to create a memory for himself; the most dreadful sacrifices and pledges ... the most repulsive mutilations ... the cruellest rites of all the religious cults ... all this has its origin in the instinct that realised that pain is the most powerful aid to mnemonics.[128]

Out of the mnemonic cruelty, and the consequent fixing of ideas, argues Nietzsche, emerges the 'nation of thinkers'. This is how Nietzsche explains the emergence of the German nation.[129]

The space of power, with its rigid boundaries – either erected with a thick wall or drawn with their abstract line on the map – might seem like the formation of an impregnable fortress. Yet, the very pragmatic logic of territorial boundary – either that of city, of state or of empire – creates an opening onto the outside.

The walled cities weren't simply containers; they were 'bent on bringing within the wall all that lay outside them'.[130] The force of this predatory desire impelled the power of the city to create numerous passages, linking the city with its outside. Henri Lefebvre, in the process of puzzling over this 'dual character' of that most archetypal city of power, Rome, characterises it as a relationship between 'urbs and orbis'.[131] This relationship does not establish amicable passages between friends; rather they are given to raids of pillage, of conquest, of slave hunt, of trade, of knowledge, through which power goes out of the enclosed city and returns with long caravan loads of booty. However, the network of roads emanating from the city also provides the passages for raids from the outside: which walled city wasn't ruined by nomadic raiders from the outside? Even if there is no destructive visitation by the nomads, the walled city is haunted by the other, always trembling at the nocturnal folding of the outside. Amos Oz, the chronicler of the uneasy consciousness of modern Israel, is acutely aware of this double-bind, to which his stories bear an eloquent testimony.

At the end of *khamsin*, when the heat waves from the desert decamp their seize on the kibbutz, the more ominous howls of the jackals penetrate into its walled inside.[132] Amos Oz writes.

> At the twilight hour our world is made up of circles within circles. On the outside is the circle of the autumn darkness, far from here, in the mountains and the great deserts. Sealed and enclosed within it is the circle of our night landscape, vineyards and orchards and plantations. A dim lake astir with whispering voices. Our lands betray us in the night. Now they are no longer familiar and submissive, criss-crossed with irrigation pipes and dirt tracks. Now our fields have gone over to the enemy's camp. They send out to us waves of alien scents. At night we see them bristling in a miasma of threat and hostility and returning to their former state, as they were before we came to this place.
>
> The inner circle, the circle of lights, keeps guard over our houses and over us, against the accumulated menace outside. But it is an ineffective wall, it cannot keep out the smells of the foe and his voices. At night the voices and the smells touch our skin like tooth and claw.[133]

No doubt Amos Oz is re-staging here, through the age-old device of allegory, the bitter dispute over territorial claims between Israelis and Palestinians, for no nation or state has been more fortress-like than Israel. But beyond local relevance, Oz's story speaks the paradox of the wall which brings to the fore the impossibility of keeping out the outside. No matter how thick the wall of the inside is, the phantom of the outside slips through it as if it were a net with enormous holes.

Even at the formal, structural plane of certainty, the foundation on which rigid boundaries rise up to proclaim their impenetrable

singularities rests on a volatile and shifting ground. Much of Jacques
Derrida's work is given over to the demonstration of this insight.
However, in *The Law of Genre*, despite his characteristic reticence for
the thematic of power, Derrida bends the question of formal division
to bear on the inscription of power.

Derrida's broaching of the binary rests on the strategic invocation of two possible readings, which are set on their course in
response to two imaginary statements: 'Genres are not to be mixed'
and 'I will not mix genres'. One possible reading of this circuit of the
general/particular, and one that normative discourse would prefer,
would tame it by placing it under the innocence of the descriptive or
constative statement. But surely there is more to the statement
'Genres are not to be mixed' than a mere description of a state of
affairs. Here, Derrida introduces his second reading: it is now a
matter of 'authoritarian summons to a law of "do" or "do not"'.[134]
The force of the law creates the enclosure called genre by erecting
boundaries around it so that 'one must respect a norm, one must not
cross a line of demarcation, one must not risk impurity, anomaly or
monstrosity'.[135] So when one says 'I will not mix genres' from
'Genres are not to be mixed' one is not simply drawing a corollary, by
the way of a simple deduction, from the general to the particular,
which, besides confirming the givenness of generic boundary,
articulates the subjection to a prescriptive force. It is under the
weight of power, as a vow of obedience, that 'I' repeats the 'truth' of
the generic space to which it belongs.

Yet, Derrida contends, in the performative repetition 'I will not
mix genres' something more than the mere confirmation of generic
boundary takes place. It gives, even though obliquely, an intimation
of 'the law of the law of genre' whose nature harbours 'a principle of
contamination, a law of impurity, a parasitical economy'.[136] For one
thing, it is the supplementary repetition 'I will not mix genres' that
provides the generic enclosure with its body. In other words, the
'identifiable trait' (the body of the genre), with which the boundary of
the genre is fixed, does not belong to the genre itself but is ascribed
to it by the repetition or the secondary statement. Therefore, the
genre itself is marked by the marks of the secondary statement,
which while supposed to belong to it, in fact follow from it. Derrida
calls this process 're-marking' – the law of the law of genre. One of the
consequences of re-marking is that the claim to belong to the genre
– with its pre-given boundary – cannot really belong to it: it can only
'participate without belonging'.[137] The secondary, the performative

statement – which is also aleatoric – through the play of re-marking, will constantly exceed the generic boundary to which it allegedly belongs. It brings to the fore that which is always already there in the structure of re-marking, the gaping holes in the walls of the generic space, thereby opening the body of the inside to the outside – allowing passages for travels and encounter with the other. Despite acknowledging the power of the law as the force behind rigid division, Derrida, unlike Nietzsche and Foucault, does not venture to trace the genealogy of the 'subject' who remains obedient to the law of the inside. His arguments draw their cogency from formal, logical demonstration, yet they confirm the paradox of the wall that Amos Oz's story narrates.

Coming back to the paradox of the city wall or the national boundary we can observe the following possibility: the passages through which power goes out, and the passages through which the outside intrudes, are also passages of travel. However, the passage along the routes of power, taken by the subjects moulded by the mnemonic or the light machine of the inside, often amounts to no more than the epistemological capture of the other, or its paranoiac folding into oneself, rather than the perilous movement of travel. For travel to take place, one has to forget the memories of the *same*, and encounter the other.

In Amos Oz's 'Nomad and Viper', the enclosed inside of the kibbutz is not haunted by the nocturnal cry of the allegorical figures of the jackals but by the voices of the nomads. Not only the nomads' voices penetrate the fence of the kibbutz, but their bodies also intrude into the inside, constantly inciting real or imaginary menace. Guela, still without a man in her life, is a dutiful daughter of the inside. On a fateful saunter to the fragrant orchards, at the edge of the kibbutz, Guela chances upon an intruder from the desert. On the face of it, this chance meeting at the border zone has all the makings of an encounter that could traverse the line and make Guela into a traveller. Yet, burdened by the memories drummed into her of the horror of the outside, she is only capable of a paranoid gesture. It folds her within herself and within the border; and she remains a prisoner of the inside. Yet, like the nocturnal cry of the jackals, the force of the encounter, of which the paranoid gesture is a symptom, affects her in the very depth of her body. When the nomad smiles and asks with rare gentleness, 'What time is it?',[38] the benign question acquires a strange power. It touches the dark interior of Guela, who fastens the top button of her blouse, and trembles at the 'repulsively handsome' face of the nomad. Guela, in the oxymoron 'repulsively handsome', feels the pulse of the libidinal as it comes up against the memories of the inside, the force of the law and the dense barrier of the border. Afterwards, away from the border zone and back in the sanctum of the inside, the real drama of the meeting unfolds. Geula's last image of the nomad before they go their separate ways presents him in his starkest otherness: the nomad suddenly stops speaking Hebrew and lapses into Arabic. More disturbingly, animal that he is in his otherness, the nomad becomes one with his goats as he disappears amidst their 'dark, a terrified, quivering mass'.[139]

Guela is so fatally marked by the 'repulsively handsome' face of the nomad that she cannot forget him, and the trace of the paradox incited by this event – the libidinal pulse and the force of the law – continues to haunt her. Facing the trace of the other, the subject of the inside finds herself before two conflicting possibilities. On the one hand, in a paranoid spasm, she experiences the trace of the nomad as a pollution that soils her purity, protected by the law and the fence. Instead of affirming the touch of the other, she seeks vengeance. Now her emotions accord well with the vengeful youths of the kib-butz who go out to raid the nomads' camps. While desperately cleansing herself with a soap, Guela tells herself: 'Yes, let the boys go right away tonight to their camp and smash their black bones'.[140] In the perverse pleasure of *ressentiment* and the passion for vengeance, Guela tries to erase the trace of the outside and to return to the fenced inside of the kibbutz. But on the other hand, the trace of the other summons Guela to the outside, and for a moment we see her poised at the threshold of becoming a traveller. While watching the green and the red lights of Israeli Air Force planes on bombing raids, Guela longs 'to get up and go to him ... and never come back'.[141]

Beyond this momentary longing, Guela, for so long a dutiful daughter of the inside, cannot take the step outside, because, like the lidless eyes of the viper that cannot be closed, she does not know how to do otherwise. The only thing to do is to expel the traces of the nomad. So deep was his touch that mere soap and the thoughts of vengeance are not enough: she vomits him out 'among the flowering shrubs'.[142]

Power cannot do without the inscription of boundary: the more rigid it gets the better it seems to like it. Yet the boundary, no matter how thick the volume of the wall, can never fully succeed in filling the fissures in its own very structure. Just as the others, through these fissures, can intrude into the inside, so the insiders can venture into the outside. Yet, as we have seen, to be a traveller is not an easy task. The eyes of power can see a long way and the mnemonic machine leaves too deep a mark.

Let us end this section, as we began, with Kafka. Kafka might simply appear as the poet of closed space; and it is true that no one has mapped the spaces of power with more scrupulous attention than he. There are so many spaces of power in Kafka, each more terrible than the last: the impenetrable threshold before the door of the law, the ominous shadow of the Great Wall of China, the cruel labyrinth of the castle, the marooned space of the penal colony which houses that most impeccable of torture machines, the tiny claustrophobic cell-like room of Gregory Samsa – they all tell infernal stories of imprisonment. Yet, or perhaps because of this, no other European writer has been so passionate a traveller as Kafka. How can one not see the obviousness of Deleuze and Guattari's position, argued against the orthodoxies of the Oedipal and theological genres of criticism, that Kafka's so-called allegories or absurdities are simply lines of escape. Entrapped within the spaces of power – a Jew in a Prague ghetto, living the nightmare of pogrom – Kafka devises two lines of escape. The first of these goes through pure intensity: the 'immobile voyage' of 'becoming-animal'.[143] This line affords absolute speed in the narrowest of confinements: it is the art of moving in a cage, and it is on this line that Deleuze and Guattari rest their case for Kafka's minor literature.

Their claim, to a large extent, is true. There are so many becoming-animal in Kafka's stories: Samsa becomes a giant bug, while the giant mole burrows its rhizomatic passage. Once one has taken to flight on this line, the molar solidity of the subject goes though a metamorphic decomposition until there remain only pure forces and untrammelled intensities. One has made the quantum leap and reached the molecular – the singular plane of forces – where one force can, following Spinoza's ethical prescription, form a 'common notion' with other forces and become other. Yet there is nothing transcendental about this line of flight: one does not go elsewhere but is carried along by the immanent speed of self-differentiating forces. The immanent speed is the force proper to the metastratal real where, argues Spinoza, there exists only a composition of forces, which he calls the body.[144] Since the bodies are defined in terms of forces alone (their velocity and their affectivity) there exist a univocity among all bodies. This is what Spinoza means when he says: 'All bodies agree in some respects'.[145]

When bodies encounter each other – be they bodies of men, animals or plants – a mutual affecting of forces takes place. In the process of this molecular encounter, 'two bodies adapt themselves to one another'.[146] If, in the event, the encounter proves to be a positive one, in so far as it enhances the force of acting, a 'common notion' is formed. This is the art of taking flight and becoming. Deleuze and Guattari develop their notion of 'a parallel evolution' out of this Spinozist notion, which I discuss in the next chapter.

In Kafka's stories, becoming-animal is an extreme line of escape, which involves 'absolute deterritorialisation'. On this line, which constantly provokes exorbitant risk, the 'subject' faces a catastrophic breakdown along with the destratification of the space of power. Movement on this line inheres within it just as many possibilities for the agreeable as for the disagreeable (poisonous) encounter – one can 'really' become schizophrenic rather than merely discovering the schizophrenic multiplicity of forces. Deleuze and Guattari rightly caution us about getting on this line too hastily.

Apart from this ultimate line of becoming-animal, there is a second line of escape. Deleuze and Guattari are not unaware of it; they call it the line of 'relative deterritorialisation', where one escapes 'by shifting and travelling'.[147] Yet despite their recognition that 'absolute D[deterritorialisation] necessarily proceeds by way of relative D[deterritorialisation]',[148] they surprisingly say nothing about Kafka the traveller.

For Kafka the motion and the speed of travel offer, even if only momentarily, a practical line of escape from regimes of the inside in their various forms of organisation: the trap of the Oedipal family, the terror of the pogrom, the petty-bourgeois life of a petty bank clerk. Of course, not all travels are the same. Some, because their movement is bound to the gridded space, prove to be just as imprisoning as the walled enclosure. And Kafka knew it very well. For 'Samsa was a traveller'.[149] He hated it; he called it 'wretched travelling'.[150] His fellow travellers, he called 'kept women'.[151] His timidity, he explains, owes its origin in being a traveller.[152] Gregory Samsa's routes are the habitual routes of work and commerce, for he is a 'commercial traveller'. More aptly, we should call him a sedentary traveller, for his movements, bound as they are by the routine of work and the circulation of commerce, are given to the stasis of repetitious circulation. For Samsa, these routes are routine passages to daily imprisonments: to repeat Michel de Certeau, they are instances of 'travelling incarceration'. On these travelling routes, if

Deleuze and Guattari do not sense a line of escape, we should not blame them. Indeed, they are the routes of 'reterritorialisation' that return the 'subject' to its fixed location or to the molar black hole.

For Kafka there is another kind of travel: the travel of speed that enables him the encounter with the outside, offering lines of escape. Late in the evening, during inclement weather, when he almost resigns himself to staying inside, Kafka suddenly slams the door of his apartment and goes out for a stroll. He discovers 'out-of-the-ordinary agility' and 'rapid change'. The speed of travel takes him out of the confinement of home, away from the Oedipal theatre. As he says, 'one has stepped completely outside one's family'.[153] On the way home, approaching the inside, he feels the urgency of even greater speed, and becomes one with the speed of the street itself. This is Kafka's becoming-passage: 'I stride along and my speed is the speed of the side of the street, of this street, of this part of town'.[154]

Home-coming always inspired dread in Kafka, because it returns one to the dreadful closure of belonging, and reminds one that one has not escaped the grinding stability of the inside. Approaching home, he ponders, 'Do you feel you belong, do you feel at home? I don't know, I feel most uncertain'.[155] The uncertainty is the symptom of the fold of the outside; Kafka's return, after having become a passage, without returning. It is the eternal repetition of the stranger in the homeless home. Or as Wilson Harris puts it, it is the 'echo of the stranger, the everlasting stranger one is despite every homecoming?'[156]

Gregory Samsa's travel has been along the mapped and gridded route. On this route the more one travels, the more one is entrapped. So Kafka wants to travel along other routes, to other places 'of impassable height' which are not 'yet traced on any map'.[157]

What does a traveller do when he gets there? Certainly he does not produce a geographical map of the un-mapped space. If he were to do so, he would only be repeating the monotonous journeys of representation, the acts of power, and the thrusts of light. The true traveller's way is the Fat Man's way: the Fat Man does not produce a map of the landscape, he encounters it and addresses it. He lets the encounter disturb his thought, as all encounter should. The movement yields to the speed and the speed gathers a furious momentum. There is no chance here for centring a fixed perspective, so that representation can overcode the landscape. The speed is the secret of encounter; it is the necessary preparation for hearing the call of the other. The landscape summons the Fat Man; his eyes are its way of becoming-beautiful. Here is what the Fat Man says: 'It makes my reflections sway like a suspension bridge in a furious current. It is beautiful and for this reason wants to be looked at'.[58]

When Kafka wants to be a Red Indian, it has nothing to do with the fascination of the exotic. Neither is it a question of mimicry. What draws him towards the Red Indian is his motion and his speed on a galloping horse. All he wants is a joyous encounter with these forces, so that the intensity of speed can be doubled to a breathless momentum that will melt away the solidity of space:

> Ah, if one were a Red Indian, on the alert immediately, and if leaning into the wind on one's galloping horse one went quivering swiftly over the quavering ground, over and over again till one stopped using the spurs, there being no spurs, till one threw away the reins, there being no reins, and one scarcely saw the terrain out in front as a well-mown stretch of moorland without even a horse's neck or a horse's head.[59]

Becoming a Red Indian is one of Kafka's lines of escape – of becoming-other in the motion of travel. It is a departure of the nth power; it erases the route of a return journey home. One cannot really travel along the route mapped by Hegelian dialectics – where the *same* moves only to return to the *same*. Kafka knew it better than anybody else. Travel means a traversal of the line of the inside, always going towards the other, moving without a telos, and without ever returning. This is the affirmative ethics of departure:

> I ORDERED my horse to be brought from the stables. The servant did not understand my orders. So I went to the stables myself, saddled my horse, and mounted. In the distance I heard the sound of a trumpet, and I asked the servant what it meant. He knew nothing and heard nothing. At the gate he stopped me and asked: 'Where is the master going?' 'I don't know,' I said, 'just out of here, just out of here. Out of here, nothing else, it's the only way I can reach my goal.' 'So you know your goal?' he asked. 'I've just told you. Out of here – that's my goal.'[60]

Kafka shows us both the imprisoning spaces of power and how to escape them. Before one can escape the spaces of power, as a way of preparation, their lines of articulation must be analysed with scrupulous precision. Of the lines of escape, there are two: one involves the catastrophic speed of absolute deterritorialisation – the line of becoming-animal; the other takes the line of relative deterritorialisation of travel. Yet the latter yields the speed of molecular intensities, forms bands of becoming (becoming-passage or Red Indian), and takes him to the outside. There is no qualitative opposition between travel and absolute deterritorialisation. The difference is rather between two types of travel: one along the route of power, through the illumined path of light, at the end of which lies the goal and the return journey home. The other breaks with the route of power, its gridded space, moves without the allure of a goal (which has often been that of the golden city); and the *same* never returns the *same*. In fact, the former hardly deserves to be called travel: it can only either be a 'travelling incarceration' or the sedentary movement of power on the adventure of conquest, knowledge and commerce (they have other *raisons d'être* than travel). Only the latter is truly travel. The way of travel is Zarathustra's way, the Fat Man's way, and Kafka's way.

The Manichaean boundary of colonial space

From the opening pages of *A Passage to India*, where Forster draws the *mise-en-scène* of a colonial city to stage the fatal tragedy of colonial relations, Chandrapore appears cut into two. Along the banks of the Ganges, along its meandering stretches of unrelieved stench, lies the lower order of the native city: it is a city of 'excrescence'.[161] Inland, perched on the hills, parallel with the green foliage, rises up the city of higher order – the beautiful city of the colonisers. Against the overwhelming disorder of the native city, the colonial city, with its passion for geometrical symmetry, is the very expression of order. They are contiguous to each other yet opposite to each other, on top of each other, as if they are rent by violent antipathy to each other. The colonial city, writes Forster, 'shares nothing with the city [of the natives] except the overarching sky'.[162] The paradox of two-cities-under-one-sky, so often repeated in the colonial landscape, led Fanon to declare that 'the colonial world is a Manichaean world'.[163]

The Manichaean order rests both on the spacing of difference and the staging of opposition. It accommodates, not without risk, the Aristotelian logic of identities and the Hegelian logic of the sublation of difference. In other words, in its Aristotelian moment, it creates clearly demarcated spaces from which their identities emerge in resplendent isolation. It provides a space without the troublesome middle term so that the purity of each identity is never endangered through the leakage of its difference or each other's identity. Each demarcated space of identity is rigorously protected from its other by an uncrossable chasm between them. It says: there is a boundary between us and them and it must not be crossed. If it is crossed the world will be plagued with disorder, and we would no longer know with clarity who 'we are' and who 'they are'. From this space of rigorous separation arose the taxonomic passion that led post-Enlightenment naturalists, anatomists and ethnologists to map human bodies in their ostensible identity and difference. From the logical space of Aristotelian identity, and the corresponding space of taxonomic order, emerge the static and the essential fixation of identity and difference. This is the first principle of Manichaean logic.

Against the statics of Aristotelian logic, Hegelian logic offers sublation through movement. In the dialectical circuit, identity (*same*) and difference (other) slide into each other, producing a sublated synthesis. On the face of it, the dialectic seems to offer unending movement for the continuous undoing of identities. Yet, if we consider the working of the dialectic, the principles through which it acts – namely the principle of subjectivity, the principle of telos and the principle of opposition – a very different image of it appears. The sublating movement between the subject (*same*) and the object (other) is a one-way process: it is the subject (*same*) who intrudes into the space of the object (other). Furthermore, any real movement never really takes place as the subject (*same*) goes to the object (other) only in pursuit of its own self-realisation. The subject (*same*) returns, after having enlightened itself, to itself. The subject (*same*) in its movement never encounters the object (other); and if it had, it would have been a movement of non-return.

Even the egological movement of sublation cannot go on *ad infinitum*. The principle of telos works as an in-built brake on the movement of the dialectic: anything – self-consciousness, state, empire, civilising mission – can serve as its goal. The adventure of the dialectic, despite its grand posturing, only takes it to its, often less than honourable, goal. So it seems that the apparent infinite movement of the dialectic, is, after all, finite.

Finally, what can we say about the principle of opposition? It is the very motor force of the dialectic – without it there would be no movement. Now we can see that the dialectical movement between subject (*same*) and object (other) is a movement between oppositional forces: it constructs the other term as a negative pole. Hegelian logic says: we and they face each other in opposition, but we must go to them if we want to fulfil ourselves. They are negatives, the site of non-values; their sole purpose is to be our shadow so that we may shine in splendour. Besides, dialectics is founded on the logic of equivalence: 'they' amount to what 'we' are not. Therefore, they are internal to the process of our own self-definition. Incidentally, the principle of opposition and the egological movement allow the dialectic to cohabit amicably with the Aristotelian logic of disjunctive identities.

Given the opposition between the *same* and the other, the dialectical movement, like the movement of the power of the walled city to its outside, can only venture out on a violent and predatory raid. It is hardly surprising that the walled city has been the archetypal colonial inside, from which power flowed out to fashion so many empires from the far reaches of other spaces.

Manichaean logic arrogates to itself the combined forces of the Aristotelian and the Hegelian logic. On the one hand, it creates neat spaces of identities with rigid boundaries that must not be crossed. On the other hand, it makes the realisation of the self conditional upon the crossing of the boundary. Between them there seems to lie a simmering contradiction. Yet, given the egological movement (non-movement) and the oppositional structure of dialectics, the contradiction is easily patched up. Because the egological movement of the dialectic is a kind of sedentary voyage, it never really crosses the rigid boundary of Aristotelian order. The colonial voyagers carry their boundaries on their back as they move. They are the opposite of Toynbee's (or Deleuze and Guattari's) nomads. Where the nomad moves without moving, the colonial voyager does not move while moving. When the Aristotelian fixed space joins forces with the self-enclosed movement of Hegelian dialectic, it leads to the Manichaean obsession with the two-cities-under-one-sky in the colonial space.

When the European colonialists, in their sedentary voyages, ventured into other places, they moved tightly folded in the inside, and replicated the same old boundaries in distant places. They created, like Robinson Crusoe, their enclosed spaces, so that they need not risk the encounter with the other or open themselves to the trace of the outside.

The Manichaean logic, contends Fanon, is embodied in the very spatial body of the colonial world. Not only is the space of the father/ motherland deemed to be eternally different from the space of the native land, but in the very inside of the alien space of the native land, the colonial power creates yet another spatial division of the inside and the outside. This is the meaning of the expression: two-cities-under-one-sky. By creating two cities in the city of the other, the colonial power strains to stave off the leakage of the outside, which it invites by leaving its homeland. In the modern colonial world, the Manichaean logic, argues Fanon, is articulated in the division of space:

> The colonial world is a world divided into compartments. It is probably unnecessary to recall the existence of native quarters and European quarters ... Yet, if we examine closely this system of compartment, we will at least be able to reveal the lines of force it implies ... its ordering and its geographical lay-out ... The colonial world is a world cut in two. The dividing line, the frontiers are shown by barracks and police station. In the colonies it is the policeman and the soldier who are the official, instituted go-betweens, the spokesmen of the settler and his rule ... he is the bringer of violence into the home ... of the native.[164]

The Manichaean division of space is at once a symbolic embodiment of the eternal separation of the *same* and the other and a technique of power. On the one hand, the spatial division is the physical expression of the logical space of binary difference. On the other, the spatial division is an essential technical arrangement of the colonial governance. Both of these forms express the relationship of force and work as an instrument of force. On the symbolic plane, as the tale of Chandrapore tells us, the geographical division of the two cities gives expression to a set of relational values in vertical order. The native city of the plains is condemned to the lower order – it is both a city of excrescence and a city of disorder. The majestic head of the colonial city of the hills soars as the city of higher order; it is both a city of elegance and order. To these symbolic values, Fanon adds the economic values: the city of the colonisers is the city of opulence; it is 'a well-fed town'. The city of the colonised is a city of misery: it is 'a hungry town'.[165]

The city of the colonised and the city of the colonisers, in their bounded division, repeat the division that organised the space of post-Enlightenment Europe. There holds more than an analogy between the 'homeland of madness' that rational Europe created within, and the city of the natives in the colonial space. In fact, it expresses the same logic of the normal and the pathological with which post-Enlightenment Europe fashioned its mode of life. Similar to the relationship that obtains between the 'homeland of madness' and the 'homeland of reason', the terms of exchange between the cities of colonised and colonisers are those of the violent language of force. When the colonial power journeys into the city of the natives, as suggested by Fanon, it is never to open itself up to it, but only to exercise power. Despite so many intrepid adventures covering so many miles, most colonial travellers only repeated the Manichaean logic of two cities. Because they hardly ever left the fold of the inside, they never became travellers. They moved through the immobile passage towards the solid wall traced by the terminus of telos, which often took the form of representation and knowledge, and consequently they hardly ever crossed the line to encounter the other. Theirs was a journey, under the imprint of the Manichaean logic, of the mobile boundary of the *same*.

Despite disclosing the pathos of the two-cities-under-one sky in the colonial landscape, *A Passage to India* is grounded in the logic of a disjunctive space that eternally separates the *same* from the other. The narrative fabric of the novel is interwoven around two distinct orders of spatial disjunction: the primary disjunction between the 'Occident' (the *same*, Europe, England) and the 'Orient' (the other, Asia, India); and a secondary disjunction between the cities of the colonisers and the colonised within the 'Orient' (the other, Asia, India). Forster's strategy of registering moral indignation against colonial rule relies on the authority of the primary disjunction. It brings the eternal division between the 'Orient' and the 'Occident' to the fore in order to abjure the secondary division of colonial space. It says: there is an eternal separation between the 'Orient' and the 'Occident', and the boundary between them must not be crossed. Consequently, the 'Occidental' colonial power, by crossing the forbidden boundary that divides it from the 'Orient', invites contamination to its own self. Forster never questions the legitimacy of the metaphysical grounds upon which the two cities under the colonial sky rest. Nowhere in *A Passage To India* is the image of the colonised's city as the city of excrescence and disorder put under question. Nor is the image of the coloniser's city as the city of order ever doubted. What Forster shows is that these two cities are placed in the wrong place – in the other space of the 'Orient'. Due to their mis-placement, their relationship takes on a pathological dimension. Forster's critique of colonialism is simply a demonstration of this logic.

Beyond the pathological mis-placement of the two cities lies the very pathology of the one sky – the immanent baseness of the other space (the 'Orient', India). This is what Forster says of India: 'there is something hostile in that soil'.[166] Or as Ronny says to Mrs Moore, 'there's nothing in India but weather, my dear mother; it's the alpha and omega of the whole affair'.[167] They express the primary division between India (the other, the 'Orient') and England (the *same*, the 'Occident'). The proper boundary line lies at the threshold between the 'Occident' and the 'Orient'. Its mis-placement within the 'Orient' – which gives rise to the pathological relationship between the *same* and the other – constitutes the impropriety of the two-cities-under-one-sky in the colonial landscape. Hamidullah's answer to the question: 'How do you like Englishwomen generally?' articulates the proper/improper placement of boundary: '[Englishwomen] they are much nicer in England. There's something that doesn't suit them out here [India]'.[168]

Since Forster's narrative rigorously upholds the rigid Aristotelian order of the essential difference between the 'Occident' and the 'Orient' with the effect of installing an uncrossable boundary between them, it is driven to treat the movement of the *same* into the other as improper. What *A Passage to India* sets out to demonstrate is both the impossibility and the undesirability of a passage to India.

Most of the old hands in the colonial regime are too well fixed in the city of the colonisers and their clubs and racecourses to avail themselves of the opportunity of encountering the otherness of India. They constantly live in the bounded space – reserved exclusively for the colonisers – which serves, like Robinson Crusoe's fortress, as home from home. They are unsuitable figures to dramatise the impossibility of the passage. So Forster brings into the scene three relatively unformed characters: the individualist outsider, Fielding, and the two newcomers, Miss Quested and Mrs Moore. They are all not quite 'pukka'.

Fielding's case is relatively straightforward. Despite his conscientious openness and generosity of spirit, he is too well-folded in the glorious civility of the 'Occident' to be a passenger into the 'Orient'. The Mediterranean waters of the Italian peninsula will always come between him and India.[169] It is more than cultural difference. For Fielding, the origin of difference lies in the very physical body of the earth itself. When his party for the amusement of the newcomers breaks up on Ronny's rude intrusion, Fielding ponders, 'It was as if irritation exuded from the very soil. Could one have been so petty on a Scottish moor or an Italian alp?'[170] At this level, if we set aside Fielding's liberal refinements, he is not all that different from McBryde, the police superintendent, who says:

> All unfortunate natives are criminal at heart, for the simple reason that they live south of the latitude 30. They are not to blame, they have not a dog's chance – we should be like them if we settled here.[171]

Fielding returns from India without having travelled: the *same* returns to the *same*, because his return only confirms the old boundary under whose shadow he ventured out. He came to India folded in the Mediterranean waters and returns only to be re-folded in them again. It is along the Mediterranean waters that Forster locates the threshold of primary division – the proper site for the eternal disjunction between the 'Orient' and the 'Occident'. It is also the originary site of the binary relationship of values – the difference of order and disorder that the higher and the lower grounds of Chandrapore repeat.

On his return journey, reclaimed by these Mediterranean waters, Fielding re-confirms the rigid boundary between the 'Occident' and the 'Orient'. It also confirms, despite his long sojourn in India, his inability to cross the boundary. Face to face once more with the originary threshold that separates him from India, Fielding rediscovers 'the joy of form'.[72] Following this well-worn epiphany the relationship between two spatial orders – between the 'Occident' and the 'Orient' – comes to be expressed in the oppositional values of form and formlessness. Lost in the rupture of the moment, Fielding remembers what he has never forgotten:

> The building of Venice ... stood in the right place, whereas in poor India everything was placed wrong. He had forgotten the beauty of form among idol temples and lumpy hills; indeed, without form, how can there be beauty? ... now, the joys of form, and that this constituted a serious barrier.[73]

In the rediscovery of the joy of form, Fielding rediscovers the proper threshold that eternally separates the 'Occident' from the 'Orient'. How can it be traversed since nature and space have marked them apart? Forever faithful to the originary mark of separation, Fielding, in the ecstasy of form, returns to the fold of the same. His has been a truly Hegelian or sedentary voyage. In the denouement of *A Passage to India*, Fielding's blocked passage is explained more by the logic of spatial/natural boundary than by the colonial inscription of difference. He could not traverse the line and come closer to Aziz, because 'the horses didn't want it – they swerved apart; the earth didn't want it, sending up rocks through which riders must pass single file'.[74]

Miss Adela Quested's inability to yield herself to the passage to India takes on a rather tortuous route. Not yet completely coded by the logic of the two-cities-under-one-sky, Adela in her innocence wants to step out of the colonial city 'to see real India'.[75] It proves to be fatal, because, despite its innocence, Adela's desire brings a tremor to the primary boundary marked by the Mediterranean waters. *A Passage to India* again and again repeats the refrain: the primary boundary between the 'Occident' and the 'Orient' cannot and must not be crossed.

There are three kinds of truth about India in the novel. First: the received wisdoms of the colonial city, which are based on the kind of truth implied by the lady in the club when she claims: 'I really do know the truth about Indians'.[76] The truth of this claim amounts to no more than the gross stereotypical knowledge of the natives and how to treat them. It is the kind of truth to which the likes of Callendar or McBryde subscribe, and which Forster endeavours to undermine through ironical exposure.

Second: there is the apparently objective truth to which the narrator's own voice gives expression. This kind of truth is grounded in the logic of primary division – the essential difference between the 'Orient' and the 'Occident' marked by the Mediterranean waters. The authority of this kind of truth establishes a series of oppositional relations – order/disorder, form/formlessness – between the 'Occident' and 'Orient'. Having set this opposition in place, the authority of this kind of truth produces generalised knowledge about 'Orientals'. For instance, the narrator's typification of Aziz's behaviour as typical 'Oriental': 'Like most Orientals, Aziz overrated hospitality, mistaking it for intimacy, and not seeing that it is tainted with the sense of possession'.[77]

Third: there is the truth of the inscrutable truth. Like the second category of truth, it is drawn from the inference of the primary division – the eternal separation between the 'Orient' and the 'Occident'. However, unlike the second category of truth, it takes the implication of the primary division to its logical conclusion. Incidentally, the authority of the second category of truth falls victim to the logic of its own inscrutable truth: it claims to know what its own logic of primary division says it cannot know. These kinds of profound, yet unwitting, self-ironic, self-destructive moments abound in colonial narrative.

The truth of the inscrutable truth issues from the figuration of India as the site of absolute otherness. Its orientalness, as we have already noted, is troped in terms of spatial and natural difference. By resonating an antinomical lore of other nature, India (as a part of 'Orient') surrounds itself with a thick wall that no 'Occidental' can traverse. It is the outside proper, of which no 'Occidental' can have any knowledge – an India that would never come, because it is 'never defined'[78] and remains undefinable.

Yet India does call '"come" through her hundred mouths, through objects ridiculous and august'.[179] It is an appeal from the inscrutable other. But the primary boundary of the Mediterranean waters and the secondary boundary of the colonial city are precisely in place, with all their rigidity, to muffle this appeal from the outside.

Miss Adela Quested's desire to see 'real India' takes her to the threshold of the third kind of truth. It opens her up, if only momentarily, to the outside; and we see her poised precariously at the threshold of becoming-traveller. Unfortunately, Adela is not ready for it; and things come to a head in the celebrated incident in the Marabar caves. Before we can see how this drama of the colonial encounter unfolds, we must ask: what are the Marabar caves? They are, for sure, more than just a giant granite structure with holes in it. Yet, they are neither purely symbolic nor incorporeal. They are the very depth of the corporeal mass of immemorial India. When we read the Marabar caves being described as 'Before time, it was before space also,'[180] the allusion does not point to the onto-theological moment of genesis. Yet it is obvious that we are directed to imagine a time beyond the metronomic time of common sense and a space beyond the *extensio* of representation. Here, in fact, we have the implicated time and space of geological sedimentation. Forster at the beginning of the 'Caves' chapter makes it abundantly clear:

> Geology looking further than religion, knows of a time when neither the river nor the Himalayas that nourish it existed, and an ocean flowed over the holy places of Hindustan ... and the India we call immemorial came into being.[181]

The Marabar caves are the living bodies of the aeon of geological formation. Conceived in this way, they lend themselves to be used as a microcosm of India's radical otherness, formulated through the tropes of spatial and natural difference. In fact, the caves are made to function as the fold of difference: they envelop the geographical difference marked at the Mediterranean threshold within the aeon of geological formation. Hence, the caves come to stand as the matrix of primary difference between the 'Occident' and the 'Orient'. They are symptomatic sites of 'Orient'/India's absolute natural and spatial otherness. It is, therefore, no wonder that they, in their dark, resonating cavities, give the purest expression to the third kind of truth: the inscrutable truth of non-knowledge. They escape the spaces of representation. The infamy of their reputation, as Forster explains, 'does not depend upon human speech'.[182] Inscrutably folded in their

dark interior, the caves offer the visitors only the murmurs of their
bodies – the terrifying echoes – the eternal repetition of boum, bou-
oum, ou-boum. Adela's quest to get to know 'real India', her move
into the outside, takes her face to face with the inscrutable truth of
the caves. In themselves, as Forster tells us, there is nothing extraordinary or terrifying about the caves – only the dull monotony of
circular chambers. Yet they affect Adela in such an extraordinary
manner that it defies any adequate explanation.

We have seen that Forster's narrative imbricates the truth of the
inscrutable truth of the caves, albeit as a limit case, with the truth of
primary difference that divides the 'Occident' from the 'Orient'. Yet
this truth breaks down the very binary division to which it is meant to
bear witness. We must not forget that the truth of binary difference,
grounded in analogy and resemblance, cannot subsist without an
epistemological plane and a representational frame. For the truth of
the cave is a truth that cannot be known: it exceeds the representational order of good sense. Here we descend to the metastable depth:
the groundless grounds of *spatium* and the timeless time of the aeon
(Greek *aion* – eternity).[183] Being restored to their essence – to their
non-sensical force of repetition – the caves undo the order of knowledge and representation. Thereby they overcome the boundary
marked by the Mediterranean waters.

Between Adela and the cave there no longer rises up the barrier
that eternally cuts her off from the 'Orient' (India). Like Alice's mirror,
the granite solidity of the caves become 'pure surface', opening passages for her to travel and encounter the other. By lifting the barrier
the inscrutable caves release the forces of eternal repetition – the
forces of self-difference and becoming-other. The only thing Adela
has to do is to say 'yes', and she will be zooming through the passage
or climbing the mountain like Zarathustra or becoming a Red Indian like Kafka. At the threshold of her venture, outside the colonial
city and the 'Occidental' inside, she cannot muster force enough for the
final move. Instead, she asks Aziz a silly question: 'Have you one wife
or more than one?'[184] It brings back both the secondary boundary of
the colonial city (crude stereotype – they have so many wives) and the
primary boundary of the Mediterranean waters (he is an 'Oriental' –
it is his nature). Obviously, the question speaks Adela's desire for Aziz,
but it is a Hegelian desire of the *same* tracing its own passion and
returning to the *same*. It has nothing to do with the affirmative desire
for the other – saying 'yes' to the other – going to the other in a
movement of self-difference without wanting to return to the *same*.

Then it all happens: Adela rushes out of the cave and rolls down-hill covered in thorns. Later, she will call it her 'hallucination'. The narrator prefers to call it 'hysteria'. But we know that it is an alleged case of rape. Whatever may have happened, the violence of the event is undeniable. We can understand the violence as a collision of forces – the forces of the inside and the outside at a moment of their, as Spinoza would say, sad and poisonous encounter. The caves, by erasing the boundary, unleash the forces of becoming-other. If Adela had said 'yes' to it, she would have been carried along the 'smooth surface' of the passage to the other side. Unable to do so, because she, like Guela, could not forget the memories of the inside, she is re-claimed by the rigid boundary and folded back into the inside. Later, in her 'double relation' to the event Adela comes to recognise her unpreparedness: 'All the things I thought I'd learned are just a hindrance, there're not knowledge at all'.[185] But it is too late. She had already felt the full impact of the collision: the violence of the sudden placement of the wall before the speed that cleaved the passage outside. It is a very sad and poisonous encounter. It is best described as a case of Manichaean malady. One of its symptoms shows a lapse into an extreme form of *ressentiment*, and a fantasy of vengeance. He raped me; he ought to be punished.

From the very threshold of the outside Adela returns to the fold. And we find her, like Fielding, by the Mediterranean waters – the thick wall that eternally divides the 'Occident' from the 'Orient'. Under the shadow of Lesseps' statue, a missionary asks her if she is returning home after a taste of the tropics. He re-phrases his question: 'Observe, I don't say to what do you turn, but to what do you *re*-turn'.[186] And adds: 'He turns to the East, he re-turns to the West'.[187] To this Adela says: 'I see', while looking at the 'Mediterranean clarity'. Her venture into India, despite being so close to a 'passage', has been a Hegelian journey: the *same re*-turns to the *same*. And the primary opposition between the 'Occident' and the 'Orient' is reaffirmed once more. How can she be a traveller under such an enduring Manichaean logic?

Only Mrs Moore, in the very simplicity of her approach, crosses the line and encounters the other. Unlike the high drama of the cave scene, this happens so untheatrically that it almost escapes our attention. It is at the mosque in the moonlight. Aziz, escaping the humiliation of colonial protocol, takes refuge in its serene inside. Forbidden to outsiders, it is the most native of the native cities. Natu-rally, Aziz feels completely at home. Then, quite unexpectedly, from the gloom appears the figure of an Englishwoman. It is Mrs Moore. Unusually for a member of the 'master race', she has taken her shoes off and quietly slipped into the mosque – a space, in terms of Manichaean logic, which stands inimical to the club whence she came. She makes the journey from the club to the mosque as if carried along the smoothest of smooth passages, as if the barrier between the two cities has melted, as if she has long forgotten the memories of the Mediterranean waters. She enters the mosque and takes it for what it is – a place of god. It is so near, yet so far, but not rent by the Manichaean machination.

Inside the mosque she takes Aziz as another summoned by the serene beauty of the mosque in the moonlight. He is neither fixed as a native nor as an 'Oriental'. She encounters him without the insistent memories of the boundaries: it is a meeting without pre-condition. Hence, Mrs Moore's passage into the mosque is the genuine passage of a traveller. It is also the only moment of encounter with the other without the paranoia of othering. Aziz is surprised, and says, 'the way you address me'.[188] Along with the evaporation of boundaries, goes the old mode of address: she is no longer addressing as a coloniser to a colonised. Aziz knows that Mrs Moore has traversed the line and touched him in joyous encounter, and that she has become other. He tells her: 'then you are an Oriental'.[189] She will have a new name, too: Esmiss Esmoor.

While Adela – facing the otherness of the cave and the eternal repetition of the 'boum, bou-oum, ou-boum' – folds back behind the barrier, becoming a victim of Manichaean malady, Mrs Moore takes it as an encounter with the infinity of the other. No doubt Mrs Moore is violently shaken by the tremors. Yet the violence of these tremors does not issue from the sudden invocation of the Manichaean boundary but from the force of being put under question, from the breakdown of her subjectivity moulded by the colonial city, and of being affected by the eruption that flattens the boundary between inside and outside. Vileness and poetry and the divine words, 'Let there be light'[190] amount to the same thing: 'boum'. In the process, she is bereft of any exclusive distinction, of any traces of boundary, of any power of representation. Yet the tremors that unform Mrs Moore also provide her with the suppleness needed to slip through the boundary; they open her up to the outside – and she becomes a traveller.

The Manichaean boundary, vengeful by nature, would not forgive her for that. She has broken through it, and violated its laws. She has touched the other, and cannot come back alive. Only sedentary voyagers, journeying through the Hegelian route, can return to the fold. On her way back to England, the primary boundary of the Mediterranean waters that eternally divide the 'Occident' from the 'Orient' lies in wait for her. It will rise up like a gorgon to strike her stone-dead with its avenging gaze. This is how Forster puts it:

> Somewhere about Suez there is always a social change: the arrangements of Asia weaken and those of Europe begin to be felt, and during the transition Mrs Moore was shaken off.[191]

She dies immediately. Does the narrative, after everything is said and done, want to reconfirm the Manichaean division: East is East, West, West – that the boundary between them must not be crossed? Forster's critique of colonialism is at least grounded on this position. Yet we know this is precisely the position which played such a central role in the self-legitimation of colonial governance. Or can we read in it that the rigid boundaries can never maintain their absolute impenetrability, they can always be breached, though the task is not an easy one, because the Manichaean order will stalk you with vengeful eyes?

The rigid and the supple lines of travellers

The geographer John Kirkland Wright observes that the Sirens' voices, with their promise of the alluring charm of *terrae incognitae*, have always laid a poetic spell on men. The call of other places has incited men to journeys beyond the limits of their horizon. Yet all journeys are not the same. Wright explains:

> The Sirens, of course, sing of different things to different folk, some they tempt with material rewards; gold, furs, ivory, petroleum, land to settle and exploit. Some they allure with the prospect of scientific discovery. Others they call to adventure and escape. Geographers they invite to map.[192]

Each object of quest defines a traveller: there are as many travellers as there are objects. They do not all travel the same route: there are as many routes as there are travellers. A commercial traveller might take the same track as a pilgrim but they would be travelling along different routes. But despite so many routes, there are only two lines of travel: the rigid and the supple lines. These two establish the qualitative difference between travellers: either one is a sedentary traveller or one is a nomadic traveller. It is not the types of movement that set them apart, rather the difference lies between movement and speed. Obviously, a commercial traveller, a geographer or a conquistador moves in space, arrives at a different place. Yet bound by the pre-set goals they never leave the point of departure: they move folded in the inside. They might travel in the fastest possible vehicle and cover a thousand miles yet they remain where they are, because they are on a rigid line which keeps them grounded in the enclosure of their home. Despite so many rituals of departure, they cannot really depart. For that, they would need the intensity of speed, since speed is the secret of the supple line of the nomadic traveller. It is not an easy task, for it is a question of becoming: 'Voyaging smoothly [supple line] is a becoming, and a difficult, uncertain becoming at that'.[193] The two lines are a rough sketch of the lines drawn by Deleuze and Guattari.

The lines of travel do not exist in isolation; they are imbricated in complex configurations. To each line of travel corresponds a particular conception of space, a particular type of boundary, a particular arrangement of power, a particular semiotic order, a particular organisation of things, and a particular mode of subjectivity. It is the weight of their aggregate effects that defines the line of a traveller. From the rigid space of geometricism, the rigid boundary of binarism, the rigid mould of subjectivism and the rigid (central) perspective of representation will emerge only a rigid line of travel. On the other hand, the supple line of travel presupposes the pre-geometric space that Heidegger's ontology reveals, the transitory boundaries of fluctuating performances, the non-binary difference of self-difference, the non-subjective individuation of the molecular, and the non-representational moments of encounter. This is Deleuze and Guattari's smooth space – the space of affects, which is more: 'Intense *Spatium* than *Extensio*'.[194]

So far I have attempted a series of interplays of these lines to explicate the grounds that immobilise a traveller and the groundless ground that enables a traveller to gather the speed to move elsewhere. My first aim, with the help of Heidegger, Bachelard and Merleau-Ponty, has been to establish, against the epistemological tradition, an alternative ontology of space, boundary and difference. We have seen that Heidegger's notion of dwelling as a non-foundational and transitory mode of habitation is not contrary to travelling. In fact, the very space of dwelling, through the fracturing of representational space, enables travel to take place. The supple space of region (*Gegend*), with its provisionality, multiplicity, and micro-locality, is both a space of dwelling and a traveller's supple line. If we prune Heidegger's region (*Gegend*) of its metaphysical excess, of its flirtation with the authentic presence of Being (*Das Sein des Seienden*), then we have a *Heterotopic* space where the fold of the outside offers passage to a nomadic traveller. Here, the neat distinction between dwelling and travel disappears. In fact, for a nomad, as Deleuze and Guattari put it, 'The dwelling is subordinated to the journey; inside space conforms to outside space'.[195] Only in the supple space can the speed of travel be gathered against the sedentary movement of a mere change of location.

Two kinds of space: striated (*extensio, strata*) and smooth (*spatium, metastrata*). Two lines of travel: rigid (inside) and supple (outside). Two kinds of travellers: sedentary and nomadic. Two fundamental attributes of travellers: movement (departure and arrival) and speed (intensity, plane of consistency, body without organ). Two secondary attributes: dimension (points, gravity, immobility) and direction (trajectory, flight). Two kinds of individuation: molar (subjectivity, black hole, faciality) and molecular (haecceities, unformed matter). Two orientations: representation (centred perspective, white wall, reterritorialisation, coding, root tree, *mots d'ordre*) and encounter (multiplicity, deterritorialisation, performance, chance, event, decoding, abstract machine, diagram, rhizome, becoming).

This proliferating series of doubles articulates some of the configurations of the rigid and supple lines as they appear in Deleuze and Guattari's *A Thousand Plateaus*. These apparently binary divisions, following Bergson's intuitive methodology, are Deleuze and Guattari's way of establishing pure differences in kind through transcendental analysis. But in fact they are composite. As Gilles Deleuze's comments on the Bergsonian practice of splitting suggest: 'composite represents the fact, it must be divided into tendencies or into pure presences that only exist *in principle (en droit)*'.[196] The kind of transcendental analysis Deleuze attributes to Bergson, and which he himself practises, does not lead to Kantian idealism. Instead, it is given to empirical specificities without the overarching syntheses of the legislative faculty:

> this going-beyond does not consist in going beyond experience toward concepts. For concepts only define, in the Kantian manner, the condition of all possible experience in general. Here, on the other hand, it is a case of real experience in all its peculiarities. [197]

Pure differences in kind only express directions and tendencies; they are virtual moments. In practice, they are not divided by a thick wall (binarism), but unfold on a singular plane in an active process of actualisation:

> Smooth space and striated space – nomad space and sedentary space ... And no sooner have we done that than we must remind ourselves that the two spaces in fact exist only in mixture: smooth space is constantly being translated, traversed into a striated space; striated space is constantly being reversed, overturned to a smooth space.[198]

The form into which actualised events are moulded may, in the process of being captured by various social powers, acquire a striated fixity and a rigid line, but the force of the virtual still throbs under their surfaces. Following Bergson's virtual force of creative evolution (internal difference), Spinoza's singular and univocal force of explication (difference in itself), Nietzsche's self-affirmative force of becoming, and Freud's libidinal force (*Thanatos*) as the ground-less ground of repetition,[199] Deleuze and Guattari develop a positive ontology. They call the pure and the virtual moment of this ontology the plane of consistency or the body without organs – a moment composed of unformed matter and pure intensities. The plane of consistency or the body without organs, characterised by the speed of deterritorialisation, destratification and decoding, knows only intensive affects (Spinoza's body, which Deleuze and Guattari call Longitude and Latitude). And the line of flight is its highest form of expression. Besides, it is the creative force of all entities, a complication of unformed matter in the *metastratum* which explicates or gives expression to the actual. The actual acquires rigidity by being formed into stable entities as a result of various forms of capture. Hence, even the rigid line or the striated space needs this force for 'propagation, extension, refraction, renewal, and ... without which it would perhaps die of its own accord'.[200]

Now we can see that rigid and supple lines, striated and smooth spaces, sedentary and nomadic travellers, and their corresponding attributes – movement and speed – are not mutually exclusive in actuality; rather they are the virtual tendencies or, as Deleuze and Guattari would say, of abstract machines: 'Voyage smoothly or in striation ... But there are always passages from one to the other, transformation of one within the others, reversals'.[201]

Living in a striated space one is enclosed by a rigid line; therefore, one can only become a sedentary traveller. A traveller, densely coded in a striated regime, moves folded in his home-made codes –

like travelling in Noah's ark. For 'the ark is no more than a little portable packet of signs'.[202] On this line of travel, one's territory moves with one's body: the 'moved body', as Deleuze and Guattari say, that serves as a 'portable territory' – 'the house of the tortoise, the hermitage of the crab'.[203] The travelling of a 'moved body' on a rigid line amounts to no more than a movement between fixed points: departure and arrival between fixed locations. The 'portable territory' guards against the speed and the intensity of the molecular and the chaos of the outside. For a 'point is always a point of origin'.[204] It serves as a force of gravity – pulling the 'moved body' towards its centrifugal direction, so that in the passage between points the 'moved body' does not become a 'moving body' and take flight to the outside, to the other. So the points and the pull of gravity are the essence of movement – the mode in which a sedentary traveller travels between fixed points in her/his 'portable territory'. The 'portable territory' guards the molarity of the molar subject as s/he moves between points in space, and dutifully carries for her/him the codes of faciality (white wall = communicative signification + black hole = subjective consciousness) so that s/he can become a subject of representation. Remaining the *same* in the 'portable territory' the immobile traveller finds a fixed perspective to centre her/his subjectivity and to gaze down upon the visual space rather than experience the intensity of speed. As a subject of representation, s/he traces a geographical map, rather than composes a performative map of intensities.[205] On the rigid line, the coded subject of representation likes nothing better than to overcode the point in space at which s/he arrives at the end of her/his journey. Her/his refrain has none of the intensity of music. It is only given to the expressive tone of signifying repetition, which returns to territorialise and reterritorialise in order to establish points in accord with the laws of gravity. The following quotation from Wilson Harris's *The Four Banks of the River of Space* is a good example of refrain as expressive line of territorialisation in the colonial travels of conquest: 'the Shadows Ross's predecessors [the colonial map-makers of the world – from botanists to cartographers] had borne in their heads and arms when they left Europe, Shadows of classical lore with which to christen orchids and flowers'.[206]

Unfortunately, it is on the rigid line that travel as a genre is located. Yet, as we have seen, the rigid and the supple lines are not mutually exclusive: they are intertwined in actuality and exist on the same plane of immanence. In fact, in the movement between the points, the speed of the supple line haunts the rigid line of travel. Hence travel literature, despite its rigidity, despite its infinite games of chess, cannot always guard against the intensity of the supple line, the musical refrain of eternal repetition, and the game of 'Go'.[207]

Before we expound the pragmatic rules of movement – the rules governing travel as a particular genre that represents movement from one spatial point to another – we should remind ourselves of the composition of the supple line of a traveller. As against mere movement between points, the primary attribute of the supple line is speed (intensity). Here, one goes through the points rather than from one point to another. Of course, no one can go through the points with a molar or 'moved body'. What is required is a 'moving body' that recovers its metastratal functions, as defined by Spinoza: what can a body do? This question presupposes the composition of the body in terms of speed and slowness, its capacity to affect other bodies and be affected by other bodies. The celerity of the 'moving body' pulls it away from the point and from its gravitational force, thus becoming a true or nomadic traveller. 'Every Voyage is intensive, and occurs in relation to thresholds of intensity between which it evolves or that it crosses. One travels by intensity'.[208]

The supple line does not possess the dimension or the border of a territory. Hence, on this line one does not reterritorialise, nor does one mark space with an expressive refrain or signify in accordance with the codes of faciality. It breaks boundaries and creates passage. We can get an intimation of this line from the novels of Wilson Harris, who in *The Infinite Rehearsal* writes: '[it] secretes a corridor or passageway through every wave and overturning of rigid expectation'.[209] It is a line of direction that ultimately takes one beyond the threshold, to the line of flight, towards becoming-other. It has no beginning nor any end – only the circulation in the middle, dwelling in the multiplicity of the in-between, given to the event, chance and encounter. Travelling on the supple line, as Deleuze and Guattari say, is:

> another way of travelling and moving: proceeding from the middle, through the middle, coming and going rather than starting and finishing ... The middle is by no means an average; on the contrary, it is where things pick up speed. *Between* things does not designate a localizable relation going from one thing to the other and back again, but a perpendicular direction, a traversal movement that sweeps one *and* the other away, a stream without beginning or end that undermines its banks and picks up speed in the middle.[210]

This is the line, following Nietzsche's eternal repetition, Wilson Harris calls infinite rehearsal. All arrivals and departures amount to the same thing: not the return of the *same* but the affirmative return of a dice-throw so that the movement of self-difference is repeated all over again to infinity. Wilson Harris, in a truly rhythmic refrain, articulates this in the double movement (departure and arrival) of the double (Robin and W.H):

> When Robin set sail I[W.H] returned to the sea whence I had come. I am the ghostly voyager in time, in space, in memory, but always I return to the vast ocean, the rolling seas and the great deeps.[211]

The pragmatic rules of movement

In this section I want to trace the pragmatic rules of the formation of the rigid line. In other words, I want to trace the pragmatic rules that constitute travel as a particular genre of literature.

In general, it is the movement between points in space that is taken as the essential trait of travel as a genre. There is a point of beginning, which is also the point of origin, from which a traveller takes her/his leave. S/he departs the spatial fold that marks her/his horizon and arrives at somewhere beyond. The point of departure and the point of destination constitute the movement from the location of the inside, or the site of origin, to the location of the outside or the site of difference. What this movement constitutes is precisely the Manichaean poles of home and non-home, or the *same* and the other. Between these two poles lies the boundary or the threshold of difference that a traveller must cross in order to effectuate the movement from one to the other. Yet, just as there are as many travellers as there are routes, so there are as many homes/non-homes or the boundaries between them as there are travellers. The parameter of the home is conditional upon the kind of journey a traveller wants to make. If, for instance, a traveller ventures into an adjacent province within her/his own country, and wishes to apprehend the space of her/his arrival in terms of the generality of a provincial reality, then the province of departure will serve as a point of origin or the parameter of home. S/he will, therefore, take her/his rightful place among 'provincial' travellers. Similarly, a traveller from one nation-state to another will be a 'state' traveller. And a traveller from a continent to another continent will be a 'continental' traveller.

Most cross-cultural travellers in post-Enlightenment Europe have been 'continental' travellers. You are a Frenchman/woman when you are in Italy, but you are European while in India. This seems rather odd, since you do not cease to be a French man/ woman. Indeed, you are very proud of your Frenchness, and even dislike Italians, Germans, or, for that matter, all other Europeans. You are not a fool, either: you know you have arrived in India. Surely, you are discerning enough to see the difference between India and China. Yet you have become a 'continental' traveller. How is this possible? Aren't you playing the strange game of the circle within a circle, devising a Chinese box in which you put boxes within boxes, or are you simply making use of the rhetorical magic of synecdoche? Of course you remain a Frenchman/woman, but your Frenchness now comes to stand, like a sail for a boat, for the continental expanse of Europe. Similarly, India still remains India, while giving its own fragment of a body to stand for the full body of the 'Orient'. It is on the plane of a conceptual symmetry that the points of movement are located.

Yet the frame of the home is not shaped by the point of departure but by the point of arrival. In other words, the kind of home you will have depends on where you are going. If your movement aims at another continent, then you will have a continent for a home. Similarly, the borderline will be set by the kind of other place you wish to arrive at. Yet the question of boundary is a good deal more complex than this. It is not simply a matter of saying that at a designated geographical point lies the boundary – for one thing, as we have seen, boundaries are neither natural nor substantial. It is not geographical lines that decide boundaries. Rather, geographical lines are assigned to space on the basis of complex discourses of difference. For instance, the simple evaluation of familiarity/unfamiliarity might serve as the practical logic of difference, in this case, the borderline will be inscribed at the limit of one's own horizon of familiarity.

There are as many boundaries as there are travellers. Each traveller, depending on the kind of difference, or the point of arrival, s/he sets as the telos of her/his undertaking, will construct her/his own border in the process of movement. The marking of spatial boundaries is secondary to the discourse of difference that a traveller wants to enact. If s/he is looking for 'savages', then the borderline, worked through with conceptual symmetry, will be placed at the limit of 'civilisation'. The spatial boundary between them will be marked by the doubling of the analogous difference fashioned in the discursive orbit.

There are some boundaries, such as the ones that exist between states, that seem to offer a ready-made threshold of difference. But does the boundary of a traveller coincide with the line of separation between two territories? Before we answer this question, let us take a detour through the territorial formations of modern and pre-modern powers.

It is generally accepted that the homogenous spatial boundary is only of recent invention, its origin lying in the territorial conception of sovereignty that emerged with the nation-state. Since the space of the nation is seen as the arch-subject that endows its inhabitants with their individuality, its identity must be secured by a clear and continuous demarcation line from the adjacent spaces of other nations. Both empirical geography and the abstract figures of geometry served as the technology for securing both the homogeneity and the transparent identity of the space of the nation. Empirical geography meticulously surveyed the territory of the nation so that its full body – which serves as the point of subjection for its national subjects – was knowable, with all of its contours clearly marked out. As a complement to geographical surveys, geometry represented the empirical body of the nation on the abstract grid of the map. But one irony of this was the production of the homogenous empty space of a nation. Perhaps it is for this reason that the map of a nation needs a permanent theatre of cruelty, so that its incorporeal body, in the rituals of blood, can impose a sense of solidity.

In pre-modern territorial formations, on the other hand, the homogenous conception of a spatial extension was not necessary. This was the case because it was the personal body of the monarch which served as the principal of sovereignty, and acted as a point of subjection for the subjects rather than space. Consequently, it was not important to have a homogenous territory. Hence the territorial formations of pre-modern powers were zonal: an ensemble of enclaves, often discontinuous, defined the domain of a particular sovereignty.[212] It was the resonance of the sovereign body and the relay of his power that bound the space of an empire into a unity. The spatial boundary was simply located at the limit to which the resonance of the sovereign's power could reach.

Since in pre-modern territorial formations the borderline was not continuously marked, the threshold of difference that a traveller placed could hardly be that of a neat geographical borderline. However, this does not mean to say that s/he did not demarcate a spatial line of difference. Rather, the spatial line was marked as a secondary effect of the discourse of difference. A traveller might want to arrive at the empire of the Great Khan, as Marco Polo once did. In this case, a discourse of difference taking an exotic sovereign body as its object, and mapping the territorial extent of its power would mark the borderline between the *same* and the other. Here, a traveller would not construct a geographical boundary by crossing a spatial line. Rather it was the other way round: the geographic boundary was drawn at the discursive disjunction between two oppositional sovereignties.

Since the nation-state has a continuous boundary, does the line of difference for a 'state' traveller lie at the meeting-point between the territories of two states? My answer to it would be the same as what we have argued in the case of a pre-modern traveller. Besides the ambiguities of the territorial meeting-points, for which the term 'frontier' is often used, the spatial line of separation is marked, as before, in the discursive space. It is by claiming to witness the 'peculiarities' of the French that the spatial boundary between Germany (if the traveller is German) and France is established. Even if the German traveller is not interested in the 'peculiarities' of French manners and customs, the very invocation of a different sovereign body will mark the territorial border between them.

Now we must ask ourselves how the movement between points in space takes place? In other words, how a traveller manages to travel from one place to another, and more importantly, how s/he crosses boundaries?

It is worth remembering Zeno's paradox: the flight of the arrow is always static. If any measurement of any one point of the arrow's flight is taken, the dimension of space is found to be equivalent to the extension of the arrow's body. We never apprehend a 'moving arrow' but only a 'moved arrow' from point to point. The arrow does not go through the between, it simply stays at one point, then at the next point and so on. Hence the moved arrow, like any 'moved body', is always static. One can only go through a point, as we have learnt from Deleuze and Guattari, by unforming a 'moved body' into a 'moving body'. In other words, one can only go through the points in a flight of speed and pure affectivity. If this happens, the body in question not only crosses the boundary, it also erases, in the process, the points and the boundary between them. Moreover, the speed and the affectivity of the 'moving body' takes place at a level that remains anterior to the apparatus of capture – beyond measurement and representation.

Now, again: how does the 'moved body' move from point to point in space? In other words, how does it remain static yet jump from point to point? The passage between the points is both a temporal process and a performative act; it is where the 'moving body' performs the aleatoric event in the flux of time. Not the linear time of the *chronos*, where discreet moments unfold in a contiguous sequence. The time of *chronos* (metronomic time) and the space of points (dimension or extension) are really the same thing: disjunctive units with rigid boundaries around them. One cannot pass through a metronomic moment in time any more than one can pass through a dimensional point in space: either one can be at a point A (or moment A) or at a point B (or moment B). No passage is possible here, except by a miraculous jump across the chasm between the points or moments.

There is another type of time: the time of infinity that Deleuze calls '*aion*'. This conception of time owes its origin to Bergson's concept of duration (both as a virtual ontological moment and as an actual apprehension of time) and to Nietzsche's eternal return. The virtual duration, as Deleuze's study on Bergson shows, 'is an internal multiplicity of succession, of fusion ... of *difference in kind*'.[213] This is the time of 'uninterrupted change' where 'transition is continuous'; it is a continuity unbroken by the discreet point of time (*chronos*) and space (*extensio*); and it is described by Bergson as 'a gentle slope'.[214] The virtual duration goes through the points in a continuous process of becoming; it is the slope of passage. How does the virtual duration becomes actual or present? In *Creative Evolution* Bergson provides us with the answer:

> For our duration is not merely one instant replacing another; if it were, there would never be anything but the present – no prolonging of the past into the actual, no evolution, no concrete duration. Duration is the continuous progress of the past which gnaws into the future and which swells as it advances.[215]

The virtual duration is actualised or made present through a double movement: one movement expands towards the past, the other contracts towards the future. The present, therefore, does not cease to pass, but only passes through the past. On the one hand, it is always some thing that *has been* – something that has just happened; on the other hand, it is something about to happen – in the process of becoming. Therefore, the present is empty. Gilles Deleuze, in *The Logic of Sense*, sums up this complex configuration of duration:

the present which spreads out and comprehends the future and the past, an unlimited past-future rises up here reflected in an empty present which has no more thickness than the mirror.[216]

The 'empty present' does not mean that it is not real. What it simply means is that the present cannot be made into a presence in the space of representation; it does not have the density of dimension or points. For that, the present needs to be neatly segmented from the point or moment before and after. The present duration, as the actualisation of the virtual duration, is the real of the event itself. In its vanishing moment, the force of the virtual duration, as the internal process of self-difference that maintains an uninterrupted continuity, comes to be repeated. The fact that the present as event cannot be represented does not at all mean that it cannot be sensed. Indeed, it is sense itself with all of its immanent force and speed – the intensive ripples of the power of what has happened and becoming. The present as event appears in the space of representation as phantasm, simulacrum, paradox, non-sense, etc. But it never stops to exude the intensity of speed which representation, by marking points, endeavours to contain. The present as event is the force of the real in which one can only act or be acted upon. Since it has neither the fixity of points nor the dimensionality of representation, it opens the smooth passage of the mirror through which one can pass as Alice once did.

The present as event is also the eternal repetition as Nietzsche conceived it. It is the aleatoric moment of the dice-throw: something that happens only once and is repeated so that it will happen only once to infinity. Hence, it is the affirmation of the force of becoming: 'Return is the being of that which becomes. Return is the being of becoming itself, the being which is affirmed in becoming'.[217]

The time of the passage is the time of the event: the chanced repetitive becoming of the eternal return and the virtual present of the moving duration. Since the time of the event unfolds at metastratal level, the distinction between time and space disappears. Space as unformed matter, *physis* and *spatium*, exists on a singular plane as the time of virtual duration and eternal return. Without this continuum, a 'moving body' cannot slide into the passage to continue moving, passage, as we have seen, which lies between the points, between arrival and departure. But a traveller intent on moving from point to point does not avail her/himself of such a passage. How, then, does s/he move from one point to another?

In the prologue to *The Divine Comedy* we see Dante already half-way along the road. He is about to cross the threshold and enter the circle of the Inferno. How does he cross the threshold?

> Half way along the road we have to go,
> I found myself obscured in a great forest,
> Bewildered, and I knew I had lost the way.
>
> It is hard to say just what the forest was like,
> How wild and rough it was, how overpowering;
> Even to remember it makes me afraid.
>
> I cannot tell exactly how I got there,
> I was so full of sleep at that point of my journey
> When, somehow, I left the proper way.[218]

Since the forest marks the threshold, its crossing enables Dante to reach the other side. Yet this passage as an event of crossing cannot itself be represented. All Dante could say about the passage is his overpowering experience of disorientation. Of the forest, the space of the passage, and the durational movement across it, Dante cannot say anything. Only the experience of disorientation remains as the trace of the intensive force of duration that the 'moving body' endures in the course of the passage. Strangely, this is the sign of the supple line that expresses the real event of the travel.

In so far as the movement from point to point is concerned, Dante simply makes a miraculous jump from the location before the forest (point of departure) to a location after the forest (point of arrival). The 'moved body' can only move from one point to another by means of an ellipsis of the passage in-between. Michel de Certeau, following Augoyard, expresses the traveller's movement by means of ellipsis in terms of the stylistic figure of asyndeton:

> Asyndeton is the suppression of linking words such as conjunctions and adverbs, either within a sentence or between sentences. In the same way in walking it selects and fragments the space traversed; it skips over links and whole parts that it omits. From this point of view, every walk constantly leaps, or skips like a child, hopping on one foot. It practices the ellipsis of conjunctive loci.[219]

If a traveller moves between points by ellipsis, how does s/he indicate that s/he has crossed a threshold? Does s/he do this by merely announcing her/his arrival in another place? But how do we know that it is another place? Simply, the answer must be that it is by repeating a discourse of the other that the traveller announces her/his arrival in another place. A traveller might make a long and difficult journey to arrive in Calcutta, but it is only by announcing the difference in discourse that s/he could signal her/his crossing of the boundary. For instance, Lévi-Strauss signals his arrival in Calcutta by cataloguing a series of qualities that supposedly constitute its 'natural environment': 'filth, chaos, promiscuity, congestion; ruins, huts, mud, dirt; dung, urine, pus, humours, secretions and running sores'.[220] Since a traveller cannot really move from point to point except through ellipsis, s/he creates her/his passage by means of the discourse of difference. Hence, a traveller who moves in gridded space can only move in a discursive space by articulating difference. By placing Calcutta in his discourse as a place of filth and chaos, Lévi-Strauss articulates his passage into another place. Strangely, his discursive othering of Calcutta not only signals his passage there, it also brings into effect the very boundary between his point of departure and Calcutta which he has supposedly crossed. The travel from point to point redoubles the points in discourse in the binary framing of differential contiguity: the disjunctive relationship between the *same* and the other. In the process of articulating his passage to Calcutta, Lévi-Strauss explicitly invokes his point of departure, or his point of origin, and the boundary that divides him from Calcutta: the 'filth, chaos' that constitute the 'natural environment' of Calcutta, says Lévi- Strauss, 'things we hate and guard against'.[221]

We who 'hate and guard against' are the point of origin, departure, and the markers of the boundary that makes Calcutta the other of the 'We'. One does not need to be overly observant to see that, in this particular case, Lévi-Strauss is bringing into play the discourse of hygiene and order to put in place the point of departure and the point of arrival. By doing so, in fact, he is enacting the opposition between Marseilles (the port of departure) and Calcutta. He travels between these two cities, or more precisely, creates a bridge over the ellipsis, by the discourse of hygiene and order. Odd though it might sound, the fact remains that the real travelling machines for Lévi-Strauss, in this case, are hygiene and order.

It is rather careless of Lévi-Strauss to show his hand so blatantly, and reveal his point of origin, and the binary frame of his movement, by invoking the oppositional discourse in the name of 'We'. He need not have done so; since the travelling between points takes place in the conceptual orbit of representation, there always exists a relationship of symmetry. One need not blatantly display the point of the 'we' in order to name or represent 'they'. The 'we' as a point of origin is implicit in the very naming of 'they'. The travel from point to point can only take place in the conceptual symmetry of 'we' and 'they'.

And it is through symmetry that difference and othering takes place. Of course, we are dealing here with the logic of 'the same'. If we go back one step further, even the predication of qualities (filth and chaos) is not necessary to produce the discursive passage from Marseilles to Calcutta. The very nomination of Calcutta, and its deictic placing in the symmetrical relation of discourse, signals a movement from the point of the same to the other. The traveller need only say: it is Calcutta and I am here. In this particular case, Calcutta, on the singular plane of the discourse of cities, stands in a symmetrical relationship to Marseilles, which plays the deictic point 'there' – the point of departure and origin. Michel de Certeau makes a similar argument in *Heterologies*, when he writes 'an image of the other and the place of the text is simultaneously produced'.[222]

There is a profound irony in Roland Barthes's *Empire of Signs*.[223] So singular was his desire to be unlike any other Westerner, to escape the major gesture of its discourse – its comparative realism – that he invented an entirely semiotic system called Japan. His travel to 'Japan', he claims, does not take him to another space or another culture, but to an orbit of signs of his own devising. These signs, in due course, come to stand for the vanishing lightness of dancing signifiers of a *'faraway'* world against the onerous gravity of Western metaphysics. Between these two oppositional points of discourse, Barthes travels through discourse from the 'West' to 'Japan'. Don't all travellers who travel between points, travel *'faraway'* through systems of signs or through discursive passages? Barthes's claim to uniqueness, his disclaiming of a passage to 'real Japan', simply confirms the lot of the travellers who travel from point to point: they all travel through the semiotic passage. If Barthes is unique, his uniqueness lies in the fact that he produced a self-conscious meta-discourse out of it.

Joseph Conrad, in his geographical essays, came to recognise the discursive nature of movement. In *Landfalls and Departure* he writes: 'The Departure is not the ship's going away from her port any more than the Landfall can be looked upon as the synonym of arrival'.[224] He calls 'Departure' a 'sea event'. Ships depart not by moving in space, but by being placed in the flow of the discourse of navigation. The 'sea event' of 'Departure', Conrad writes, consists of 'precise observation of certain landmarks by means of the compass card'.[225] Similarly, the arrival at a 'Landfall' is not effected by the visual recognition of the landscape but by the sailor's cry of 'Land ho!'

The movement between points, the departure and arrival, can only take place through ellipsis, over a discursive bridge. However, the discursive bridge of the movement varies from travel to travel, depending on the kind of differential space the traveller wants to arrive at. And the passage, to remind ourselves again, is always in the middle, in between the points, in the uncharted and the unbounded *spatium*. Conrad is well aware of this. In *The Nigger of the 'Narcissus'*, the narrator writes:

> The passage had begun, and the ship, a fragment detached from the earth, went on lonely and swift like a small planet. Round her the abysses of sky and sea in an unattainable frontier. A great circular solitude moved with her, ever changing and ever the same, always monotonous and always imposing.[226]

Between points, between embarkation and disembarkation, between departure and arrival, lies the boundless middle of the passage: the unrepresentable horizon of the sea as the simmering force of the outside. It is here, folded in the 'dark mass' of the sea, that the real or nomadic travel takes place. The 'moved body' of the ship becomes the 'moving body' of the passage.

The movement of the sedentary traveller from a point of departure to a point of arrival, as we have seen, takes place through conceptual symmetry, and within the framework of representation. Since the point of departure is equivalent to the discursive point of representation, the origin of sedentary travel lies in the place of her/his enunciation. Michel de Certeau has clearly seen this in his writing on Montaigne: 'In short they [referential testimonies] signify not the reality of which they speak, but the reality from which they depart, and which they disguise, the place of their enunciation'.[227] The place of enunciation, then, is the real point of origin of a sedentary traveller. And upon this place is constituted Travel as a particular genre of literature. What is now clear is that Travel as a genre, founded as it is on the movement into other places, makes its move by the displacement of the place of enunciation. In other words, it is through the repetition of the *same* that the other takes its place in discourse. Vico calls it 'Poetic Geography'. The principal mechanism of 'Poetic Geography' is analogy or metaphoric similitude. In describing the Hellenic mapping of the world, Vico writes:

> within Greece itself accordingly lay the original east called Asia or India, the west called Europe or Hesperia, the north called Trace or Scythia, and the south called Libya or Mauretania. And these names for

the regions of the little world of Greece were (later) applied to those of the world (at large) in virtue of the correspondence which Greeks observed between the two. [228]

The face of the other mapped, and the attendant movement into the other through analogy or conceptual parallel amounts to the displacement of the place of enunciation. It is simultaneously the point of origin of travel and its source of representation.

Italo Calvino, in *Invisible Cities*, has made very similar points to the ones we have been arguing. Kublai Khan,[229] the guileful master of the semiotic game, soon discovers that Marco Polo's movement from point to point in space is anything but a passage through space. Calvino writes: 'Kublai Khan had noticed that Marco Polo's passage from one to another involved not a journey but a change of elements'.[230] Obviously, the elements are not occurrences in space but are drawn from the surfaces of 'leafy discourses'. Since a traveller enacts his passage from point to point in discourse, he need not undertake arduous journeys in 'real' space to say: I am a traveller and I have travelled to so many cities. It is all a matter of playing a semiotic game, of taking hold of the discursive rules for forming cities. Once this is done, the rest is easy: their innumerable combination and permutation will zoom you through countless cities. That is why, after a while, when Kublai Khan has fathomed the rules of cities, he does not send Marco Polo to distant places anymore. Now the Great Khan engages Marco Polo into endless games of chess and invents endless numbers of cities to which Marco Polo, as an adept at the game, merely gives his assent. The moral of the story is: one does not need to move in space to enact a journey in space.

Calvino offers us another interesting insight which has an important bearing on the study of travel as a genre. When Marco Polo has exhausted drawing vivid tableaux of distant cities, the wily emperor of the Mongols gently prompts his emissary to name one last city, which is also the first. There lies the secret city from which Marco Polo speaks, which Kublai Khan must unveil in order to decipher the map of the cities of which his empire is composed. Under Kublai Khan's persistence, Marco Polo reveals his first city, his point of departure, his place of enunciation: 'to distinguish the other cities' qualities, I must speak of a first city that remains implicit. For me it is Venice'.[231]

Since the representation of other cities hinges on the displaced repetition of the first city – the discursive place of enunciation and the site of origin – any critical engagement with accounts of travels must not begin with the scrutiny of other cities. Rather, the focus of our critical attention should be the first city itself. In other words, what is needed is a genealogy of the traveller's point of departure.

Although the travellers of travel accounts remain mainly sedentary as they jump from point to point in space or draw their representational maps of distant places, they are always haunted by the speed of nomadic travel and the possibility of an encounter with the outside. In the in-between the points of movement, between departure and arrival, every traveller risks the speed of nomadic passage, the openness of the encounter with the other and the process of becoming. Yet most travellers' accounts desperately try to suppress the speed of passage and to block the path of encounter with the other with dense walls, so that they can conjure up the authority to represent the world at which they arrive.

Let us finish our long passage through this chapter with a reading of Coleridge's *Kubla Khan*,[232] which will enable us to glimpse once more the simmering underside of the discourse of the other: the molten and the plastic moments of encounter that haunt the equanimity of representation.

It is said that on waking from an opium dream and still lingering in the reverie, Coleridge composed his celebrated poem 'Kubla Khan'. This poem might have been a part of a larger epic, as has been claimed, but the structure conforms to the classical closure of a completed work. In Kenneth Burke's words: 'Whatever may have got lost, the three stanzas in their overall progression tick off a perfect form, with beginning, middle and end respectively'.[233]

The apparent linearity of the poem has a more Hegelian structure to it than one of simple accumulation. The frame, the two extremities of the poem – the beginning and the end – is bound by the enactment of a sign of sovereign will and its power of effectuation that realises the ineffable telos. Between the sign of the will that decrees, and the telos that culminates in paradise, the epicentre of the poem is swallowed up in a dark cavern. One could say that the sovereign will, following an impeccable Hegelian logic, overcomes the wound in its heart and reaches the goal it sets in motion. Or does it? We will soon see. The sign of the sovereign will, echoing Marco Polo's Kubili Khan, bears the name Kubla Khan. Not only a mere resemblance of names. Coleridge, in the brooding whirlpool of romantic lyricism, repeats many of the enduring figures Marco Polo had put into circulation – and none more abiding than the figuration of Kubili as an utopian ideal, who despite being absolutist, holds the key to order. Here, against the prevailing figure of the despot, who served as the very negation of the Western democratic self-image, we find an idiosyncratic representation of another monarch which, nonetheless, is far from accidental, and articulates the tortuous drama of Western body-politics. We will have occasion to reflect on it in the later chapters of the book. Now let us stay with Coleridge.

Coleridge, following Marco Polo's narrative, preserves the image of Kubla Khan as an awesome machine of power, who functions by decrees – the characteristic juridical mode of the One – the absolute appurtenance of power to a singular, sovereign will:

> In Xanadu did Kubla Khan
> A stately pleasure-dome decree

Marco Polo's narrative, as we shall see, constructs the figure of Kubili Khan, in a complex web of cross-cultural discourse, as a model absolutist power, and pours into it an intense utopian longing. The power of the decree in the second verse, which affects both rational order and pastoral plenitude: an engineered order with its 'walls', 'towers' and 'girdles', and an archaic dreamscape à la garden of Eden with its 'blossomed ... incense-bearing tree' and 'Enfolding ... greenery'. This is the ideal blend of the rational and the natural: the perfect image of utopia. However, the telos of the poem, if we insist on a Hegelian reading, is the repetition of this utopian moment in the 'I' of the poem who 'drinks the milk of paradise'. As if the power of the decree, announced in the second verse, channels its way through a labyrinthine course to affect the 'I's' own utopian quest. This is the dream Marco Polo nurtured in iconising Kubilai Khan, so that the utopian longing for order in Christendom would find a perfect model for its own self-realisation. It is a plausible narrative. However, we have not yet grappled with the labyrinth and the chasm that haunt the middle of the poem. This question of the demonic middle, in concurrence with Marco Polo's own narrative, is to do, I would suggest, with the problematic nature of cross-cultural representation, and with the devouring monster that lurks in the encounter with the other.

The presumed consummation of the 'I's' journey to 'the milk of paradise' by way of the salutary force unleashed by Kubla's decree involves a double movement: representation of the other and becoming-other. After having depicted the luxurious enclosure, the unfolding of an earthly paradise from the seething power of Kubla, the poem undergoes a violent cut announced in the disquieting exclamation 'But oh!'. This cut that opens the second stanza not only blocks the flow of Kubla's benevolent power, it puts radically into question the unproblematic representation of the first stanza. Within the ordered space of the first stanza, or rather simmering within its fold, lies the virtual plane, in Deleuze and Guattari's words, of 'pure relation of speed and slowness between particles',[234] where the representation of the other gives way to the encounter with the other. The sacred river Alph which, from its Olympian provenance, so compliantly surrenders its space to Kubla's command, turns back to repeat its elemental force of speed and slowness: it recovers its being as *physis* or intensive *spatium*. In the process, it ruptures the ordered container that Kubla's power has decreed, and short-circuits the representational project Marco Polo so assiduously undertook and Coleridge so deliriously repeated.

Folded within the placidity of utopia stirs 'a savage place' which contains the 'chasm, with ceaseless turmoil seething'. Following its own ineluctable rhythm, the seething particles gather speed and traverse the membrane that holds it together to form 'huge fragments vaulted like rebounding hail' which become the sacred river. Its sudden speed, in the course of a few miles, gives way to absolute slowness as it sinks into 'a lifeless sea'. This elemental movement of celerity and entropy not only ruins Xanadu, it reveals its little secret – no more than a simulacrum: 'The shadow of the dome of pleasure' – and leaves it suspended in thin air, 'Floated midway on the waves'.

The solidity of the representation of the other in the first stanza now melts away. It cannot be otherwise, since the representation of the other must accept, even though grudgingly, its lot as simulacrum.[235] Amidst the molecular flow of the second stanza, we also see a movement away from the desire for the other as an object of knowledge to the encounter with the other. The molecular movement, which exceeds the containment of the other in representation, clears the blockage, opens a supple line or a pure surface, so that the encounter with the other as Infinity may take place. Coleridge eloquently delineates the image of Infinity in the 'caverns measureless to man'.

The fatal moment has arrived for the attempted capture of the other in representation to yield to the eternal separation of the encounter, where the subject gets decomposed in the 'holy dread' of the Infinity. The other is now the 'demon-lover' beyond a boundless chasm, where the desiring subject becomes an abject lover – a 'woman wailing for her demon-lover'. Could this be a metamorphic process of Coleridge's becoming-woman and Kubla Khan's becoming-demon-lover?

Near the end of the second stanza the proper name Kubla Khan is once again cited. This time the man of power, who draws rigid boundaries with his monolithic decree, and so imprisoning himself and others, is released. He is now in the throes of becoming a man of war again: the nomadic wanderer of his ancestral past – the impeccable enemy of rigid boundaries. The Hegelian movement is already killed in its tracks: the power that created the earthly paradise at the beginning of the first stanza cannot grant the same to the desiring subject at the end of the poem. This is because Kubla Khan is no longer the sovereign with a juridical force which violently impinges upon things. He has become a 'demon-lover' and a nomadic warrior. His proper domain is the simulacrum, 'the shadow of the dome ... on the waves'. If Coleridge wants to continue with his odyssey, he has to renounce all claims to representational mastery. For one thing, the object of representation itself has disappeared: Kubla Khan, the sovereign has become an Infinite (demon-lover) and a nomadic man of war (who always moves elsewhere). Either way the other reveals its absolute alterity, and in its wake does violence to representation by exceeding its grids of placement. Henceforth, Coleridge's odyssey needs to cross the threshold and enter the process of becoming-other. This can only be done by entering into the orbit of the simulacrum.

The simulacrum immediately reveals its nature as a paradox – the disjunctive synthesis of heat and cold – imaged precisely as 'A sunny pleasure-dome with caves of ice!' Now we can see that the simulacrum, being a phantasmic copy and a bearer of paradox, savagely undercuts the authority with which representation (or mimesis) is secured in the first stanza. When the poetic interlocutor repeats the simulacrum by implanting it on its own 'self', he is already in the process of becoming-other:

> I would build that dome in air,
> That sunny dome! those caves of ice!

If the repetition of the phantasmic copy, grounded in paradox, disempowers the 'self' of its representational drive, it allows it to come face to face with the other. The other as Infinity will always undo and exceed any representational capture by the rapacious ego. However, it shows a pathway to self-difference, a secret of becoming otherwise than itself. By fastening its desire on the simulacrum, by repeating it, the discursive subject meets the other. We must not forget that the other is no longer the supine object to be depicted, nor is he the sovereign who decrees and erects boundaries. The molecular explosion of the second stanza, which already signals the encounter with the other, sweeps away the benevolent icon and reveals its dreaded nature: a demon lover and a man of war, whose proper home is the simulacrum. By repeating the simulacrum, the 'self' enters the house of the other, and thereby comes into proximity with the other. From here on there is no turning back: the 'self' is ready to take flight, to become otherwise than itself, to become the other. The pathfinder to be followed is the demonic lover (Infinity) and the nomadic man of war. On the way the 'Abyssinian maid' and her 'symphony', in the doubling of the archetypal sign of otherness – the Homeric Siren – helps overcome the residual pull of the molar subject, and sends it on the inexorable track of becoming-other.

Of course, as Deleuze and Guattari have shown, becoming-other is not a question of mimicry, nor is it a literal embodiment. However, it is neither an empty metaphor nor is it unreal: it is a process of self-transformation in the proximity of the other. It is a matter of being traced by Infinity and of following the speed of the wandering man of war. The sign of this becoming is registered in the sudden displacement of the 'I' into 'he' in the last stanza. Between what has happened (dome that floated away) and what is about to happen (the floating dome that will be repeated), between the irretrievable time of the past and the virtual time of the future, the self-presence of the 'I' – the immobile being in the present who masters and represents – loses its ground and becomes 'he' – the signature of the other. The charmed circle of subjectivity – the illocutionary frame of I-thou – is broken. Consequently, it brings to an end the panoply of configurations belonging to the subjective mode: the dialectics of mutual self-confirmation, the self-appropriation of the other in translation or representation, and the desire for the other grounded in Ressentiment. Instead, it provokes a form of individuation, termed by Deleuze and Guattari 'haecceity'.[236] 'He' as 'this thing' is no longer a subject of enunciation but part of anonymous statements. He has become, in other words, the other – the 'holy dread'.

Coleridge's poem helps us establish the visible and the invisible sides of the discourse of the other: on the one hand, there exists the obsessive drive to represent and master; on the other, the turbulent moment of encounter. However, the subject, in order to sustain his authority to represent, represses the haunting memories of encounter – which are the unconscious and the molecular plane of the discourse of the other. Coleridge's poem reveals, by staging representation and undoing it with the forces of encounter, the double-sided nature of the discourse of the other.

Travellers, who live in walled castles, move on gridded space, along rigid lines, cross boundaries only in the orbit of representation, travel from point to point without travelling, do so by forgetting how to dwell, how to move on supple space, how to encounter, and how to become. Yet, as we have seen, dwelling is ontologically primordial; beneath the surface of a rigid boundary and the visible frame of representation, there lie the primordial forces of shifting difference, ever-changing boundaries and the speed of becoming. The force of this positive ontology is always active in the passage between points and can, when least expected, break through rigid lines, metamorphosing the 'moved body' of a sedentary traveller into the 'moving body' of a nomadic traveller. When this happens the map of representation falls into ruins as the galloping speed of encounter takes the traveller away. This is how a truly ethical performance of travel takes place. There, under the orchestration of Wilson Harris, one dances to the secret music in the palace of the peacock, becomes a peacock and is 'instantly transported to know and to hug to himself his true otherness and opposition'.[237]

2

OTHERING

AND THE OTHER

When Prospero, the deposed Milanese 'prince of power' and a Renaissance man of learning, voyages to another island, he immediately frames the other within the familiar orbit of master/slave relationship. This is how Prospero's first meeting with the other proceeds:

> *Prospero* Come away, servant, come. I am ready now. Approach, my Ariel, come.
> *Ariel* All hail, great Master! grave sir, hail! I come[1]

Instead of allowing an encounter to take place, Prospero turns his first meeting with Ariel into a repetition of dialectics. He hails Ariel as his servant; Ariel responds in recognition of Prospero's mastery; and thereby the deposed 'prince of power' regains his self-conception as a lord. One cannot do without the other in the specular regime of self-mastery. Frantz Fanon, meditating on the specular drama of colonial dialectics, writes: 'There is a quest for the Negro, the Negro is in demand, one cannot get along without him'.[2]

The other, positioned in the economy of need, can only emerge as an effect of othering. The true locus of this othered-other is the discursive monologue of the *same*. Ariel is not an interlocutor in dialogue any more than he is a subject of his own enunciation. His voice is emplaced in a mock dialogue to service Prospero's desperate need of recognition. Apart from playing the specular foil to the self-mastering subject, the othered-other, being a plastic figure without resistance, can assume any form to suit the requirement of the master. It would not have been that terrible if the othering of the other were no more than the forlorn pleas of the master for the recognition of his selfhood. Sure, we would have had wretched masters full of pathos, slaves in master's clothing, as Nietzsche saw them. Even Hegel would have felt pity for them, as he did in *The Phenomenology of Mind*. Unable to sublate authentically the othered-other, because the exteriority of the negated object cannot close the self-alienating distance, the master cannot gain the truth of his essential consciousness. Hegel draws the consequences of the master's hapless dialectical move:

> But it is evident that this object [slave] does not correspond to its [master's] notion; for, just where the master has effectively achieved lordship, he really finds something has come about quite different from an independent consciousness. It is not an independent, but rather dependent consciousness that he has achieved. He is thus not assured of self-existence as his truth.[3]

We would not shed any tears for Prospero if his quest for self-recognition through the mediation of the othered-other fails. The master may never be able to emerge from the deep chasm of alienation into which he invariably falls in the face of the eternally distancing object. Moreover, the master's own desire, as it is negatively articulated through the mimetic process, is mediated by the other; Gilles Deleuze explains:

> it is always through others that my desire passes and receives an object. I desire nothing which may not be seen, thought, possessed by a possible other. This is the foundation of my desire [negative desire]. It is always other people who fasten my desire down onto the object.[4]

Yet the incurable alienation, the negativity of mimetic desire, nourished as it is in the dank pool of *Ressentiment*, only fuels the master's ego-mania for possessing the other: the other's body, gold that is moulded by the other into gods, distant places where the other dwells, and so on. However, in order to create the condition for possessing the other the master necessarily subjects the other to his othering. Prospero is no exception: in order to possess the other island, he renders a number of otherings. We have already seen how Ariel's othering serves Prospero with the specular surface of recognition. But what othering must he render in order to claim the island as his own? Whatever form it takes, the othering must effect a deterritorialisation of the existing order of the island on Prospero's arrival. Prospero others Sycorax, the founder of the ruling line of the island, by calling her a 'foul witch' and inscribing in her person the resentful paranoia of a despot. The othering of Sycorax, positioned as the negative pole of sovereignty to Prospero's benevolence (who rescued Ariel from Sycorax's unjust imprisonment), deterritorialises the island, emptying it of any legitimate authority, and thereby clearing the way for Prospero's territorialisation of the island.

What about Caliban? Hasn't he been othered as a deformed monster? Of course, yet he need not have been subjected to the discourse of othering in order to deterritorialise the legitimate authority of the island. Since the legitimacy of Caliban's claim to the lordship of the island depends on his being a rightful descendent of the ruling filial line, the delegitimation of Sycorax, the origin of the line, automatically deterritorialises him.

We must not lose sight of the fact that the destinies of Sycorax and Caliban and Ariel are not simply an enactment of a speculative scenario but are in fact what has befallen the 'natives' of all colonised spaces. Europe, from the Renaissance onwards, has othered many cultures and races in order to mediate its self-identity and to deterritorialise the other places, thus creating a vacancy of governance, so that colonial powers can legitimately territorialise them.

Othering does not produce the other; it only produces an othered-other. One cannot produce the other. The other is so radically inscrutable in being an outside or infinity that it eludes the othering of the subject (the master). In other words, the other remains beyond the representational capture – designation or predication – of the subject. As Deleuze and Guattari say: 'The outside [the other] has no image, no signification, no subjectivity'.[5] Only the act of othering produces a relational point, a surface of reflection, an oppositional or negative pole in representation. It is by wrenching the other from the outside and turning it into an object of designation and predication that the othering is accomplished. If the other were to remain the other, it would remain beyond representation. It is in the process of questioning the authority of the discourse of othering and bearing witness to the other that the ethical question of justice is raised.

Hegel, in *The Phenomenology of Mind*, writes:

> First it has lost its own self, since it finds itself as an *other being*; secondly, it has thereby sublated that other, for it does not regard the other as essentially real, but its own self in the other.[6]
>
> Each is the mediating term to the other, through which each mediates and unites with itself.[7]

Hegel's dialectic not only represents the philosophical apotheosis of the Western discourse of othering, it also reveals its egological and representational basis. The other is never a difference in kind, but rather a conceptual differentiation set in motion by the subject for its own self-realisation: it is the self that others the other for the mediation of its own unity. Furthermore, the other produced in the oppositional movement of othering remains within the *same*, in the ambit of its self-relation. Hence, the othered-other is no more than a relative difference that the self sets up to give meaning to its own identity. Moreover, as we have seen, the othering of the other deterritorialises the other, opening space for the master's mastery and territorialisation. It is a discursive manoeuvre that effects, in Emmanuel Levinas's words, 'the concreteness of egoism'.[8]

The othered-other is the other of being that constitutes the relationship of the *same* and the other within a totality.[9] The marking of the other as a relative difference within the structure of totality (of which the dialectic is a classic instance) is what produces the 'imperialism of the same'.[10] Moreover, Levinas argues that the process of egological othering is not something that happens incidentally but is inherent in the very ontology that has dominated Western thinking since the classical Greeks.[11] The dominant thrust of Western thinking, which is orientated by the consciousness of being, is driven by the obsession of capturing otherness in knowledge. Levinas writes:

> Here [in the Western epistemological and ontological tradition] the known is understood and so *appropriated* by knowledge, as it were freed of its otherness. In the realm of truth, being, as the *other* of thought becomes the characteristic *property* of thought as knowledge. The ideal of rationality or of sense (sens) begins already to appear as the immanence of the real to reason; just as, in being, a privilege is granted to the *present*, which is presence to thought, of which the future and the past are modalities or modifications: re-presentations.
> But in knowledge there also appears the notion of an intellectual activity or of a reasoning will − a way of doing something which consists precisely of thinking through knowing, of seizing something and making it one's own, of reducing to presence and representing the difference of being, an activity which *appropriates* and *grasps* the otherness of the known. A certain grasp: as an entity, being becomes the characteristic property of thought, as it is grasped by it and becomes known. Knowledge as perception, concept, comprehension, refers back to an act of grasping.[12]

By translating the other into knowledge, by turning the other into an object for the mediation of self-consciousness, by using the other as a foil for achieving self-consciousness, the 'imperialism of the same' is established. The othering of the other produces a relational difference so that the self-mastery of the subject can glorify its own meaning. The othered-other is self's own other, rather than the other. It does not bear testimony to a difference in kind but to the relative difference, which is a numerical point that articulates the differences in species within a genus. The othered-other is a mediated difference within the plane of representation, whose four principles are defined by Gilles Deleuze in *Difference and Repetition*:

> There are four principal aspects to 'reason' in so far as it is the medium of representation: identity, in the form of the *undetermined* concept; analogy, in the relation between ultimate *determinable* concepts; opposition, in the relation between *determinations* within concepts; resemblance, in the *determined* object of the concept itself. These forms are like the four heads or the four shackles of mediation. Difference is 'mediated' to the extent that it is subjected to the fourfold root of identity, opposition, analogy and resemblance. [13]

Beyond mediated difference, beyond the closed circuit of totality, lies pure difference and the other as infinity, which gives rise to the ethical question of how to relate to the other without compromising its otherness. Before I engage with this question, however, the lines of articulation internal to the discourse of othering requires further exploration.

The parameter of othering

Frantz Fanon in *Black Skin, White Mask* recounts the calamitous aftermath of the othering gaze of the white man:

> On that day, completely dislocated, unable to be abroad with the other, the white man, who unmercifully imprisoned me, I took myself far off from my presence, far indeed, and made myself an object. What else could it be for me but an amputation, an excision, a haemorrhage that spattered my whole body with black blood? [14]

By othering the black man, the white man not only places him in an empty conceptual relationality that affirms his own self-identity, but also fixes the black man's so-called essence. The black man is dragged from his alterity to coincide with the concepts that the white man forms of him. These concepts, which express the essence and the truth of the black man, are concepts whose origins, predictably, lie in the innermost sanctum of the white man's world. Hence, the essence of the black man is no more than the displacement of concepts with which the white man represents the totality of his own world. Once the black man is fixed with the displaced concepts, he is translated into a term within. He is no more than an internal other with the function of completing the binary circuit of dialectical totality that consigns him to the role of white man's other. This is the ontological foundation of racism. Deleuze and Guattari in their own way also reach the same conclusion:

> From the viewpoint of racism, there is no exterior, there are no people on the outside. There are only people who should be like us and whose crime it is not to be. The dividing line is not between inside and outside but rather is internal to simultaneous signifying chains and successive subjective choices. Racism never detects the particles of the other; it propagates waves of sameness.[15]

Not only is the black man othered in the 'waves of sameness' – mediated through identity, analogy and resemblance of concepts – he is also burdened to bear the load of opposition within the white man's totality, and, thereby, made to serve as an open container for the white man's negativities. The black man is what the white man is not: the black man's essence is what the white man lacks and abhors within himself. This is how the 'imperialism of the same' of Europe inscribes the world with its own narcissistic passion, whose 'amputation', 'excision', and 'haemorrhaging' of othered subjects Fanon's writing so eloquently articulates.

Despite apparent concordance with existential humanism and the acceptance of the reciprocity of recognition of the Hegelian dialectic, Fanon's thinking traverses both of these positions. For one thing, the mutuality of recognition is destined to remain a hopeless ideal in the colonial scenario. Moreover, Fanon comes to question both the mimetic desire and the self-realisation through lack. He writes:

> The dialectic that brings necessity into the foundation of my freedom drives me out of myself. It shatters my unreflected position. Still in terms of consciousness, black consciousness is immanent in its own eyes. I am not a potentiality of something, I am wholly what I am. I do not have to look for the universal. No probability has any place inside me. My Negro consciousness does not hold itself out as a lack.[16]

The affirmative 'Negro consciousness' must say no to mimetic desire, to the totality of the universal, to the pathos of the 'lack'; otherwise the 'Negro consciousness' would remain reactive and be plagued with *Ressentiment*, and the cycle of the dialectic would be repeated once more. Towards the end of *Black Skin, White Masks*, Fanon clearly restates, in concurrence with Nietzsche, his affirmative ethics of the black man's becoming:

> I said in my introduction that man is a *yes*. I will never stop reiterating that. *Yes* to life. *Yes* to love. *Yes* to generosity. But man is also a *no*. No to scorn of man. *No* to degradation of man. *No* to the exploitation of man. *No* to the butchery of what is most human in man; freedom. Man's behaviour is not only reactional. And there is always resentment in a *reaction*. Nietzsche had already pointed that out in *The Will to Power*. To educate man to be *actional*, preserving in all his relations his respect for the basic values that constitute a human world, is the prime task of him who, having taken thought, prepares to act.[17]

Despite the lingering traces of the universality of humanism, Fanon shows that the positive ethics of becoming and social justice are only possible through the overcoming of the mimetic desire of *Ressentiment*, egocentric othering, and the pathos of negativities. Although he clearly shows the way to be taken, the nature of ethics and justice, *vis-à-vis* the other, needs further discussion to be clarified. Before that, however, we should analyse the lines of articulation internal to discourses that conduct the process of othering.

Although the discourse of othering firmly belongs to the 'imperialism of the same', its line of articulation is far from unitary. The figuration of the other as the site of opposition and negativities also serves as the focus of mimetic desire. In the circuit of dialectics, as we have seen, the othered-other serves as the necessary point for the articulation of the relational totality of sameness and otherness, or identity and difference. And within this totality, in the process of representing relational otherness and difference, negative or mimetic desire is articulated. Yet this negative desire is far from one-dimensional; it is strangely double-edged.

Sigmund Freud, in his essay *Taboo and Emotional Ambivalence*,[18] charts the 'ambivalent' nature of negative desire. Freud argues that when the considerations of order and the law of the normal forbid the tabooed object, libidinal impulses seek it out in 'transgressive' desire. Freud writes:

> Taboo is a primeval prohibition forcibly imposed (by some authority) from outside, and directed against the most powerful longings to which human beings are subject. The desire to violate it persists in the unconscious; those who obey the taboo have an ambivalent attitude to what the taboo prohibits.[19]

Even if transgression is no more than a mode of negative desire, in its very ambivalence, it symptomatically articulates the internal force of positive desire, which eludes representation. Freud writes 'desire ... is unconscious and the subject knows nothing of it ... [It is] an internal necessity inaccessible to conscious inspection'.[20] Yet the unrepresentable force of positive (unconscious) desire makes its dissonant sense felt in the very representation of negative desire. Ambivalence is therefore a symptom of the unrepresentable positive desire in the representational plane of negative desire. In other words, it is the 'mask' of the unconscious – the groundless ground of desire and the libidinal force of eternal repetition – put on the surface of the signifier. Gilles Deleuze, in the process of explicating the disguised presence of repetition as the dissonant sense in representation, writes: 'The mask [a figure of simulacrum and ambivalent sense] is the true subject of repetition [the transcendental force of the unconscious]. Because repetition differs in kind from representation, the repeated cannot be represented: rather, it must always be signified, masked by what signifies it, itself masking what it signifies'.[21]

On a different tack, Freud reworks the ambivalence of mimetic desire in his essay *The Uncanny*,[22] which explicates the dialectics of cultural identity and difference. Freud's etymological exploration of the German word for uncanny, *Unheimlich*, reveals it to be the opposite of *heimlich* and *heimisch*. Although the word *heimlich* carries a wide variety of connotations, its dominant sense is that of being 'at home' or 'homely'; and *heimisch* is equivalent to the English word 'native'. We can, therefore, see that *das Unheimlich* stands for both being unhomely and for foreign; it is the negation of being at home surrounded by the law of the normal. Freud, furthermore, interprets *das Unheimlich* with the repetition compulsion, the return of the libidinal from the groundless ground of the unconscious. As such *das Unheimlich* is aligned with the transcendental principle of *Thanatos*; it harbours a form of ambivalence whose effect is more perilous than the object of a mere taboo. On the one hand, *das Unheimlich* entices the homely to take flight into the unknown, the outside; on the other hand, it dramatises the risk involved in such a flight. Furthermore, *das Unheimlich*, at once, expresses the mimetic desire and the dialectical circuit of home/not-home, and in its ambivalence and disruptive sense, bears testimony to difference in kind – the other. If we tread further beyond the immediate focus of Freud's essay – which is limited to the theorisation of the disruptive effects of fantastic literature – some interesting insights into cross-cultural discourse are offered. Being a native and at home are the necessary markers of identity in a cross-cultural space, because the identity thus acquired is made possible by a binary relation, whose other terms are being unhomely and a foreigner.

Das Unheimlich, Freud explains, is not an encounter with the outside but a return of the aspects of the inside that the ego has lost and found again. He writes: 'the uncanny is in reality nothing new or alien, but something which is familiar and old-established in the mind and which has become alienated from it only through the process of repression'.[23] On this account the uncanny conforms to the dialectical model of self-relation: the uncanny object or narrative inspires dread not because it forces an encounter with the outside, but rather a meeting with the displaced representation of the inside. Hence, the unhomely and the foreigner are the self's own others, which are othered by the law of the normal. On the other hand, if being at home means to live securely with the ego endowed by the law, and the unhomely is the sign of the libidinal forces that compel to repeat, then their meeting brings out the daemonic. Freud writes:

> For it is possible to recognise the dominance in the unconscious mind of a 'compulsion to repeat' proceeding from the instinctual impulses and probably inherent in the very nature of the instincts – a compulsion powerful enough to overrule the pleasure principle, lending to certain aspects of the mind their daemonic character.[24]

The 'compulsion to repeat' that brings out the daemonic character by overruling the principle of *Eros* with the force of *Thanatos* explodes the ego. Hence, there no longer remains a 'self' with its desperate need for identity, to which the othered-other serves as a foil, but it can now open itself up for the encounter with the outside. Because it is a risk that haunts all egos, the imperial self uses all manner of ruses to deny or suppress it. The unhomely and the foreigner remain the displaced representation, through analogy, of the imperial self's already othered impulses. For instance, the tabooed incestuous impulses (already othered), through displacement, produce the incestuous foreigner (othered-other). Yet the othered-other as a displaced representation of mimetic desire is not free of ambivalence. Nowhere is this more graphically illustrated than in Homer's *Odyssey*.[25] After the Trojan war, all Odysseus wanted was to go home, but that proved to be rather tortuous because there is no homecoming without the dialectical interplay with the unhomeliness of the other. Yet all figures of unhomeliness are not the same: some incite pleasure and some dread. If Calypso, the Siren and the Lotus Eaters represent the figuration of the other as pleasure, then the Cyclops, the Laestrygonians and the Phaecians represent dread. But, in fact, it is the figures of pleasure that prove to be more insistent in preventing Odysseus's homecoming. Odysseus could easily deal with Polyphemus the Cyclops – the anthropophagy who 'care nothing for Zeus and his aegis'[26]- with his 'craft'. But his guile and prowess prove redundant before 'the strange power and beauty'[27] of the nymph Calypso; the powers of the gods are needed to disenchant him and set him on course for home again. The sweet savour of lotus has no less power of enchantment than the sensual Calypso in preventing Odysseus's homecoming: 'Those of my men [Odysseus's crew] who ate the honey-sweet lotus fruit had no desire to retrace their steps ... and put aside all thought of a voyage home'.[28] And the bewitching power of the strange melody of the Sirens casts such a spell that 'if a man in ignorance draws too close and catches their music, he will never return'.[29] However, both poles of otherness have the same function: to prevent Odysseus's homecoming.

This contradictory mode of othering can be understood in two different ways. On the one hand, the displaced representation of the other as horror and dread enables the homeliness of the home to emerge. Here the double-sidedness of the other is no more than a variety of displaced repetition – the figuration of the other with forbidden pleasure and horror. As such, despite the contradictory representation, the other remains an othered-other within the empire of the *same*. On the other hand, the contradictory representation of the other can be seen as the 'mask' of the 'daemonic character' – the sign of the repetition compulsion – that refuses to play the foil in the dialectical game of the *same*. Only in the latter does the other assume its true nature as being *das Unheimlich*: not mere figuration of the other, either as pleasure and dread, produced as they are through displaced and negative desire, but the very force of the outside masked in its contradictory representation. This is the force that insists that Odysseus 'will never return' home.

Response to the other

Now that we have explored some of the configurations of the discourse of othering, we can ask how can one respond to the other without compromising its otherness? I will attempt to address this question by taking the ethical meditations of Levinas, Lyotard, and Deleuze and Guattari as my guide.

The ethical sayings of Emmanuel Levinas

Among contemporary philosophers, Levinas is most singular in his insistence that the ethical response to the other cannot be formulated in the cognitive, totalisable language of mediation. The other cannot be said (*le dit*), but only responded to in the language of saying (*le dire*). The former represents the 'other of being', the latter bears testimony to the 'otherwise than being'. The privileged mode in which the language of the 'said' appears in the West is ontology: the consciousness or self-knowledge of the subject. Since ontology grasps the other by illuminating it in terms of its own concept, it invariably reduces the otherness of the other. Levinas explains:

> The relation with Being that is enacted as ontology consists in neutralising the existent in order to comprehend or grasp it. It is hence not a relation with the other as such but the reduction of the other to the same.[30]

Levinas goes on to call ontology 'a philosophy of power'.[31] Moreover, under the conceptual power hides an egological passion that violently appropriates everything to meet its gluttonous need:

> My being-in-the-world or my 'place in the sun', my being at home, have these not also been the usurpation of spaces belonging to the other man whom I have already oppressed or starved, or driven out into the world; are they not acts of repulsion, excluding, exiling, stripping, killing?[32]

Totalising thought, egological passion and the cognitive, or representational, language of the 'said' aspire to the same thing: the reduction and the appropriation of the other. What about the language of the 'saying' – how does this work? It is by breaching the totalising relationship with the other that the language of 'saying' 'calls into question my freedom',[33] and opens the way for a 'non-allergic' or ethical relation with the other. But if the other is not an other within ego's own totality, and the ego can have no knowledge of the other, how, then, is it possible to have a relationship with the other? This is precisely the question that Levinas addresses throughout his *oeuvre*.

Following Descartes' *Meditation*, Levinas calls the other 'infinity': 'What remains ever exterior to thought is thought in the idea of infinity'.[34] It is an absolute outside, whose exteriority exceeds ego's own idea of it: it is that which resists absolutely. 'Infinity' has many different names in Levinas's work: the Other (*l'Autre*), the other person (*d'Autrui*), the stranger (*l'étranger*), alterity (*alterité*), the holy (*le saint*), illieity (a neologism for the impersonal third person), the face (*le visage*), good (from Plato), and even God. Whatever name Levinas gives it, it is always otherwise than being, and comes from beyond (*au-dela*). Although the other is not an entity, it is not 'nothing' either. Like the overpowering silence of an empty shell as if it were full of noise, and between absence and presence, 'it is something one can also feel when one thinks that even if there were nothing, the fact that "there is" [*il y a*] is undeniable'.[35] *Il y a* is that which affects the subject when the representation of the being, or even the meaning of Being, is transcended. *Il y a* is impersonal and without any disposition. Levinas is, therefore, insistent in making a distinction between *il y a* and Heidegger's notion of *es gibt*. For Levinas, *es gibt,* which apart from signifying 'there is' also carries the meaning of generosity (from the verb *geben*), carries a trace of reciprocity and egocentricity. For Heidegger, *es gibt* of Being, once the clearing has been done, reveals its meaning as a gift to *Dasein*, even if that gift comes in the face of the finitude of death. The ethical relationship with the other, argues Levinas, is absolutely unconditional. The subject relates ethically with the other without desiring reciprocity, gift, and without even knowing anything about it. The other remains radically separate, and with which the subject can never coincide: neither with its idea nor with its time. For the temporality of the other is that of an immemorial past, which Levinas also calls anarchy. It never comes to pass as present or 'memorable time' which can be represented as recollection; before its pastness, the present is always delayed and disturbed. Levinas writes: 'Incommensurable with the present, unassemblable in it, it is [anarchy] always "already in the past" behind which the present delays, over and beyond the "now" which this exteriority disturbs'.[36] The other as infinity and anarchy guarantees its transcendence – its radical separation and irreducible difference. However, this radical separation must not be confused with essence, for essence can only be fixed in a totalisable representation where the other is opposition. How then is it possible to have ethical relationships with irreducible difference? Doesn't it free me of obligation – which would surely do if it were a case of relativism? But it is not. The other, who is irreducibly different, is also my neighbour, the other person who is in close proximity to me. It is precisely from the proximity with the irreducible difference that the ethical relation of obligation arises. It is not in my freedom to ignore the proximity of the other, for my very subjectivity is constituted by having to respond to it: 'it is the fundamental structure of subjectivity'.[37] Levinas clarifies the matter when he writes: 'the identity of the subject comes from the impossibility of escaping responsibility, from taking charge of the other'.[38] Hence ethics is the first philosophy: the question of obligation and responsibility precedes ontological and epistemological undertakings.

Do not proximity and irreducible difference stand in a paradoxical relationship? Of course, they do if we consider them from a cognitive point of view. But ethically it is precisely the irreducible difference that brings the other closer. For here, the other is not othered in representation or mediated through concepts which create the distance between ego and its other. Levinas writes: 'Proximity as suppression of distance suppresses the distance of consciousness ... The neighbour excludes himself from the thought that seeks him, and this exclusion has a positive side to it: my exposure to him'.[39] To put it simply: without othering, the other would appear without the protective shield of mediation. Hence it is a face-to-face relationship: the other appears in its naked face and I am immediately exposed to it and have to respond. The epiphany of the face that summons me does not form a complicitous circuit of 'the self-sufficient "I-Thou" forgetful of the universe'.[40] Despite the proximity, the other as my interlocutor retains its absolute inscrutability and impersonality. In order to convey the impersonality of the other in proximity, Levinas, in *Otherwise than Being and Beyond Essence*, coins the neologism 'illieity', which, he says: 'lies outside the "thou" and the thematisation of the object. A neologism formed with il (he) or ille, it indicates a way of concerning me without entering into conjunction with me'.[41] Hence the face of *illieity* that summons and obligates me is so naked that in its epiphany it appears 'denuding itself of its skin'.[42] In other words, the face appears before me not as an expressive face of physiognomy, but simply as an *il y a* that puts me into question before infinity. Although the other in the nudity of its face appears 'destitute' before me, and as such calls me out to attend to its poverty, it is, however, not below me, not even equal to me, but higher than me. My relationship with the other is asymmetrical where it speaks to me from heights and in the language of command. Therefore, the subject *vis-à-vis* the other, maintains Levinas, is always passive. The subject is commanded from the heights and obligated to respond, but without any intentionality or having a goal in mind. In fact, the command and the obligation to respond is constitutive of subjectivity: it is always already passive. Levinas writes: 'the most passive, unassumable passivity, the subjectivity or the very subjection of the subject, is due to my being obsessed with responsibility for the oppressed who is other than myself.'[43] Passivity also emphasises the non-cognitive and non-ontological relationship with the other. It safeguards against the mastery of the other through conceptual capture; it undoes the legitimacy of Kant's active faculty of understanding on which transcendental idealism is founded.

There is no limit to obligation: not only in the temporal sense, one is always already obligated and will have obligated, but everything about the other also concerns the subject. In fact, I am a hostage of the other; I even have 'to answer for the death of the other'.[44] My obligation to the other is so total that I become its substitute – everything for which the other is responsible becomes my responsibility – but nobody can substitute my responsibility. Levinas says: 'I can substitute myself for everyone, but no one can substitute himself for me'.[45]

How does the other reveal itself, and how do I articulate my response to the other's command? Levinas insists, as we have seen, that the ethical response cannot be formulated in the cognitive or propositional language of the 'said' but only in the language of 'saying'. Moreover, the other does not reveal itself to me. If I make the other reveal itself by representing it or conveying it in the language of the 'said', I would be betraying its otherness. As Levinas says: 'We have been seeking the *otherwise than being* from the beginning, and as soon as it is conveyed before us it is betrayed in the said that dominates the saying which states it'.[46] The face that summons me in its nudity is not an expressive presence, but the trace of *il y a* which as an interlocutor presents itself in the impersonal mode of *illieity*. From the height and the immemorial time of anarchy, the face commands me and puts me into question, and I bear witness to it and respond. My response to the other simply involves presenting myself before the other unconditionally and for whatever the other requires of me: I simply say *Me voici* (Here I am). *Me voici* expresses the ethical saying by not saying anything about the other. Levinas explains: '"Here I am" as a witness of the Infinite, but a witness that does not thematise what it bears witness of, and whose truth is not the truth of representation, is not evidence'.[47] The other who does not reveal itself cannot be designated or represented but only performatively borne witness to in my enunciative act.[48] By saying

Me voici I do not say anything about the other but simply perform my obligation to the other. So the 'saying' is not a language of signification, for it does not produce knowledge or even understanding of the other, but indicates my performance of the other's prescription or command which binds me in responsibility. It is a language of obedience without asking any questions.

Yet there is a paradox in the very saying of the language of 'saying'. Jacques Derrida, in his essay *Violence and Metaphysics*,[49] alerted Levinas to this paradox. His deconstructive reading of Levinas's counterposition of the Hebraic language of prayer to the Greek *logos* shows the untenability of this position. One cannot do without the rational or the representational language of the 'said' even in the case of simply bearing witness to the 'saying'. Derrida writes: 'that it is necessary to state infinity's excess over totality in the language of totality; that it is necessary to state the other in the language of the same'.[50] For his part, Levinas came to acknowledge this double-bind in *Otherwise than Being or Beyond Essence*. The unrepresentable ethical response of 'saying' can only be presented 'unfaithfully' at the price of a 'betrayal' in the language of the 'said'. Levinas writes: 'We have been seeking the *Otherwise than being* from the beginning, and as soon as it is conveyed before us it is betrayed in the said that dominates the saying which states it.[51] Since this betrayal is unavoidable, the task of philosophy, argues Levinas, is to find a way of bearing testimony to the 'saying' in the 'said'. The double-bind of the dilemma calls for a double-bound strategy: 'The *Otherwise than being* is stated in a saying that must also be unsaid in order to thus extract the *Otherwise than being* from the said in which it already comes to signify but a *being Otherwise*.[52] Here Levinas's position comes very close to the deconstructive strategy of Derrida.

Levinas sets out the transcendental condition of ethics only within a closed-circuit of two – the face-to-face encounter with the other. But what happens when there are more than two? In other words, how do the transcendental principles of ethics apply to communal or societal or political situations? They do not apply: the ethical circuit is broken with the coming of the third (*le tiers*). In the relationship with the third party, says Levinas, 'My anarchic relationship with the illieity is betrayed'.[53] I am not only contemporary but also equal with the third party: it betrays my asymmetrical and passive relationship with the other. With the coming of the third party the relationship is no longer ethical; however a new question arises: 'What do I have to do with justice'.[54] Justice is not possible in the language of 'saying' since it requires the mediation of the language of the 'said'. Hence, in the matter of justice, all the apparatus of the *same* returns, for:

> justice is necessary, that is, comparison, coexistence, contemporaneousness, assembling, order, thematisation, the visibility of faces, and thus intentionality and the intellect, and thence also a copresence on an equal footing as before a court of justice.[55]

At this point one might ask: since I live with a third party, and so does everybody else, what then is the point of ethical principles? Levinas endeavours to address this question by invoking a double-bind strategy similar to the one with which he negotiates the relationship between the language of the 'saying' and the 'said'. In fact, the paradoxical relationship between 'saying' and 'said' already indicates the relationship between ethics and justice. Although in justice ethics is betrayed, justice needs ethical principles to be just. In other words, in the rational, representational order of politics and society only the trace of the transcendental grounds of ethics can prevent the immanent drift of justice from becoming unjust. For that Levinas needs to show the trace of the anarchic other in the relationship with the third party. In other words, the third party must be considered more than just one of many who do not concern me. Levinas does this when he says: 'The third party is other than the neighbour, but also another neighbour, and also a neighbour of the other, and not simply another fellow'.[56] Although the third party does not come from the immemorial time of anarchy, as s/he is synchronous with me, s/he does not become my belated concern: 'the others concern me from the first. Here fraternity precedes the commonness of a genus. My relationship with the other as neighbour gives meaning to my relations with all the others'.[57] Now we can see the importance of the transcendental principles of ethics.

Let us remind ourselves of the discussion so far: as against Western ontology, which appropriates difference by translating the other in terms of its consciousness and need, ethics, as defined by Levinas, insists that the other remains absolutely unknowable yet situated in a concrete face-to-face proximity with me, which obligates me to it and individuates my subjectivity. Then Levinas goes on to say that this position does not hold as far as society and politics are concerned, where the ontological preoccupations are not only unavoidable but necessary. In his third move, he brings back ethics into politics and society to say that unless these dimensions are shot through with ethics we cannot have a justice which is just. Only then can I take up my place as a just member of a community. To put it in Levinas's words: 'justice can be established only if I, always evaded from the concept of the ego, always destituted and divested of being, always in non-reciprocatable relationship with the other, always for the other, can become an other like the others'.[58]

I have avoided a number of difficult aspects of Levinas's ethical philosophy. Obviously much of it is informed by a particular brand of Talmudic philosophy which has much in common with Sufi and Vedantic mysticism, where the infinity of 'God' is not subject to rational theology but is the object of performative devotion and love. Moreover, Levinas's own political position, especially his apology for Zionism and the state of Israel, is highly troubling. Finally, the transition from ethics to justice remains very sketchy: apart from saying that justice can be just because of the trace of ethics, Levinas does not have much to say about it. However, despite all these limitations, Levinas's ethical 'saying' can serve as a yardstick for the just principle of justice in cross-cultural relationship. He shows how the representation of the other, and the consequent othering, is inherently violent – only serving the mastery of the *same* at the expense of the other. And a just relationship with the other must begin with the acceptance of the irreducible alterity of the other, which would question the cognitive capture of the other in representation with the ethical performance of obligation towards it.

Lyotard's Differend

Jean-François Lyotard's 'philosophising' in The Differend[59] takes on board the task of rigorously working out Levinas's rather sketchy transition from ethics to justice. Whereas Levinas slides off the page by simply saying that justice must be traced by ethics to be just, Lyotard tries to elaborate the pragmatic rules under which justice works to settle disputes. In the course of it he aligns Levinas's ethical justice with Kantian judiciousness and turns it into a move within Wittgenstein's language game. Furthermore, Wittgenstein's language game itself then is shot through with Roman Jakobson's pragmatics of semiotic circuit, and transformed into 'phrase universe'. The complex interlacing of all these strands forms the disputed arena of Differend (différend) from which the idea of justice emerges.

The elementary particle in Lyotard's analysis of justice is 'phrase'. The idea of phrase he has in mind, however, is not that of a grammarian, but of the Levinasian sense of *il y a*: 'there is',[60] an event, which in *The Differend* he prefers to call 'Is it happening'. More precisely, though, it is a move in a language game – a pragmatic circuit composed, like Jakobson's semiotic circuit, of 'the addressee, the referent, the sense, the addressor'.[61] However, unlike Wittgenstein's language game, the moves in the phrase universe do not presuppose human agencies as players of the game. A phrase is simply a move within a given set of rules: it indicates no more than that something has taken place. Although it has an addressor, it remains, along with the other three components of pragmatic circuit, empty. It is the next phrase that fills in the slots reflexively. Since the sense is not already fixed in the first phrase, the pragmatic circuit, unlike Jakobson's semiotic circuit, does not exchange predetermined codes. Just like the addressor, the sense is a contingent, reflexive judgement of the next phrase. The next phrase does the linking between phrases, thus forming the genre or the universe of phrases. Although a phrase connects with another to form genre, the nature of connection remains contingent. Lyotard says: 'To link is necessary, but a particular linkage is not'.[62] The contingency of linkage maintains the internal indeterminacy of a phrase universe. There are many regimes of phrases, such as 'reasoning. knowing, describing, recounting, questioning, showing, ordering, etc'.[63] Each has its own singularity and is not translatable into another. They are performative in nature; that is to say, they are a way of doing things, or affecting outcomes, which are specific to the genre in question. For instance, the cognitive genre performs knowing and the ethical genre performs obligation. It is when heterogeneous genres come face to face, and have to reckon with their mutual untranslatability, that Lyotard introduces the idea of *Differend* (*différend*). When irreducible differences encounter each other, the dispute can only be settled 'judiciously' without compromising each other's alterity and without any privileged and pre-set criteria.

A *Differend* as a site of dispute between heterogeneous phrases must not be equated with a litigation. Litigation is a settlement of dispute within the orbit of the *same* where the rules of one genre impose themselves on others to mediate justice. The result is precisely the opposite: injustice. The distinction between a litigation and a *Differend* is so central to Lyotard's argument that his preface (which he calls Reading Dossier) to *The Differend* opens by showing how they differ from each other:

> As distinguished from litigation, a Differend (*différend*) would be a case
> of conflict, between (at least) two parties, that cannot be equitably
> resolved for lack of a rule of judgement applicable to both arguments.
> One side's legitimacy does not imply the other's lack of legitimacy.
> However, applying a single rule of judgement to both in order to settle
> their differend as though it were merely a litigation would wrong (at
> least) one of them (and both of them if neither side admits this rule).
> Damages result from an injury which is inflicted upon the rules of a
> genre of discourse but which is reparable according to those rules. A
> wrong results from the fact that the rules of the genre of discourse by
> which one judges are not those of the judged genre or genres of dis-
> course.[64]

If a *Differend* is judged as if it is a case of litigation then a damage
(tort) is incurred by one of the parties. The consequence, however, is
even more radical, for it involves the loss of means for the damaged
party to prove that it has been wronged. Hence, a damaged party
before the court of litigation is no longer a plaintiff who failed to
prove its case, but a victim. Lyotard explains: 'It is in the nature of a
victim not to be able to prove that one has been done a wrong. A
plaintiff is someone who has incurred damages and who disposes of
the means to prove it. One becomes a victim if one loses these
means'.[65]

When the other is judged in terms of the rules of the *same*, then
the otherness of the other is denied, and the other becomes a victim.
Since the other as victim loses the legitimacy of its own discourse, it
is reduced to silence. As a plaintiff before the court of the *same*, it can
only defend itself in the language of the *same*, and thereby suffers
victimage even if it succeeds in proving its case. It is like playing a
game by someone else's rules, where one loses even by winning. For
the plaintiff to cease being a victim, it must find its own expression
for the language of its irreducible difference. In so far as my own
discourse is concerned, I can prevent my victimisation of others in
two ways: first, by stopping judging others by my rules; second, by
bearing testimony to others' differences. This involves finding a new
idiom that lies outside of my game because 'phrases obeying different regimes are untranslatable to one into another'.[66] The other
phrase can only be translated by drawing an analogy between it and
my phrase with the effect of reducing the other's alterity into the
same. It is now clear that Lyotard's *Differend* is a reworking of
Levinas's alterity in terms of the pragmatics of the language game.
However, there are some areas of difference between Levinas and
Lyotard which I will explore in a moment.

In so far as Western thinking is concerned, Lyotard, not unlike Levinas, complains about the hegemony of speculative, cognitive and ostensive phrases which form epistemological and ontological genres. These genres, argues Lyotard, install themselves as the universal court of all judgements. As a result, the difference, say, of the ethical genre is reduced to the ostensive proof of the epistemological genre. In other words, it judges 'the good or the just upon the true, or what ought to be upon what is'.[67] For Lyotard the totalising thrusts of Western ontological (speculative) and epistemological (cognitive and ostensive) genres not only capture the ethical genre but produce a totalitarian discourse. The speculative and epistemological genres do not allow any outside – they mediate everything with categories of consciousness, and subject them to the procedures of ostensive proof.

When Lyotard comes to describe the ethical *Différend* he calls it obligation. Since he follows Levinas's arguments very closely, I will not describe them, except to offer a few comments on how he phrases them in pragmatic terms. The ethical phrase for Lyotard, as it is for Levinas, is prescriptive and performative. The other, the addressor, phrases its command and thereby obligates the addressee, who performs it by responding to it. But if the addressee asks 'what do they mean?', s/he not only betrays the ethical genre with the cognitive, but turns her/himself into addressor. Moreover, this move turns the 'subject of uttering' (*sujet de l'énonciation*, enunciation) into a 'subject of utterance' (*sujet de l'énonce*, statement). In other words, the other as a place of prescription is made into an object of cognitive or constative discourse. The result is the mastery and imprisonment of the other in the empire of the *same*. In the prescriptive genre of obligation, Lyotard argues, the 'I' cannot remain itself but must be displaced into 'you' – the place of the addressee – who can only respond to the phrase 'you ought to'. 'I', as an ethical interlocutor, cannot be a subject of experience but only a witness to a prescriptive phrase who never stops being an addressee. So far it seems that Lyotard is in complete agreement with Levinas. However, Lyotard wants to push Levinas's arguments to their limits and prune them of any subjective traces. In so far as 'I' as an addressee experiences the other as 'somebody', Lyotard argues, the ethical obligation is betrayed with the cognitive phrase. For him, the invocation of the first-person, who is a subject of experience, invariably brings into play a self who exercises cognitive judgement. Lyotard likens the other, or the addressor of the ethical phrase, to 'event' (Is it happening?), and as such is '"absolutely" not marked,

not even by a silence'.[68] Even the slightest alteration of this absolute
inscrutability would betray the other, and the ethical phrase stops
being ethical anymore. It seems that Lyotard interprets Levinas's
ethical sayings as dislocating the other from *Is it happening? (Arrive-
t-il)* to *Are you coming? (Arrives-tu)* by making the other 'somebody'.
Levinas phrases the other as *Are you coming?*, as if the other needs
the experience of 'I' to reveal itself. Here Lyotard sees a profound
irony in Levinas's work. Levinas, we may remember, critiqued
Heidegger's egologism partly for his preoccupation with the disclo-
sure of the meaning of Being. Lyotard thinks that Levinas is repeating the Heideggerian folly when he figures the other as if it wants to
be 'somebody' through my experience. As Lyotard puts it: Levinas's
addressee, as the site of the subjective experience of the other,
behaves as if 'the foreign phrase wants to phrase itself through you
as its go-between, that it wants something from you because it would
like to be itself'.[69]

By questioning Levinas's addressee as the 'go-between' of the
ethical phrase, Lyotard questions both his subjectivism and religiosity. Levinas, to remind ourselves, conceived ethical relationship as a
face-to-face encounter, where 'I' is directly addressed by the other in
the prescriptive language of command, and where the ensuing obligation defines 'I's' subjectivity. Lyotard's arguments contest the
aspects of face-to-face where 'I' is the chosen addressee of the
addressor who is 'somebody'. The face-to-face that addresses the
addressee as 'you' cannot avoid the implication of subjectivism.
Beneath the subjective structure of the face-to-face, Lyotard sees the
presence of the divine whose divinity, like Heidegger's Being, strives
to reveal himself by calling the addressee into being. He calls this
'edifying confusion' characteristic of religious, mystical thinking. In
the ensuing laughter of the pagan, Lyotard wants to maintain the
absolute anonymity and impersonality of the ethical phrase. For
him, the addressor of the ethical phrase is not 'somebody', nor is it
addressed to anybody in particular. What he wants to show is not my
unavoidable obligation, but how obligation works in an ethical
phrase. It has nothing to do with my personal responsibility, but is
internal to the ethical genre as a phrase universe. However, if I want
to take part in an ethical genre I cannot do so without being obligated
to the other about whom I cannot know anything. So for Lyotard, I
am not always already responsible for the other – which is only possible in a religious or mystical mode of discourse that presumes the
presence of a primordial other as 'somebody' who needs me – but

only responsible if 'I' want to phrase an ethical phrase. The consequence of their difference is this: for Levinas, one cannot avoid being obligated to the other – it is the very core of one's subjectivity; for Lyotard obligation is contingent, in so far as one is implicated in the ethical genre. Whether one should be implicated in the ethical genre or not, is a question Lyotard cannot answer.

For Lyotard, the question of justice can only be posed in terms of the heterogeneity of regimes of phrases: after everything is said and done, justice amounts to no more than respecting the irreducible difference of each genre of phrases. Primarily, it is the genre of a phrase that suffers wrong when it is prevented from expressing its own case in its own language and is mediated by another. A 'human subject' suffers wrong only secondarily, and only in so far as s/he is a plaintiff by virtue of being implicated in the wronged genre. A worker suffers wrong in so far as s/he has to appeal in the phrases belonging to capital. Since the phrases of the worker (say, the language of surplus value) do not get a hearing as they are made illegitimate, the worker is a victim no matter how well s/he is treated by the tribunal of capital.

Given the fact that phrases are incommensurable with each other and there does not exist a common language to settle disputes between them, how does one proceed without victimising others? In order to answer this question Lyotard turns to Kant. The mode of presentation (*Darstellung*) of ethical phrase, argues Lyotard, is not representation – characteristic of the cognitive phrase – which requires ostensive demonstration. The object of the ethical phrase, like the object of the aesthetic phrase, is the object of an Idea, and not an object of cognition. The latter involves determinant judgement, and as such is representable in terms of 'what is the case'. The ethical phrase as an object of Idea cannot be formulated into a concept of knowledge or determined as 'what is the case'; hence, neither can it be determined nor represented. It is an 'intuition without concept' which is only signalled by a 'feeling' without origin or destination, but like *il y a*, it cannot be doubted. In fact, doubting does not come into it at all since to doubt 'feeling' is to judge it in terms of cognitive phrase which would betray it. Hence the 'Idea can be neither proved nor refuted'.[70] In the ethical phrase, 'the Idea is signalled by the feeling of respect and constitutes the situation of morality or obligation'.[71] Since the ethical phrase as Idea cannot be judged using the determinant judgement of the cognitive phrase, how is it to be judged? Here the Kantian 'judiciousness' comes into play.

Lyotard has a high regard for Kant's *Critique of Judgement*; for him it presents an exemplary case of 'judiciousness'. The basic premise of a judicious move, Lyotard argues, is the separation of the universe of phrases into heterogeneous genres, of which Kant's disjunction of faculties stands as a pre-eminent precursor. In other words, a judicious move, which prevents the committing of injustice, must accept as its precondition the incommensurability of phrases characteristic of the *Differend*. In a judicious move, as Lyotard puts it, 'judgement must recognise and bring to light the abyss that exists between ... sentences: their incommensurability'.[72] Once the judicious move has accepted the incommensurability of phrases or faculties, it cannot use an overarching criterion of judgement, or a predetermined law, to judge any of them. How does one judge without universal or determined criteria? Lyotard turns to the Kantian sublime for an answer, which 'judges without a rule'.[73] The sublime as a non-representable paradox not only represents the highest point of aesthetic judgement but also serves as a sign of social and political 'judiciousness'. Lyotard writes:

> the feeling of the sublime as an affective paradox, the paradox of feeling publicly and as a group that something which is 'formless' alludes to a beyond of experience, that fleeing constitutes an 'as-if presentation' of the Idea of civil society and even of cosmopolitan society, and thus an as-if presentation of the Idea of morality, right where that Idea nevertheless cannot be presented, within experience.[74]

In the end, Lyotard prescribes the imaginative experiments of the sublime as the only way to approach the irreducible difference of the other without doing injustice to it. This is the aesthetic 'judiciousness' of the pagan. Since the pagan can accept neither the pre-ontological obligation nor the face-to-face subjective mode of address that obligates him, he invents an anonymous language-game to phrase the ethical genre, where the addressor and addressee positions remain empty. Unlike Levinas's obligation, for Lyotard the obligation is not obligatory. If I want to play the ethical game, or want to behave justly, I must make myself obligated to an unknown other, whom I cannot represent but only bear testimony to in my discourse by conducting an imaginative experimentation analogous to the aesthetic art of the sublime. The problem with this position is that it reduces ethical response to the other to the modernist aesthetics of avant-gardist creativity, because for Lyotard ethics remains simply a problem of representation rather than a practical problem. In other words, he reduces the question of 'how do I act towards the other?' to 'how do I express it?' Moreover, if Lyotard succeeds in erasing Levinas's subjective traces, he does so by neutralising the force of Levinas's ethical saying. For Lyotard, there is no good reason why ethics should be obligatory, and consequently it lets the 'subject' off the hook of her/his responsibility towards others.

For its implications for a cross-cultural ethics, Lyotard's the *Differend* does not represent a major advance over Levinas's 'saying', except in its analysis of victimhood, which, by clearly delineating what is only implicit in Levinas, provides us with a useful critical tool. For Lyotard, as we have seen, the victim is not a wronged plaintiff before a court of litigation, but one whose language does not get a hearing. This is precisely what happened to the colonised other of Europe. Moreover, the universalist and cognitive discourse of the West, whose unjust hegemony Lyotard bemoans, is the means by which the West represented its other, and thereby inflicted further wrong on it.

Deleuze and Guattari's 'a-parallel evolution or involution'

Michel Foucault is right to see *Anti-Oedipus* as 'a book of ethics'.[75] Indeed, individually or together, much of Deleuze and Guattari's work is driven by the ethical imperative of a life without a 'totalising paranoia'. Hence much of what Deleuze and Guattari do should not be seen as mere theoretical exercises; on the contrary, they are ethical performances that dramatise affirmative values. However, unlike Levinas and Lyotard, Deleuze and Guattari do not reject the Western philosophical tradition in its entirety. Instead, Deleuze, in particular, traces a minor ontological route from the Stoics via Spinoza and Bergson to Nietzsche, which, while being affirmative, manages to stay free of a 'totalising paranoia'.

Deleuze's early works, most notably *Nietzsche and Philosophy* and *Difference and Repetition*, carry out a thoroughgoing critique of totalising thought, on whose apex sit Hegel's dialectics. Where the dialectic, by means of conceptual analogy, only displays negative or relative difference, Deleuze endeavours to dramatise a positive and absolute difference. Moreover, against the mimetic desire and the pathos of *Ressentiment* characteristic of dialectics, Deleuze proposes affirmative desire and joyous becoming. In *Nietzsche and Philosophy* Deleuze, in contrasting Nietzschean transvaluation with Hegelian dialectics, sets up the course of his own ethical project:

Not all the relations between 'same' and 'other' are sufficient to form a
dialectic ... [It] depends on the role of the negative ... In Nietzsche the
essential relation of one force to another is never conceived of as negative element in the essence. In its relation with the other the force
which makes itself obeyed does not deny the other or that which it is
not, it affirms its own difference and enjoys this difference ... For the
speculative element of negation, opposition or contradiction Nietzsche
substitutes the practical element of *difference*, the object of affirmation
and enjoyment.[76]

Deleuze, in order to arrive at an affirmative ethics of joyous
becoming, makes two basic moves: in one, he stages a speculative
drama that enacts a positive or dynamic ontology of self-difference
that differs from itself; in the other, he presents a practical
'diagram' of becoming-otherwise in the encounter with the outside.
Deleuze articulates the former by drawing on the internal movement of Bergsonian virtuality and the Spinozist efficient difference
of singular and univocal being. However, his interpretation of
Nietzsche's dynamics of internal force and of Freud's *Thanatos* as
the groundless ground demonstrates a productive process of self-
difference which accords with Bergsonian and Spinozist ontologies.
Deleuze's arguments on positive ontology, rehearsed through the
reading of the works of these philosophers, are rather complex, and
often shot through with concepts borrowed from medieval philosophy. It would be an interesting exercise to trace his course through
these philosophers in pursuit of a positive ontology – but this book
is not the place to do so. For our purpose here it suffices to note
that the positive ontology that Deleuze establishes as the speculative ground for ethics insists on the internal productivity and movement of being which differs from itself. Hence, unlike dialectics,
positive ontology does not require mediation for its determination.
Consequently, the positioning of relative difference, negation and
opposition are not required: in positive ontology, the concept of
being determines itself by its own internal causation. Therefore,
the determination of being can neither be permanent nor be aiming towards permanence, but is in permanent flux. In fact, it is with
the question of determination of being that Deleuze moves from
ontological speculation to the practical ethics of joyous becoming.
This is what, following Foucault, Deleuze and Guattari call 'actuality', where the self-differentiating being, in the process of becoming, encounters the outside. In *What is Philosophy* they write: 'The
actual is not what we are but, rather, what we become, what we are

in the process of becoming – that is to say, the Other, our becoming-other'.[77]

Deleuze, in his essay on Michel Tournier,[78] shows how the structure of othering works, and indicates a world without it which would allow the world of the other to emerge. He begins by showing how 'the Other' functions, like the Lacanian symbolic order, as the *a priori* structure of the 'possible world', which distributes relational positions to self and its other.[79] The 'possible world' not only brings with it a subject capable of stable perception, it also offers its subjects a world of totalising significations:

> Other people relativise the not-known, the not-perceived; since for me, the other people introduce the sign of the not-perceived into what I perceive, causing me to grasp what I don't perceive as perceivable for others.[80]

The structure of 'the Other' causes the opacity of the world to vanish, and thereby offers an illumined totality where everything is potentially knowable and intelligible. The 'possible world' is also a world of 'commonsense' and 'good sense' where the specular subject seeks to master the other in representation. Michel Tournier's Robinson, still mimicking Defoe's Robinson in the early chapters of *The Other Island*, writes in his journal:

> I demand, I insist, that everything around me shall henceforth be measured, tested, certified, mathematical and rational. One of my tasks must be to make a full survey of the island, its distances and its contours, and incorporate all these details in an accurate surveyor's map. I should like every plant to be labelled, every bird to be ringed, every animal to be branded. I shall not be content until this opaque and impenetrable place, filled with secret ferments and malignant stirrings, has been transformed into a calculated design, visible and intelligible to its very depths![81]

Even though the island, before the appearance of Friday, is without another subject, Robinson behaves as if the structure of 'the Other' is still in place, and sets about the representation of a 'possible world' that will secure his mastery over it. However, Robinson of 'the Other Island' soon stops mimicking his model and overcomes 'Other-as-structure' which releases the absolute other, whom Deleuze variously calls 'double', 'completely-other than the Other', 'beyond the Other', 'Other (*Autre*) than the Other (*autrui*)' and 'real others'. With the disappearance of the structure that drives the othering, the process of mediation disappears, resulting in direct encounter with the other. Now, instead of being trapped in the mimetic desire and the pathos of *Ressentiment*, Robinson of *The Other Island* discovers the 'upright desire' of self-affirmation and becoming-other. This is the 'actuality' of the ethical moment that expresses the 'virtuality' described in the ontological speculation. In a nutshell, Deleuze-Guattarian ethics prescribe the overcoming of negative desire and the pathos of *Ressentiment* so that being can actualise its self-difference. This, they argue, cannot be carried through as long as the 'subject' continues to harbour relational difference. In other words, the 'subject' who still does the othering remains trapped in mimetic desire, and is in no position to affirm its own self-difference. For Deleuze and Guattari the freeing of the other from representational capture and becoming-other in the immanent movement of self-difference is a simultaneous process. In order to grasp this process we must further explore how their idea of 'the a-parallel evolution' works.

Deleuze and Guattari drew the notion of 'the a-parallel evolution' from the work of Rémy Chauvin, and which Deleuze explains in his conversation with Claire Parnet as:

> becomings: it is not one term which becomes the other, but encounters the other, a single becoming which is not common to the two, since they have nothing to do with one another, but which is between the two, which has its own direction, a block of becoming, an a-parallel evolution.[82]

Deleuze insists on qualifying this evolution as a-parallel because for him the encounter that leads to becoming does not take place between two molar identities which appropriate or imitate each other. If the evolution were parallel, the *same* would have appropriated the 'other' by turning it into a relative difference through the analogy of concepts. By invoking the idea of 'the a-parallel evolution', Deleuze wants to signal the encounter between multiplicities which maintain their absolute difference from each other. When an encounter takes place, one does not recognise the other but repeats the other to form 'a single becoming'. However, we must not see this as a process where one gets absorbed by another or mimics another. For mimicry does not indicate 'doubling', but rather a form of repetition in the manner of tracing where one molar subject imitates another. Hence Deleuze and Guattari are right to view 'mimicry [as a] bad concept, since it relies on binary logic to describe phenomena of an entirely different nature'.[83] Instead the repetition resulting in 'doubling' takes the form of the simulacrum, which by overturning the model and the copy, unleashes the force of becoming otherwise, which Nietzsche calls 'eternal repetition'. Far from being a mimetic repetition, 'the a-parallel evolution' signals a mode of repetition which effects a 'block of becoming' in the encounter between multiplicities who remain outside of each other.

Perhaps the term 'evolution' is rather misleading because it indicates a line of descent and filiation, where a genus evolves towards a teleological point of growth. Since becoming, in the encounter with the other, takes place 'between heterogeneous terms' involving the composition of 'alliance', Deleuze and Guattari, half-way through A Thousand Plateaus prefer to call it 'involution'.[84] For the process of becoming in encounters is a form of folding, where the outside folds into the inside producing an 'in-between' that cannot be either.

Although, as we have noted, Deleuze and Guattari borrow the term 'the a-parallel evolution' from Rémy Chauvin, its philosophical provenance, despite sharing common ground with Nietzsche and Bergson, decidedly lies in Spinoza's 'common notions'. Deleuze's interpretation of Spinoza emphasises the paradoxical ontology which is simultaneously both singular and univocal: singular in substance and univocal in attributes. The singularity of substance indicates that everything complicates or folds into one substance; and the univocity of the attributes indicates the expression or the unfolding of the substance in everything. Moreover, the singularity and the univocity present being as internally caused and immanently productive without external determination. However, against the backdrop of this ontological speculation (geometric method), it is when Spinoza comes to define body and its power of affection that we enter the arena of practical ethics. On the one hand, the body is defined as pure function – what can the body do? – which amounts to no more than a 'set of relations of speed and slowness, of motion and rest, between particles that compose it from this point of view, that is, between unformed elements'.[85] The body thus defined is what Deleuze calls 'longitude'. On the other hand, the body is defined as a site of affection 'that occup[ies] a body at each moment, that is, the intensive states of anonymous force (force for existing, capacity for being affected)'.[86] The effect of affection determines the variation of bodies' capacity for acting, which Deleuze calls 'latitude'. Together they form the plane of immanence or consistency – the plane on which all becomings take place.

How is a 'common notion' formed? In order to answer this question we have to gather several building blocks. But we must begin with the body, since it is through this that 'common notions' are formed. Once bodies are shed of their molar forms, such as genre or species and we define them in terms of the functional traits of their *unformed elements*, the rigid distinction between them disappears. Instead, we discover something common to all bodies – namely, extension, motion and rest. When a body, given the commonality of *unformed elements*, encounters another a common notion between them is formed. However, the process is a good deal more complex than this. For the common characteristics causing bodies to join each other in practice require an agency, which is provided by the power of affection. However, the power of affection itself has two sides to it: the *power of acting* and the power of *being acted upon*. Spinoza defines the former as *actions* and the latter as *passions*. Deleuze explains:

> one needs first to distinguish between two sorts of affections: *actions*, which are explained by the nature of the affected individual, and which spring from the individual's essence; and *passions*, which are explained by something else, and which originate outside the individual. Hence the capacity for being affected is manifested as a *power of acting* insofar as it is assumed to be filled by active affections, but as a *power of being acted upon* insofar as it is filled by passions.[87]

The power of affection in its active mode (*action*) is internally caused by a body's own essence, thereby producing an 'adequate idea' – the force of becoming. The power of affection in its passive mode (*passion*) is determined externally. In other words, a body is made to suffer an affection by another body outside it, which separates the body from its power of acting, producing only an 'inadequate idea'. These two powers of affection roughly correspond to Foucault's two relationships of forces: 'the power to affect other forces (spontaneity) and to be affected by others (receptivity)'.[88] It should now be clear that encounters between bodies take place in the passive mode, i.e. the plane of passion. Therefore, it seems that all encounters reduce a body's power to act, and consequently, keep in check the force of becoming. However, all passive affections are not the same. In fact, there are two types of *passion*: sadness and joy. Deleuze writes:

> when we encounter an external body that does not agree with our own (i.e., whose relation does not enter composition with ours), it is as if the

power of that body opposed our power, bringing about a subtraction or a fixation; when this occurs, it may be said that our power of acting is diminished or blocked, and that the corresponding passions are those of sadness. In the contrary case, when we encounter a body that agrees with our nature, one whose relation compounds with ours, we may say that its power is added to ours; the passions that affect us are those of *joy*, and our power of acting increased or enhanced.[89]

It is only with joyous encounters that 'common notions' are formed, when two bodies join forces to compose a more powerful body. Although formally the joyous encounter remains *passive*, it produces a result which is active, as it increases the power of acting. Consequently, despite external determination, an 'adequate idea' is produced because a joyous encounter 'expresses the effect on us of a body that agrees with ours, it makes possible the formation of a common notion that comprehends the agreement adequately from within'.[90] Hence a common notion leads to a joyful becoming of multiple bodies in encounter. Now that we have followed through the stages of conceptual elaboration that Spinoza carried out to formulate 'common notions', we are perhaps in a better position to understand Deleuze and Guattari's 'a-parallel evolution or involution'.

Although they formulate the concept of 'the a-parallel evolution or involution' on the basis of Spinoza's 'common notions', they do not simply repeat it. Instead, Spinoza's insights provide them with the tools for 'diagramming' their own practical ethical imperatives. We have already seen that for Deleuze and Guattari 'the a-parallel evolution' is a process of mutual becoming through the valency of forces in the event of encounter. It is worth emphasising once more that the parties involved in an encounter are neither models nor copies of each other: they are radically different from each other. Neither can their relationship be conceived through analogy nor as parallel. For parallel relationships can only exist between stable identities formed by a molar organisation in a rigid strata. The encounter takes place at the molecular level or on the plane of consistency; and the encountering bodies are Spinoza's bodies of pure function and affection. So the encounter takes place behind the masks of bodies rigidified with received meaning and immobile subjectivities (white wall and black hole); hence the bodies in encounter become de-stratified or deterritorialised. Once a body is de-stratified and becomes a body in encounter it discovers its outside which allows it to enter the 'plane of consistency' where the distinction between interior and exterior disappears, making it possible for the body in question to conjugate with forces of the other body and become-other. Hence becoming-animal is not a question of imitating a molar animal but conjugating with the molecular animal (Spinoza's body again) which shares certain pure functions (common notions) with my body. This is a practical strategy of performative becoming. Deleuze and Guattari say:

> You become animal only molecularly. You do not become a barking dog, but by barking, if it is done with enough feeling [joyful affection], with enough necessity and composition, you emit a molecular dog. Man does not become wolf, or vampire, as if changed molar species; the vampire and werewolf are becomings of man, in other words, proximities between molecules in composition, relations of movement and rest, speed and slowness between emitted particles ... do not look for a resemblance or analogy to the animal, for this is becoming-animal in action, the production of the molecular animal.[91]

This is how the mutual becoming of two bodies in 'the a-parallel evolution or involution' takes place: my body reaches the outside and 'I' experience the other body as the outside (intensities without an image or representation), then two forces of the outside are combined to produce a powerful new body which is 'neither one nor two, nor the relation of the two; it is the in-between'.[92] Before we evaluate Deleuze and Guattari's ethics in relation to that of Levinas and Lyotard, we need to explore the practical 'diagram' of becoming that Deleuze and Guattari prescribe.

For Deleuze and Guattari 'there is no becoming-majoritarian; majority is never becoming. All becoming is minoritarian'.[93] Minority, however, should not be seen as a numerical figure. Rather minorities articulate the gap from the axioms that serve as the molar principle of stratification. Moreover, minorities are not models to be copied but, like simulacrum, unfetter the force of becoming. In fact, minorities represent multiplicities of contingent connection without the axiomatic of subjection, where the principle of the 'one' functions as the transcendental principle, the subject of enunciation, and the point of repressive power. Although for Deleuze and Guattari minorities represent the anonymous multiplicity of the outside, they do not deny the concrete particularity of the majority/minority relationship. Hence in Deleuze and Guattari's joyful politics there is no becoming-man, becoming-Whitman or becoming-European; only becoming-women, becoming-black or becoming any other subaltern. Yet they also argue that 'even blacks ... must become black.

Even women must become women'.[94] This apparent antinomy needs an explanation. First, the numerical or subaltern minorities, despite being oppressed by the majority, do not automatically become nomadic or molecular minorities or form rhizomatic multiplicities. Second, by being contingently exterior to the stratified regime, or being its othered-others, minorities harbour not only a dissonant force but the virtual force of the outside. Third, the subaltern minorities must actualise the virtual force of the outside to become rhizomic multiplicity. If minorities do not become minorities they will be trapped within mimetic desire, reactive politics, and the sad passion of *Ressentiment*. Consequently, even if the current majority is vanquished, a new majority will be born from the minorities. Fanon knew it well: it is worth remembering his ethical prescription to the colonised minorities caught in the mimetic trap: 'do not imitate Europe ... so let us stop envying her'.[95]

Deleuze and Guattari's position of becoming-minority of minorities has been controversial, feminist writers especially having taken exception to it. For instance, Luce Irigaray writes of 'becoming-women' as that 'which has been long been familiar to women. For them isn't the organless body a historical condition?'[96] Among others, Rosi Braidotti shares Irigaray's views when, engaging with Deleuze's work, she writes: 'one cannot deconstruct a subjectivity one has never been fully granted'.[97] More importantly, these writers see the danger of giving up sexual difference for an ethics of self-difference that prescribes the overcoming of all notions of binary or essential differences. However, if it is a strategic move for achieving rights or even demanding power, Deleuze and Guattari would not object to it. Rather they see the need for it; they write: 'It is, of course, indispensable for women to conduct a molar politics, with a view to winning back their own organism, their own history, their own subjectivity: "we as women ..." makes its appearance as a subject of enunciation'.[98] The voiceless must have a voice, the subaltern must speak, Caliban must retort in the mastery of his own discourse. Alas! after all, there cannot be a completely un-Hegelian way. To overlook this, paradoxically, amounts to deafness to the call of concrete minoritarian others. Aimé Césaire has given the most poignant expression to this insight:

> I want to rediscover the secret of great speech and of great burning. I want to say storm. I want to say river. I want to say tornado. I want to say leaf, I want to say tree. I want to be soaked by every rainfall, moistened by every dew. As frenetic blood rolls on the slow current of the eye, I

want to roll words like maddened horses like new children like clotted milk like curfew like traces of a temple like precious stones buried deep enough to daunt all miners. The man who couldn't understand me couldn't understand the roaring of a tiger.[99]

However, if essential difference – of which the notion of experiential plenitude of sexed or racial bodies has been a persistent expression – is not rejected as an ethical principle, it will only mimetically repeat the absolutism it opposes. Apart from reproducing essentialism, which the asserting of experiential valorisation of sexual and racial bodies are driven by their own logic to embrace, this position also loses the ethical ground for critiquing the existing structure of power. Politics based on essential difference can, in the end, only claim injustice on the ground that we do not have what they have. Hence it is important to retain the ethical postulate in which minorities must also become minorities, even though strategically a molar politics claiming a share of the majoritarian power is a historical necessity. The relevance of Deleuze's minoritarian becoming to the politics of subalterns needs much more careful discussion than I have given it here. Moreover, Deleuze and Guattari's notion of Minor Literature, argued in relation to Kafka's work, offers an interesting account of subaltern literary/linguistic practice as a kind of burrowing into the majoritarian bodies both to decompose them and to recompose a new line of becoming, which can have wide implications for subaltern politics in general. However, since the politics of the subaltern, although bearing on the concerns of the present book, does not constitute its main focus, I will leave it at that.

For Deleuze and Guattari 'the a-parallel evolution or involution' as a framework of ethical relationship with the other *diagrams* the mutual process of becoming-other. I become other by decomposing my molar shell and the other whom I encounter also comes into my proximity in its true otherness (as a Spinozist body without a representable identity). When this happens the distinction between us, which is imposed by the essentialist gesture of opposition integral to the binary logic, disappears and we discover the 'common notions' between our bodies. Now we can become, without the ominous shadow of the root-tree, other than our molar selves, and joyfully conjugate with each other by contingently adding forces that agree with us, and compose a powerful collective body of moving multiplicities (not the copular 'to be' of molar and fixed identity but in the anonymous mode of the indefinite article and the infinitive verb 'to

...' of virtual future). How about my obligation towards the other? Perhaps the best way to answer this question is by comparing Deleuze and Guattari's ethical prescription with that of Levinas and Lyotard.

All four philosophers, as we have seen, agree on one thing: relational difference, negation, opposition, and representation capture the other for the 'imperialism of the same'. They all want to overcome a tradition of Western philosophy that culminated in Hegel. The ethical question that faces them is: how to respond to the other without compromising its otherness. Levinas argues for 'anarchic' (pre-ontological) obligation to the other about whom I know nothing. This obligation gives me my subjectivity with the implication that the other, despite being absolutely or irreducibly different from me, is in close proximity to me. Moreover, my relation with the other is passive as I am commanded from the heights and have to obey. Despite the fact that the ethical relationship, as it is formed in a face-to-face relationship between two, breaks down in the arena of societal and political justice, it is important, argues Levinas, to keep the sense of ethical obligation in mind when dealing with justice, otherwise a just justice cannot be effected. Lyotard more or less endorses much of what Levinas argues, except that as a self-proclaimed pagan he has difficulties with Levinas's religiosity and subjectivity. Lyotard cannot accept 'anarchic' obligation as an existential condition tied to the constitution of subjectivity, so he poses his ethical question in terms of the pragmatic and impersonal games of phrase regimes. Within the ambit of phrase regimes justice works in two different ways. First, Lyotard seems to argue that if one wants to be ethical then one is obligated in the manner prescribed by Levinas. This move, as I have argued, although it frees Lyotard's position of religiosity and subjectivism, makes obligation unobligatory, thereby taking away much of the force of Levinas's argument. It is now no more than a genre of phrases which one should follow if one wants to be just. Secondly, Lyotard re-articulates alterity as the irreducible difference between phrase regimes. Injustice is committed if the rules of one phrase regime are used to judge another. A just response to the other without any common criteria can only be attempted, case by case, through innovative experimentation in the manner of the sublime arts. The upshot of Lyotard's position is that all phrases or multiplicity of differences must get a legitimate hearing, and none must judge, suppress the others, or put itself up as the arbiter of all others.

Deleuze and Guattari's ethical response to the other is quite different from both Lyotard and Levinas. However, they would share Lyotard's paganism as their ethics of becoming embraces radical impersonality and total anonymity. For them, obligation is a moral rather than an ethical issue, and as such belongs to the subjective mode, which they endeavour to overcome. Following Nietzsche and Spinoza, they see ethics as dealing with the question of how being can affirmatively become, which involves the overcoming of the pathos of the subjective mode. Driven by the need to articulate this affirmation, and unlike Levinas and Lyotard, they necessarily spend a great deal of intellectual energy in devising an appropriate ontology. Instead of resorting to the logic of the negative, or being dependent on the othering of the other and *Ressentiment*, Deleuze and Guattari propose an ontology, founded on the idea of positive force, where one becomes unceasingly through the internal movement of one's own self-difference. In other words, they conceive of a being whose nature is to become other than itself. The other, if not othered in representation, is simply the outside – the molecular force that functions, affects and is affected without an image. This outside, they argue, is precisely the force that folds the inside of the subject, which consequently erases the distinction between interior and exterior (this distinction is the essential difference characteristic of the oppositional logic of representation). After everything is said and done, their position implies that the other is simultaneously within and without: it is without in so far as there are multiple quanta of forces of other bodies that affect me, but within in so far as my body discovers its forces beneath its stratified or molar form. If there is any obligation, if we can still use the expression, it amounts to renouncing the egological drive of othering the other and capturing it in representation. To put it in a Nietzschean language, it amounts to saying 'no' to the passion of *Ressentiment*. However, saying 'no' to the negative passions, for Deleuze and Guattari, does not amount to a criterion for moral conduct, but forms a stage towards positive ethics – the affirmative moment of saying 'yes' to the eternal repetition – which involves becoming in the encounter with the other. In an encounter my forces of the outside conjugate joyfully with the other who is entirely outside and create a mutual becoming of 'in-betweens'. The upshot of this ethics is the constant co-mingling of anonymous bodies, where each is becoming-other. So Deleuze and Guattari's ethical response to the other is not obligation but the discovery of forces for reaching a proximity with the other so that a band of becoming can be formed. Levinas is sure to object to this. For him, by conceiving the other as the fold of the inside, Deleuze and Guattari would be turning the other, like the Freudian unconscious, into the unknown within, and thereby compromising the other's radical separation. Moreover, in so far as the other still serves as a vehicle of my becoming, Levinas would see their ethics as a form of egocentricity, characteristic of ontology. Deleuze and Guattari would perhaps respond to this charge by arguing something like this: only if the ontology were structured with notions of ego and molar identity, would this charge then be a legitimate one. But theirs is not. Moreover, they would argue, since my becoming through the encounter with the other involves the decomposition of the subjective mode (my ego and molar identity) – the structure of egocentricity – then it cannot be seen as egocentric. Moreover, unlike the Freudian unconscious as it is subjected to psycho-analytical hermeneutics, the outside that folds into inside remains unknown and unrepresentable.

So far as the 'historically determined' human assemblages (say, molar aggregates of racial, gender and national identities) are concerned, they would argue that becomings must pass through minorities (subaltern, dominated, subjected to enunciative author-ity). For a majority there is no becoming without betrayal, without becoming-traitor, without becoming-minority. This is the 'active betrayal' of which Juan Goytisolo, becoming the living ghost of Count Julian – the arch-traitor of the Spanish majoritarian culture – speaks:

> the pleasure of betraying: of freeing oneself of that which identifies and defines us: of that which converts us, against our will, into spokesmen of something: of that which pins a label on us and fashions a mask for us: what homeland?: all of them: those of the past, the present, and the future: large and small, powerful or miserably poor and helpless: sell-ing one's homeland into bondage, an endless chain of sales, an unend-ing crime, permanent and active betrayal.[100]

If a majority becomes a minority by 'active betrayal', a minority too must become a minority by actively resisting the mimetic desire of majoritarian principles. However, in order for an effective deterritorialisation of the majoritarian assemblages to take place, the traitorous majority and minorities must conjugate with each other or evolve or involute in an a-parallel way to compose a powerful body of 'in-between', so that the becoming-minority of everybody would be possible. For cross-cultural relationships, this is perhaps the best ethical prescription to follow. Aimé Césaire has already formulated this ethics in his *Return to My Native Land*:

> As there are hyena-men and panther men,
> so I shall be a Jew man
> a Kaffir man
> a Hindu-from-Calcutta man
> a man-from-Harlem-who-hasn't-got-the-vote.[101]

However, for the actualisation of this ethics of becoming-other certain precautions must be taken, because becoming in encounter does not take place as if the 'subject' is already destratified. Since all becomings must negotiate the assemblages of molar identities (both individual or larger aggregates like race, gender, class, etc.) and of the politics of power, certain ethical (in the moral sense) principles are needed for the preparation of this process. They are: (1) the irreducible alterity of the other must not be compromised as Levinas insists (and Lyotard, Deleuze and Guattari imply in their different ways); (2) the other must not be translated unjustly by the rules of my discourse as Lyotard insists (and Levinas, Deleuze and Guattari also imply in their different ways). Furthermore, these ethical (moral) conducts cannot be sustained without binding them to the obligation towards the other. Anselm, the dreaming narrator of Wilson Harris's *The Four Banks of the River of Space*, in his ethical journey of cross-cultural becoming, knows it well. He asks in his dream-monologue: 'What balance divides heroism into sheer possession of the other, the sheer hunt, on the one hand, and necessary burial of the stranger one bears who brings news of the chains that bind us[?]'. He answers, 'To break those chains we need to see ourselves as captives in the hand of the stranger'.[102] Being active and passive are not contradictory but a part of the same process at two different levels. The molar or the rigid subject must assume passivity in relation to the other as a way of preparing her/himself for the active becoming (molecular) in the encounter with the other. Only a passive molar subject can undertake the a-parallel evolution or involution in a joyful conjugation with others. Only Anselm, who breaks the molar chain by becoming a captive of the other, can actualise the virtual 'cross-cultural capacity to bear the dual, triple (sometimes self-reversible) content'.[103]

Finally, we must ask how the ethical responses to the other bear on the discourse of othering? The ethical principles that I have outlined – namely, the obligation for the irreducible alterity of the other, the just conduct of not making a victim of the other by de-legitimising its phrases, and becoming-other in encounter – should serve as the prescriptive imperative of any cross-cultural relationship or discourse. The discourse of othering, as I have shown, has two sides to it. On the one hand, it serves as the specular or dialectical mechanism for installing relational identity and difference, it displaces the negativities within to shape the other as what the *same* is not; and it lustfully turns on the other as the site of mimetic or negative desire, with the consequence of incorporating the other within the *same*, fixing the other with immobile essences, and deterritorialising the other of its own speech, body, land, etc. On the other hand, the discourse of othering masks the 'demonic' force of the compulsion to repeat, which betrays the mask in paradox, in the figure of the Siren (lure, pleasure and doom all at the same time). The paradox, or more appropriately the simulacrum, not only fractures the discourse of othering, but from its midst turns the destructive force of repetition-compulsion into eternal repetition – the affirmative force of becoming. In other words, the virtual force of becoming, despite the attempts of the master (the Hegelian master, not the Nietzschean master) to deny it in order to sustain its authority of othering, simmers in the very discourse of othering. To put it another way, the discourse of othering masks the virtual encounter with the other. However, in order to actualise the virtual encounter, and become-other, it is necessary to follow the threefold ethical prescription that I have outlined.

PART II

Marco Polo: travelogue as a machine of othering

3

MARCO POLO

AND HIS TRAVELS

So many have trodden the trail blazed by Marco Polo. To do so once more may seem like repeating a well-worn cliché: haven't we had enough of the alibis to relive that wonderful romance with the exotic? Yet there is much to be said about the way in which the Venetian's *Travels* churn the age-old question of the other that haunts us today as it did in the late thirteenth century. Even though Marco Polo's text is singularly obsessed with devising a discourse of othering, this luminous surface has drawn scant attention from all those rapturous *habitués* interloping in its pleasure dome. This part of the book harbours the modest aim of resonating this surface of Marco Polo's text, making a journey along its discursive route, so that the internal lines of articulation of an othering machine, on which Europe has spent such a long time and so much energy, can be glimpsed at one of its crucial moments. Since Marco Polo's text registers the originary process through which the modern discourse of othering emerged in the West, its narrative discloses the ambivalence that subsequent discourses of othering so resolutely hide.

Before we undertake this task, let us follow some of the travellers who have taken flight, tracing the invisible footprints left by Marco Polo in the late thirteenth century. Why, one wonders, should the opening shot of Orson Welles' *Citizen Kane*, which has nothing to do with distant Cathay, unfold with the towers of Xanadu, its cupolas and domes, mysteriously shrouded in the mist? Is the lord of the castle, the citizen himself, following the figure of Kubilai Khan, a man of indomitable force, or is he a true despot, whose singular pursuit of possession knows no bounds? Perhaps we have noticed that there is an eerie silence before the lonely figure of the despot, which, owing to a long Western expectation, does not require filling with the ominous epithet 'Oriental', as even the least discerning can smell it miles away. The question we put to Orson Welles' film, whether the citizen is benevolent master or a despot, should emerge as we untangle the ambivalent narrative of Marco Polo's *The Travels*. Whether Orson Welles read Marco Polo or not we do not know. Yet there is little doubt that the enigmatic figure of Xanadu came to *Citizen Kane* via the opiate reverie of Samuel Taylor Coleridge:

> In Xanadu did Kubla Khan
> A stately pleasure-dome decree[1]

It is said that Coleridge himself was drawn into the magic of Xanadu at the precise moment of his encounter with Samuel Purchas's *Pilgrimes* through Marco Polo's text. Coleridge is by no means the first English poet to be caught in the seductive topoi bequeathed to the West by Marco Polo. In Book XI of John Milton's *Paradise Lost*, Adam, on the threshold of fall, beholds the future glories of earthly kingdoms. The first of the visions that his eyes command echoes the empire and the city Marco Polo had woven in his narrative:

> of seat
> Of mightiest empire, from the destined walls
> Of Cambalu, seat of Cathian Can[2]

One can go on, and on the way the images like Xanadu, Kubilai, Cambalu, Cathay, whose provenance lay in Marco Polo's text, are repeated, with the result of turning them into enduring signs of the exotic. When one dreams of venturing beyond humdrum normality, Xanadu or Cathay provide the perfect lure of the other; they have become the signs of flight and escape for the West. No wonder, therefore, that their pre-eminent role is in the imagination of travel. Bruce Chatwin, the most self-reflective of contemporary travellers, in *The Songliner*, recounts the nascent moments of his vocation as a traveller. Young Chatwin was enthralled by the way his aunt Ruth 'lingered over such words as "Xanadu"',[3] and his vision repeats once more the vision in the words of Coleridge, 'caverns measureless to man'.[4]

It is not only in our times that Marco Polo spreads his alluring charm. Ever since the publication of *The Travels* in the fourteenth century, it never failed to draw attention to itself and incite readers to innumerable journeys. One of these journeys, in the fifteenth century, was to change the map of the world. It is said that on reading Marco Polo, Christopher Columbus first dreamt of his voyage – not to discover new lands but to arrive by an opportune sea-route at the old Orient. Moreover, the Genoese voyager was so convinced by the veracity of the tableau enacted in Marco Polo's text that he made a meticulous study of it as a way of preparing for his momentous undertaking. For the object of his quest – El Dorado – did not reside in the land of the Incas and Aztecs but in Cipangu of the far Orient. Consequently, when Columbus finally reached his destination, he could hardly fathom the novelty of his voyage. It was reported that Columbus instructed his translator – Luis de Torres, a man adept at Oriental languages – to convey his words of topographical inquiry to the natives. Luis de Torres relayed it in Hebrew, 'Do you know the kingdom of the Great Khan?'[5]

Perhaps no other text, with the possible exception of Homer's *The Odyssey*, representing other places and cultures has exerted such an enduring appeal to the Western imagination as Marco Polo's *The Travels*. Not only has it been the subject of endless commentaries, and a lure for travellers, but it continues to be a source of fascination for literary artists; two recently published, highly acclaimed English texts testify to that.[6] And we must not forget Italo Calvino's gem of a text – *Invisible Cities*[7] – which, using the figures of Marco Polo and Kubilai Khan, re-enacts much of the contemporary discussion on the relation between language, narrative and representation. If one wishes to venture beyond the textual circuit, one can always fly in the Marco Polo class to the Orient, or return to the hyper-textual world via 'Xanadu' – a computer programme that plans to link libraries from all over the world into a mega-informational network. Indeed, Marco Polo and the figures that sprouted from his text have become a mega-cultural monument.

It was at the end of the thirteenth century, when the passage to the 'Orient' opened to the West, that Marco Polo made his remarkable journey. Yet, if it were not for the narrative of the journey, Marco Polo simply would have added his number to countless others who, by the grim fatalities of time and memory, disappeared without leaving any traces. Indeed, we would never have had the iconic figure of Western travel lore that Marco Polo duly became. Despite the long sojourn in the mysterious East and all the adventures that had befallen him, it is through the prosaic narrative of his text that Marco

Polo has continued to exert his fascination on so many for so long. The enduring popularity – especially in the aftermath of its massive circulation with the advent of the printing press – of Marco Polo's text testifies to the Western longing for flights from home, to venture into the world of others. Besides the quest for pleasure in otherness, and almost submerged in its voluptuous exoticism, Marco Polo's text, along with *The Odyssey*, has been a crucial cultural text for the staging of Western discourse of cultural identity and difference. Therefore, if one is to deconstruct the Western discursive technology of othering, it is important to re-visit this cultural monument, to delve into its discursive architecture, and diagram the ground rules of its operation. Before we take the plunge in this genealogical exercise, a few textual questions need to be addressed.

It is true that Marco Polo was born in Venice, but the whole of Europe claims him. Scholars have spent inordinate numbers of hours settling the truly scholastic question – was or was not the original manuscript written in French? Although most Marco Polo scholars agree on Gothic French being the original language of *The Travels*, it is by no means a settled question. Ramusio, in the sixteenth century, claimed it to be written in Latin. Naturally, Venetian dialect has its strong claimants. In fact, there exist one hundred and forty-three known manuscripts in almost all the European languages, which makes it a truly European phenomenon. Even if the original language of the text was French, it raises some interesting questions. It is said that while Marco Polo the Venetian and Rustichello the Pisan were languishing in a Genoese dungeon, they wove the text we know as *The Travels*: Marco Polo recounted his tales and Rustichello scribbled them down. Already we have a translation from the oral discourse to writing. I wonder in what language Marco Polo the Venetian, whom no commentator credits with knowledge of French, told his stories to Rustichello the Pisan? If the language of Marco Polo's oral discourse is anything other than French, then the so-called original French text is already a translation. To complicate the labyrinthine provenance of the text, there is an added final ironical twist. The only Marco Polo text in print in France now is the popular La Découverte edition *Le Devisement du Monde*, which is a translation from English.[8] In this case English is the original language of the text. However, all these do not really concern us here as the orientation of my work makes the exegetical issue somewhat secondary. What I am really interested in is the emblematic status of the text: the way it has been relayed over the centuries, its continuous popular appeal, and the whole of Europe's claim on it. However, it is not simply on account of the fact that Marco Polo's *Travels* has charmed so many over such a long period that makes it a crucial text for the West. Rather, it is the presence, in the midst of a carnivalesque display of exotic charms, of a discourse mapping cultural identity and difference that accords the text its monumental importance.

François Hartog, commenting on another emblematic text of Western tradition, Herodotus' *The Histories* says: 'Culture (ours at any rate) develops by ceaselessly returning to the "texts" that constitute it, chewing them over as if their reading were always already a re-reading'.[9] This comment could just as well have been made on Marco Polo's text. Yet the range of reading has been rather limited: either celebrating Marco Polo's text as the narrative of a fabulous adventure, or treasuring it as a compendium of geographical and historical knowledge. It is the latter perspective which forms the dominant mode of Marco Polo scholarship. Needless to say, empirical scrutiny is the chosen method of much of the Marco Polo scholarship. It characteristically attempts corroboration and tirelessly fills in the missing threads of the text. Not surprisingly, Marco Polo's itinerary comes under intense scrutiny: had he really visited the places he claims to have done, or what possible route could he have taken to cover the places named in his text? Apart from establishing the veracity of the routes, the commentary, in its empirico-cartographic mode, endeavours to illuminate the obscure toponyms of the text. The commentary of this mode, however, has spent most of its energies in supplementing the knowledge of the text. If Marco Polo has dropped, in casual anecdote, one of those exotic nominals, say, Gog and Magog, Prester John or The Old Man of the Mountain, the commentary provides elaborate histories to complete the knowledge of the text. The editors of Marco Polo's text, notable scholars such as Ramusio, Benedetto, Marsden, Yule and Cordier, Moule and Pelliot, have provided an enormous amount of geographical and historical knowledge on the referents of the text. Leonard Olschki[10] has systematically ordered much of the empirical knowledge amassed by successive generations of scholars and put them into perspective.

This part of the book does not aim at writing yet another commentary to add to the considerable geographical, historical and biographical knowledge already accumulated, seeking corroboration with the opaque referents of the text. Rather, the endeavour is to trace a genealogy of the Western discourse of othering, of which Marco Polo's narrative is an exemplary instance. Not only is Marco Polo's text a truly pan-European phenomenon, but it registers the full range of the tropes of othering that shaped the Western sense of identity and difference. Moreover, the location of Marco Polo's text at the threshold of medieval hermeneutics and the emergent empirical taxonomy provides a telling index of the contradictory strategies for the representation of other places and other peoples. In the interstices of these two modes of discourses, Marco Polo's text, apart from negotiating a diverse encounter with other cultures, invents some novel discursive logic of its own. Apart from charting the novelty of this discursive logic, this part of the book will endeavour to fathom the matrices of Marco Polo's narrative that forged the Western sense of cultural identity and difference in the closing days of the Middle Ages. For Marco Polo's text has been a great travelling machine of othering: it inaugurated the modern sedentary voyages through which Europe brought the world beyond it into its orbit of sameness in representation.

Marco Polo travelled to tell a fantastic story. He is singularly obsessed with difference and the desire to represent it. The world that sprouts from Marco Polo's pen is as strange as the dreamscape of old fables. The text authorises its vocation to capture this world by invoking the imperial command of the Great Khan himself, who, Marco Polo says, 'would rather hear reports of these strange countries, and of their customs and usages, than the business on which he had sent them'.[11]

The gathering of cultures that Marco Polo unleashed would be the tepid beginning of a European drive to secure the rest of the world for its epistemological mastery. Marco Polo, the emissary of the Great Khan, betrays the knowledge he had gathered to a very different world. Even though Marco Polo underwrites his enterprise with the authority of Kubilai Khan, he is never accorded the privilege of being the addressee of the text. It is a knowledge gathered about others to be carried over the boundary to the world from which Marco Polo ventured out seventeen years previously. For the others remain no more than the object or referent of his discourse. Hence, the pragmatic framework of its discourse stays close to a monologue: the West talking to itself about others who never enter the illocutionary circuit. The addressees of the text, as the prologue informs, are the 'Emperors and kings, dukes and marquises, counts, knights, and townfolks'[12] of Christendom. Marco Polo, as an authoritative addresser with seventeen years of travel experience in other places behind him, would charm his readers by displaying 'the novelties and curiosities ... all the remarkable things ... in these outlandish regions'.[13]

In Marco Polo's narrative the exotic difference of a strange world, apart from the presence of old fables, is conveyed through the taxonomic presentations of other cultures and places. It is to be a veritable compendium of 'the various races of men and the peculiarities of the various regions of the world'.[14] No doubt the traces of old romance and fables haunt Marco Polo's text, but the novelty lies in its ethnographic preoccupation. Moreover, the text exudes a sense of specialist knowledge about other cultures that would be the hallmark of Orientalism in its institutional phase, which Edward Said has so scrupulously mapped.[15] Marco Polo is well aware that the presence of fables that incited the Western imagination about distant places might dent the credibility of his narrative. In order to extricate himself from any possible misrecognition as no more than a teller of tall tales, Marco Polo insists that his text is 'an accurate record, free from any sort of fabrication ... contains nothing but truth'.[16] However, the procedure for arriving at truth for Marco Polo is rather different from the monolithic scopic regime of the post-Enlightenment period. Apart from the ostensive genre of empiricist knowledge, of which Marco Polo is a true originator, he was unable to be free of medieval consubstantiality – where words and things or eyes and ears had equal status as epistemological protocols for ascertaining truth. This is what Foucault calls the world of 'similitude'.Then the truth was carried along the very act of enunciation; it was accorded legitimacy by the fact that it had taken place at all. In describing the epistemic formation of the Renaissance, Foucault highlights its enunciatory foundation, which can just as well be said about Marco Polo's discourse:

> none of these forms of discourse is required to justify its claim to be expressing a truth before it is interpreted; all that is required of it is the possibility of talking about it.[17]

Since truth flourishes in the act of enunciation, its legitimacy hangs on the subject that speaks the discourse. Marco Polo establishes his legitimacy as the purveyor of truth by exhibiting his credential as 'a wise and noble citizen of Venice'.[18]

Even if the subject is worthy of the truth, only the eye can offer it to him without mediation. What is heard can only be taken for truth if all the previous relaying points are credibly negotiated by equally worthy subjects. Truth heard, therefore, is legitimate only if previous enunciatory subjects are legitimate. Marco Polo assures his readers what came to his ears came from 'men of credit and veracity'.[19] Hence Marco Polo conveys a truth which is not only seen but also heard. No matter how strange and fabulous a reportage might seem, it is accorded the status of truth as long as it is heard from a credible speaker. For example, Marco Polo tells the charming tale of King Facfur of Manzi and his 1,000 damsels. The events the tale relates took place long before Marco Polo's visit to Manzi. He could not claim to have witnessed them. Yet the truth-value of the tale remains untarnished because, Marco Polo tells us, 'a rich merchant – a man of ripe age who had been intimately acquainted with king Facfur and knew all about his life had seen the place in its full glory'.[20] It comes as no surprise that a fellow merchant would duly take his place among the legitimate speakers in Marco Polo's discourse. Incidentally, it also signals the mercantilist pulse that throbs throughout the text. The strange discursive protocol – the consubstantiality of seeing and hearing – does not sit comfortably with the modern empiricist discourse of othering, which is grounded exclusively in the scopic regime of truth. Yet Marco Polo, as we shall see, faced with a series of practical demands, was impelled to usher in a new empirical, taxonomic discourse of othering in the West. Apart from the consubstantiality of seeing and hearing, Marco Polo's text happily accommodates old fables with precise, firsthand information. On the one hand, there are the reportings of fabulous creatures of all sorts: gryphons, unicorns, dog-headed men, and the like; on the other, there is no shortage of precise information about the military organisation of the Mongols, the communication networks and the produce of each region covered, the production process of asbestos, mining technology, and so on. For instance, two widely different types of mining happily coexist in Marco Polo's narrative: the empirically precise description of pearl gathering on the coast of Malabar and the report of the fabulous harvesting of diamonds from the serpent-infested caves in the kingdom of Motupali.[21]

The coexistence of the exact and the fabulous in Marco Polo's narrative announces an important threshold in the Western mode of discourse. It is the crossroad between medieval hermeneutics and the modern empirical discourse of othering. Marco Polo endeavours to bring to bear the monumental labour of his long sojourn at the behest of the latter, but is always stumbling into the age-old traps of the former. The presence of these variegated modes of discourse in Marco Polo's text affords us a unique opportunity to trace the long and contradictory Western constructions of its other.

The medieval discourse of othering had two interrelated strands: on the one hand, there was the fabulous tradition of popular mythologies, encyclopaedias and bestiaries; on the other, the allegorical splendour of the Christian hermeneutical tradition. The narrative of the journeys, undertaken within the ambit of the medieval discourse of othering, either repeated the exorbitant signs of otherness made tangible by the encyclopaedic tradition, or followed the allegorical route of a pilgrim envisioned by St Augustine in his *City of God*. These narratives endlessly reproduced a circular topography by repeating the signs of similitude; and trod an allegorical pathway through a sacred world. In the discourse founded on similitude, the mapping of empirical otherness, in terms of measurable distance and difference, remains unworthy, if not an impossible task. If empirical difference made an appearance, it was no more than incidental. Only in the post-Enlightenment discursive regime, where scopic protocol came to dominate, and words and things were finally made to go their separate ways, could the otherness of the other be measured empirically. James A. Boon sums up the contrasting strategies of representing otherness on either side of the great rupture unleashed by the Enlightenment: 'Earlier interpretation construed diversity as revealing traces of resemblance to divinity/diabolicalness. Enlightenment method construed diversity as conforming to taxonomies of measure'.[22] Marco Polo's text, as we have already noted, lies at the threshold of these two modes of discourse: it both constructs otherness allegorically by implanting signs of resemblance, and by arranging empirical observations into taxonomic order. Yet the empirical ordering of otherness is not without its own allegorical scaffoldings. The allegorical frame of the new taxonomic discourse of otherness is simply pushed from the ostentatious surface to an invisible depth. However, the latter remains just as, if not more, regulatory than the former. The difference between the two types of discourse of othering is not simply due to presence/absence of allegory. Rather the difference lies in the modalities of allegory – between visible and invisible frames of mediation. However, the claim that they are both equally allegorical does not amount to denying their differences; between the ostentatious and the invisible allegory there is a great deal of difference: one is content by repeating the signatures of similitude and the other restlessly observes and measures difference. The interesting thing about Marco Polo's text, due to the presence of these two modes at once, is its bringing to the surface of their mutual relationship, which the post-Enlightenment discourse of otherness obsessively represses. We will have more occasions to elaborate on these ideas in the next few chapters.

Long before Europe's empirical mapping of the world, beginning with the age of discovery, Marco Polo had already taken tentative steps towards it in the late thirteenth century. In fact, Marco Polo was beaten to it by other Catholic emissaries to the Mongol courts. When the Mongols rode from the Central Asian plains to the centre of the global theatre of power, Christendom both trembled at what it considered a sign of cataclysm and gleefully celebrated the ruin of its arch-rival Islam. In this highly charged but ambivalent atmosphere Pope Innocent IV launched the mission 'Ad Tartaros' by sending Friar Caprini (1245-1247) to the Mongol court. Following the Pope, King Louis IX of France sent William of Rubruck on a similar mission. Both men were sent to spy, make diplomatic alliances, and seek possible converts. The accounts they left of their missions show remarkable alacrity for empirical observation; and both downplay the fabulous iconography of the mysterious East. Marco Polo's text carries the pragmatic taxonomy, inaugurated by Caprini and Rubruck, to a full-blown representational practice, while framing his narrative with the allegories of medieval hermeneutics. However, the difference between them, owing to their different conditions of production, is significant: whereas Caprini's and Rubruck's were diplomatic reports, Marco Polo wrote to present the world of others to Christendom in general. Hence Marco Polo's text aspires to be a general compendium of other worlds and a cartography of encyclopaedic proportions. The novelty of Marco Polo's text lies in its struggle to find spaces for the empirical discourse of othering in a book of general cultural representation written when the fabulous iconography had not yet lost its grip on the Western conception of the world.

As we travel on the trail of Marco Polo our aim is twofold: to trace, using Marco Polo's text as a harness, the genealogy of the Western discourse of othering; and to explore the matrices of cross-cultural representation, especially within the parameters of travelogue as a genre.

It must be said that Marco Polo's text, like Coleridge's, and unlike most of post-Enlightenment travelogues and the discourse of othering, is more open in its narrative, and registers the contradictory moments of representation and encounter with considerable energy. It is a text, I would argue, eminently suitable for tracing the internal lines of articulation of cross-cultural discourse of othering in general, and in particular, the drama of a crucial historical moment when the West began fashioning its other for the age of modernity.

How does Marco Polo cross his boundary?

Marco Polo, intent on becoming a traveller of other places, yet not wishing to tread the sacred pathway of pilgrimage, needs to cross the geographical line that divides the space of another world from his own. Where does he locate his boundary, and most importantly, how does he cross it? Of course, like all sedentary travellers, in order to move from point to point in space, he has to cross the chasm of an ellipsis, which he does by erecting a conceptual bridge arranged in symmetry. Before we can untangle Marco Polo's strategy of crossing a boundary, however, we need to know where precisely that boundary is located. For that we have to follow, between his departure and arrival, the passage that marks the contour of his own world and the beginning of another. Moreover, this passage, set in motion by the binary framing of the world, and the sameness and otherness that surreptitiously issue from its tabular arrangement, enables Marco Polo to draw his own *mappa mundi*. Where is his world of sameness which has already been drawn, from which he departs to avail himself of the other half, the drawing of which will complete the map of the world? His own world, despite providing him with the means of representing otherness, albeit by means of displaced repetition, is absent from the surface of his narrative. Yet there are odd slippages that reveal the outline of his chosen home, his point of origin, from which he departs without departing. In the prologue we see the older Polo brothers, Marco's father Niccolò and uncle Maffeo, stopping in Acre on their way from the court of Kubilai Khan to meet the Pope. At Acre they present themselves to the papal legate, who, we are told, 'was filled with wonder, and it seemed to him that this affair was greatly to the profit and honour of Christendom'.[23] When Marco Polo describes the geography of the frontier space of Lesser Armenia he says on its west lies 'the sea that is crossed by ships sailing to Christendom'.[24] Again, in describing the destination of the pearls traded in Baghdad, he says 'it is in Baghdad that most of the pearls are pierced that are imported from India into Christendom'.[25]

It is rather odd, for we know that Marco Polo was a Venetian, and that most of the goods of the 'Oriental' trade came into Marco Polo's world via his own native city. Yet Marco Polo did not name Venice as the place from which he departed. Instead, Venice was subsumed under the overarching parameters of Christendom. As a map-maker of the world, following the orbit of conceptual symmetry, Marco Polo had to choose Christendom as a pole of the *same*, because he wished to arrive at the other pole that covered the vast surfaces of the rest of the world. For he had given himself the destiny of a globe-trotter, and the basic line of division in this globe was informed by that of Christendom and the rest. Yet he was not a continental traveller. For Christendom was not a geographical continent but a spaceless regime of signs that might have taken geographical locale as a site of its territorialisation. How, then, did he cross the geographical boundary to become a traveller of other places?

In fact, in so far as the crossing of the boundary is concerned, the space of geography only comes into play as the after-effect of the conceptual boundary set in a relationship of symmetry. If we follow the geographical trails of Marco Polo's travel, he sails from Venice, crosses the Mediterranean, and lands on the continent of Asia. More precisely, he arrives in Acre, the remaining Christian enclave in the Holy Land, won by the crusaders. From Acre, accompanied by Niccolò and Maffeo Polo, he travels to Jerusalem in order to procure oil from the Holy Sepulchre, as Kubilai Khan has instructed. Then they go back to Acre, where they are summoned back once more by the newly elected Pope, Gregory X, the previous Papal legate of Acre, Tedaldo Visconti. Finally with the official blessing from the newly elected Pope they set off for Khanbalik, the imperial court of the Mongol overlord, Kubilai Khan.

Since Marco Polo never wishes to be a continental traveller, his geographical passage between continents, the crossing of the Mediterranean, and the movement from Venice to Jerusalem, does not take him to another place. For the point of Marco Polo's arrival is not the continent of Asia as the site of geographical unity but the other of Christendom. Hence Marco Polo's continental movement across the Mediterranean only takes him to the centre of his own world. It is not from Venice but from Acre that Marco Polo's passage for the strange world of others begins. In order to understand why Marco Polo departs from Acre rather than Venice we need to delve into the very composition of Christendom itself.

When Marco Polo meets Rustichello the Pisan or languishes in a Genoese prison cell, he is a Venetian. But when he ventures out to a faraway world, which he labours to map as if he is an explorer to an uncharted *terra incognita*, the differences between Venice, Pisa or Genoa disappear under the universal sameness of Christendom. Hence, like Odysseus the Ithacan, who in his wanderings in the unhomely world identifies himself as an Achean (the earliest common name for unity of the Greek world before the Hellenic age), Marco Polo the Venetian passes himself as a traveller from Christendom. We would do well to remember: the place one is coming from depends on where one is going.

But in order to become a traveller of other places Marco Polo needs to cross a geographical boundary. Since Christendom is a disembodied regime of signs, where does Marco Polo find its spatial contour to cross it? Despite its incorporeal nature as a regime of signs, Christendom is not consigned to remain disembodied; it can give itself a spatial body through the inscriptive force of territorialisation. However, when Marco Polo set out on his travels, Christendom did not have a territorial body worthy of its name. In the erstwhile western territories of the Roman Empire, where Constantine and Charlemagne established their holy empire of Christendom, there mushroomed innumerable principalities, autonomous cities and kingdoms. But Christendom as a universal regime of signs had a forceful presence in the Christian territories of the West. Denys Hay observes that among the guiding notions of the Christian West of the Middle Ages 'the widest ... was Christendom'.[26]

We can easily understand, given the prevalence of Christendom as the dominant system of signs, that Marco Polo would choose to travel under its banner. However, he still needs a territorial point of departure to venture into other territories. This, as I have argued, he locates in the movement from Acre. On the one hand, we can simply say that Acre, following the rules of synecdoche, stands for the whole of Christendom. However, it is more than that; a complex configuration of factors must be taken into account to make it intelligible. Foremost among them are the considerations of the principle of territoriality and sovereignty that existed in pre-modern state formations.

In a pre-modern state formation, as we have seen, the principle of sovereignty resided in the regal body itself rather than in the geographical territory characteristic of modern nation-states. Consequently, territorial identities were secondary to the primary fullness of the regal body which inscribed it with its power of resonance.

Territorial identity, therefore, was less important than the identity of the regal body that functioned as the principle of territoriality. Since a regal body, owing to the fortunes of conquest and defeat, often moved, the territory subjected to its power of resonance also moved. Moreover, since territorial identity was secondary, the physical homogeneity characteristic of the linear boundary of the nation-state was not necessary. Furthermore, since the presence of a regal body functioned as the sole principle of unity, the territory of a state or an empire could exist as an ensemble of discrete fragments or parts without losing its coherence. In this mode of territoriality, one fragment always functioned, depending on the regal body's time and the place of residence, as the arch zone or the centre. It was from the arch zone that the power of the sovereign resonated over the discrete territorial fragments, tying them into a whole. Now we can understand why Marco Polo began his journey from Acre and not from Venice.

When Marco Polo first arrived in Acre, it was an isolated Christian zone surrounded by Islamic territories; however, it was soon to become the arch zone of Christendom itself. When the Polos were summoned back to Acre by Tedaldo Visconti a metamorphosis had already taken place. Tedaldo Visconti, having become a Pope in the meantime, transformed Acre, by the sheer presence of his newly acquired body, into the eternal city, the veritable Rome, the centre of Christendom. For Marco Polo, intent on becoming a traveller from Christendom, where better to start a journey for other places than from Acre? Hence Acre is not simply a rhetorical fragment (synecdoche) standing for the whole of Christendom, it effectively becomes both the symbolic and the veritable centre of Christendom.

There is, however, another reason why Marco Polo wants to begin his journey from Acre: for his destination is Khanbalik – the imperial court of Kubilai Khan. In order to arrive at the arch zone of another place he needs to depart from the arch zone of the *same* place. Moreover, the strange world of others that Marco Polo wants to venture into and represent is framed by the universal kingdom of the Mongols. It is between Acre and Lesser Armenia that Marco Polo crosses the boundary between the *same* and the other, for Lesser Armenia is the starting point of his travelling narrative. As soon as he arrives in Lesser Armenia he tells us that the territory is 'under the suzerainty of the Tartars'.[27]

Since Marco Polo is caught in the binary orbit of representation, it is only through the invocation of a triple symmetry that he can

effect his passage from the *same* to the other: he moves from Chris-
tendom/the Pope/and Acre to Mongol empire/Kubilai Khan/and
Khanbalik. To put it another way: since Marco Polo wishes to
represent the Mongol empire he needs an empire of his own –
Christendom – with an arch zone and a sovereign body. The fact that
when Marco Polo set out on his journey for other places Christendom hardly existed as a territorial empire did not matter much. It
was enough for it to be a regime of signs to which, as a pragmatic
necessity, he would assign a territory and a sovereign body.

No doubt Marco Polo is a Christian traveller who travels folded
in the thick carapace of Christendom. Yet he wants to avoid the
sacred, allegorical passage of the pilgrimages littered with signs of
Christendom, so that he can become a rational, empirical cartographer of other places. How can he resolve this paradox: how can a
Christian traveller from Christendom travel without treading on the
path that Christianity has laid for him? In fact, he does not resolve it.
Instead he resorts to a clever strategy that allows him to travel in the
fold of Christendom and yet avoid its prescribed routes. The move is
articulated by the silence with which he passes through the Holy
Land. For Marco Polo sets out to map the empirical wonders of
another world. But we know, as the prologue makes it abundantly
clear, that he travelled through the Holy Land. But why doesn't it
form a part of his narrative? The answer lies precisely in the paradox
or the double-bind in which he gets entangled but without knowing
how to escape from it. Marco Polo, on the one hand, travels in the
cocoon of Christendom, whose signs, in mediation and displacement, enable him to represent the relative difference of other places.
He, on the other hand, wants to flee from its onerous signs to
become an empirical annalist of the world. The first confines him in
the resplendent orbit of Christian hermeneutics; and the latter
makes him a precursor of the rationalist future which is still a long
way off. Since he was not yet in possession of the rationalist protocol
of knowledge that post-Enlightenment Europe would assemble,
Marco Polo could not afford a confrontation between the two. Faced
with this dilemma he opts for the most economical strategy open to
him: silence. If he were to describe the Holy Land empirically he
would have been forced into a confrontation between the sacred
signs of Christian hermeneutics and the secular signs of empirical
annals. If, on the other hand, he had followed the signs of Christian
hermeneutics across the Holy Land, his travel would have been no
more than a pilgrimage. Consequently, his narrative journey would

have been a repetition of the cosmic journey to the city of God: the sacred pathway through shrines and miracles would have led the pilgrim to blessed Jerusalem. As a result, Marco Polo never could have become an empirical describer of the world. So by passing Christendom in silence he is both able to create an empirical passage into other places and mediate their representation with the signs of Christendom. Hence Marco Polo is that strange thing: a secular, empirical but Christian traveller.

During his long sojourn in the world of others Marco Polo comes upon many territorial signs belonging to the sacred pathway of the pilgrimages: sites of numerous miracles, Noah's Ark, the tomb of St Thomas the Baptist or the three Magi, etc. However, they appear in Marco Polo's text as instances of wondrous curiosities met by chance, and in the course of secular wanderings, rather than as signs of textual performances of a devotional journey.

There is another reason why Marco Polo omits the Holy Land from his narrative. Marco Polo, as we have seen, wanted to visit a strange world of difference as if he were on a voyage of discovery to a *terra incognita*. In other words, he wanted to travel into an unfamiliar world from the familiar orbit of Christendom. For the Holy Land, with the blessed city of Jerusalem at its centre, was not only the symbolic focal point of Christendom but also a thoroughly familiar place. Following the sacred pathway to the city of God, numerous pilgrims had already made their way to the Holy Land. Although these journeys were given to devotional performances rather than empirical observations of landscapes or cultures that lay on their path, they accorded the Holy Land with a strange familiarity. But for Marco Polo, who was singularly set on the quest for gathering signs of unfamiliarity, the Holy Land proved doubly unsuitable for his discourse: not only was it saturated with signs of familiarity (belonging to the Christian hermeneutic tradition and its regime of signs) but it was made familiar by frequent visitations. Perhaps if he were able to enact an empirical passage through the Holy Land, he could have gathered enough signs of otherness. But, as we have seen, he was unable to do so, and consequently, he passed it in silence.

Marco Polo's passage through the discursive symmetry of familiarity/unfamiliarity is strikingly marked by his admitted omission of Asia Minor or the area around the Black Sea from his representation of otherness. In the epilogue, Marco Polo tells us, he had thoroughly explored the aforementioned area but its familiarity makes it unworthy of a place in his text.[28] By the time Marco Polo arrived in Asia Minor on his journey east, which began in 1271, its position as a long familiar place was firmly established. Ever since classical antiquity Asia Minor had been regarded as a place ambivalently placed at the frontier of the 'Occidental' world. It provided the Greeks with their earliest territories for colonisation, where they duplicated their mother-cities. Furthermore, long after the collapse of the western Roman Empire, Asia Minor continued to provide territories for the Byzantine empire centred around Constantinople. Even when Asia Minor did lie within the direct sphere of 'Occidental' influence, it remained a not-that-far, not-that-distant, not-that-unfamiliar area of a frontier in the amorphous zone between the 'Occident' and 'Orient'. Unlike the clear demarcation line of the boundary, the frontier provides only blurred difference at the betwixt and between regions. As such, as Ladis Kristof says, the frontier remains:

> an integrated factor. Being a zone of transition from the sphere of one way of life to another, and representing forces which are neither fully assimilated to nor satisfied with either, it provides an excellent opportunity for mutual interpenetration and sway.[29]

Although geographically Asia Minor lies on the other side of the continental divide, by being a frontier zone it had made itself open, as we have seen, to 'Occidental' appropriation and sway since the classical Greeks. When Marco Polo passed through the region around the Black Sea, this sway and appropriation reached new heights. The area was intensively colonised by the Venetian mercantile companies. Moreover, they were the real power brokers of the region after the infamous Fourth crusade of 1204 which overran the Byzantine empire. It was the Venetian mercantile classes who sponsored this crusade, and installed a titular Latinate Frankish monarchy on the throne of Constantinople. Even before the Fourth crusade the Venetian merchant classes had a considerable presence in Constantinople: there were approximately 20,000 of them managing their business houses, dealing with 'Oriental' goods across the Islamic barrier. Not surprisingly, enterprising businessmen as they were, our elder Polo brothers had their own trading house in Constantinople. Obviously, all these elements put together make Asia Minor and the region around the Black Sea thoroughly familiar. Marco Polo, intent on travelling to a *terra incognita*, enacted by the boundary between the familiar and the unfamiliar, naturally could not find a place for these regions in his discourse.

In order to become a traveller of other places, Marco Polo, as we have seen, does not so much cross a geographical boundary. Rather he crosses conceptual differences to enact a movement from one geographical locale to another. Moreover, these conceptual differences are articulated by the symmetrical relationship between Christendom and its other, variously configured as a relationship between the Pope and Kubilai Khan, between Acre and Khanbalik, between familiarity and unfamiliarity, etc. As we continue with Marco Polo, we shall see these configurations proliferate to cover as many differences as there are samenesses. Despite crossing a geographical boundary through conceptual differences, Marco Polo, as we have also seen, wanted to be an empirical describer of otherness. More precisely, he wanted to flee from the coded landscape of Christian hermeneutics, so that he did not have to tread the pathway of sacred signs, and describe the empirical multiplicity of otherness. For that he strategically bypasses over the Holy Land in silence in his narrative. Yet, not only does he invoke Christendom – the incorporeal regime of signs – to manoeuvre his passage into the empire of the Great Khan, but he mediates the representation of other places through the displacements of these signs. Between abandonment of the old signs of Christendom and re-invocation of them as codes of representation, Marco Polo inaugurates the sedentary voyages from the West that would map the world in relation to itself. It is, however, important to distinguish two different dimensions of these sedentary but empirical voyages. The first dimension concerns ontology, and seeks to answer the question 'what is the being of the other?', which, in other words, amounts to saying 'how does the other exist in relation to me?' Consequently, this dimension entails the othering of the other. The second dimension does not ask 'who the other is' but how does the other act? how does the other's world function? and how is it composed? Consequently, the second dimension provides a practical map for functional dealings with others. For instance, to pick a random sample from the text, the following description of the road to Cathay articulates what I mean:

> When the traveller leaves this castle, he rides a fine plane and a fine valley and along fine hillsides, where there is rich herbage, fine pasturage, fruit in plenty, and lack of anything. Armies are prone to loiter here because of the abundance of supplies. This country extends for fully six days' journey and contains villages and towns whose inhabitants worship Mohomet. Sometimes the traveller encounters stretches of desert fifty or sixty miles in extent, in which there is no water to be

found. Men must carry it with them; the beasts go without drinking till they have come out of desert into the places where they find water.

After these six days he reaches a city called Shibarghan, plentifully stocked with everything needful. Here are found the best melons in the world in very great quantity, which they dry in this manner: they cut them all round in slices like strips of leather, then put them in the sun to dry, when they become sweeter than honey. And you must know that they are an article of commerce and find a ready sale through all the country round. There are also vast quantities of game, both beasts and birds. [30]

This functional map provides a practical ambit for dealing with others; it tells any would-be traveller who wishes to cover the places where others inhabit, either for amusement or commerce, that such are the compositions of the landscape, the population, and the produce. This functional mapping also serves as a practical technology of power: it shows the addressees of the text that such are the compositions of other habitudes which must be taken into account for any effective engagement of commerce, conquest, governing, and tourism in other places. Although this dimension of empirical travel has a separate articulation, in practice it is inseparable from the ontological dimension. This is because, in sedentary travel, the functional mapping of other places is subordinated to the ontological question of 'who is the other?' Consequently, the functional mapping produces no more than a map of internal composition of the being of the other, which, as we have seen, is produced through the othering of the other. So the practical map of the other, in sedentary travel, produces a composition of an other who is already incorporated in the orbit of the *same*. In the next two chapters I will turn my attention to Marco Polo's ontological question: 'who is the other?' and explore his process of othering of the other.

Marco Polo needs, however, to make one further move to complete his movement from Christendom to other places. As we have seen, he does not so much cross a geographical threshold to enter other places, as makes his passage by availing himself of a series of conceptual substitutes, such as that of universal monarchia or the tropes of familiarity/unfamiliarity, etc. These conceptual substitutes, however, like the stamping of a passport at a border checkpoint, provide him only with the formal means of crossing a boundary: they simply indicate that a transition from one bounded domain to another has taken place or the limit of one horizon has ended and another begun. Yet riding on these formal markers of boundaries, and their attendant discourses of difference that render the othering of others on his behalf, Marco Polo signals his departure from Christendom to its others. In other words, it is by representing the otherness of other nature and culture that Marco Polo indicates that he has crossed a spatial boundary. Hence it is more appropriate to say that it is by moving between the representation of one habitude[31] to another that Marco Polo enacts his passage through differential space. Now we can see that Marco Polo arrives in Armenia – the beginning of his narration of difference – not simply by declaring the 'suzerainty of the Tartars' but also by depicting the inhabitants, 'the Turcomans themselves, who worship Mahomet and keep his law, are a primitive people, speaking a barbarous language'.[32]

4

EXORBITANT OTHERS
AND TRANSGRESSIVE TOPOI

Marco Polo set himself a fantastic task: to capture the awesome dimensions of the *oikoumene* in a single text. This prodigious undertaking is unashamedly flaunted in the original rubric *Le Divisement du Monde*. Diligently, and piece by piece, Marco Polo assembles all the signs he can lay his hands on, of places and beings covered by his equally prodigious sojourn in the continuous flow of his narrative, so that their syntagmatic assemblage can construct *L'Image du Monde*, yet another rubric for his text. It is indeed a monstrous undertaking. Yet the task he sets himself is not unprecedented. Medieval encyclopaedias, etymologies, and cosmographies, all aspired to capturing the orbicular totality of the world by their sheer density of compilations; all enunciations, no matter how 'real' or imaginary, took their proper places in a chronological order as the veritable map of the world. Pliny's *Natural History*, Pompus Mela's *De Situ Orbis*, Julius Solinus's *De Mirabilibus Mundi* and Bishop Isidore of Seville's *Etymologiiae*, in their attempt to represent the unknown (*terra incognita*) of the habitable world alongside the known, were texts saturated with fabulous creatures and monstrous races of people. Marco Polo, intent on constructing the virtual mirror of the world by mapping the unknown, repeats the structure of the encyclopaedia: its vast global scale, its successive and repetitive enumerations of places and peoples to fill in the blank spaces on the atlas, its co-mingling of the 'real' and the imaginary as the mode of representation, etc. However, there are some important differences: the encyclopaedias were entirely textual in character, as Margaret T. Hodgen points out, they were 'a compilation of compilation'.[1] They were the gathering machines given to the accumulation of textual signs belonging to the received wisdoms of cultural archives. For instance, as Hodgen noticed, Bishop Isidore of Seville in his *Etymologiiae* quoted Solinus alone two hundred times.[2] Apart from Solinus, Bishop Isidore alludes to earlier encyclopaedists like Pliny, Mela, teratological fragments in Herodotus' *Histories*, Alexandrine fables, and most importantly to biblical passages. The combined reassemblage of these textual citations produced yet another encyclopaedia: *Etymologiiae*. Marco Polo, on the other hand, wanted to flee the closed world of textual signs and see the world for himself, and only then he would compile what he had seen. Yet he could not avoid falling back onto the age-old signs of the encyclopaedias in order to fill in the gaps in his map, rather than rely on the empirical observations he had made on his long sojourn. It is with the signs from the encyclopaedias that Marco Polo constructs his 'outlandish' world of others peopled with monstrous beings.

There is something odd about Marco Polo's *Mappa Mundi* because he represents the habitable world only by speaking of others. His own self-chosen world of Christendom is noticeable in the text only by its scrupulous absence. How, then, is it possible to produce an image of the world when the surface of the text passes the world of the *same* in silence. Having projected a binary frame on the world the totality of habitable space for Marco Polo ceases to be an undivided unity: it is now composed of two segmented parts – Christendom and its others. Consequently, the others take their places in Marco Polo's map as no more than instances of relational difference, mediated by his point of departure and origin – Christendom. In other words, the segment of the *same*, despite being absent from the surface of the text, is the presence itself, since it is the agent of mediation on whose behest the map of the world comes into being. Moreover, since Marco Polo is the 'speaking subject' whose monologue gives the world its map, the presence of the *same* is all too prevalent to be in need of being spoken. Marco Polo speaks and through him speaks his point of origin, which gives shape to its other part. In fact, in the ambit of a relational difference, when Marco Polo speaks of others he only speaks of the *same*. Hence in order to complete the map of the world Marco Polo only needs to speak of the others because the *same* is doing all the talking. Marco Polo's world is there, present through presence in the authority accorded to it in the very act of speaking. Marco Polo's *Mappa Mundi* is still incomplete but from a different point of view: not because the representation of Christendom is absent but because there is nothing other than Christendom. This is the plight that befalls all binary representations where one segment speaks of another.

Since Marco Polo sets out to produce a complete compendium of a binarily fragmented world, he attempts to assemble, corresponding to each variety of sameness, as many forms of otherness as he possibly can – ethnographic others, geographic others, floral and faunal others, political others and so on. Yet all others are not the same: there are degrees of variation among them: some differ radically from their *sameness*, and some others vary only slightly. Paradoxically, as we shall see, the more radical the otherness appears the more it tends to remain the *same*.

'Nature [is] some ultimate term of otherness or difference'.[3] In order to dramatise the onto-genesis of human consciousness much of the philosophical discourse sets up binary oppositions such as nature/mind, body/soul, subject/object, and so on. Similarly, anthropological discourses on the formation of the human domain rely on the nature/culture opposition as if the otherness of nature would bring home to the humans their humanness at its most rudimentary level. But the same binary frame also casts its shadow on nature, dividing it into segments with a rigid boundary line, marking 'our' nature apart and 'theirs'. If nature is the ultimate term of otherness in anthropogenic discourse, then nature belonging to others holds up the mirror in which the perceiving subject experiences the double distance, and thereby convinces her/himself of the fantastic difference between 'us' and 'them'. Hence Marco Polo assembles a great many signs of natural otherness to dramatise the exorbitant difference between Christendom and its others. However, except on a few rare occasions, it is not nature as landscape but rather the emblems of birds and beasts that are mobilised to represent the natural otherness of other places. For instance, he represents the Quilon region of India by writing that:

> the country produces a diversity of beasts different from those of the rest of the world. There are black lions with no other visible colour or marks. There are parrots of many kinds. Some are entirely white – as white as snow – with feet and beaks of scarlet. Others are scarlet and blue – there is no lovelier sight than these in the world ... Then there are peacocks of another sort than ours and much bigger and handsome, and hens too that are unlike ours ... Everything there is different from

what is with us and excels both in size and beauty. They have no fruits the same as ours, no beasts, no birds.[4]

And 'indeed throughout India, the beasts and birds are very different from ours'.[5] For Marco Polo the differences of birds and beasts are the glaring signs of environmental difference, and as such, they are ultimately reducible to the trophospheric difference of heat/cold. So the extravagant difference of the floral and faunal varieties of Quilon, explains Marco Polo, is due to the 'consequence of the extreme heat'.[6] Since, as this view implies, there exists a natural sympathy between a particular form of floral and faunal variety and the environmental setting it inhabits, so different birds and beasts in their otherness speak the antinomical lore of a different world. The signs of exorbitant animals articulate an exorbitant world, because they are equivalent, and therefore, analogically exchangeable for one another.

Marco Polo's environmentalist fixity is not something new: since Hippocrates it had become an analytical orthodoxy for explaining difference.[7] Marco Polo even recounts an anecdote of environmentalist experimentation that supposedly proves the Hippocratic doctrine. The inhabitants of the kingdom of Kerman are 'good, even-tempered, meek, and peaceable, and miss no chance of doing one another a service'. But in the neighbouring kingdom of Persia the inhabitants are 'so unruly and contentious that they are for ever killing one another'. Puzzled by this difference the king of Kerman summons his sages for an explanation. The sages are of the opinion that 'this was due to a difference in soil'.[8] Still not entirely convinced, the king, like any good empiricist, puts the proposition to the test. He orders seven ship-loads of earth to be brought over from Persia and has them spread under the carpet of the royal banquet hall. Then he invites all the good-natured Kermanians to a banquet. No sooner have they trodden on the carpet than they begin to metamorphose into brutish types like the Persians. Such incontrovertible evidence before him, 'the king agreed that the cause did indeed lie in the soil'.[9] Although the Christian regime of signs did not endorse a materially deterministic metaphysics such as that of Hippocratic environmentalism, it easily accommodated it by overcoding it with theocentrism. Thus the environmentalist logic of difference became a sign of God's miraculous workings. St Augustine, while meditating on the chosen role of the power of combustion in God's design, writes: 'many animals live and flourish in the heat ... it happens to suit their nature'.[10]

Having been convinced of the natural difference of others' nature, Marco Polo launches himself into a frenzied invention of stranger and stranger emblems of otherness by means of a grotesque mixture of bodily parts and pigments, hyperbolation and diminution of sizes, and so on. In Tangut 'wild cattle [are], as big as elephant'.[11] In the city of Kien-ning-fu there is a species of hen whose hair is like that of a cat.[12] If you want fish, there is one 'fully 100 paces long'.[13] If one happens to visit the province of Kara-jung, one may find 'huge snakes and serpents of such size that no one could help being amazed even to hear of them'.[14]

As if mere change of appearance, colour and size were not enough to represent the staggering difference of others, Marco Polo inscribes other bodies with the truly fantastic creatures of Western imagination – unicorns and gryphons. Admittedly, the unicorns he portrays are not exactly those of old fables, as they are not 'captured by virgins'.[15] Neither are the gryphons 'half bird and half lion'.[16] No doubt, these questionings of the encyclopaedic archive with the authority of first-hand observations are a sign of Marco Polo's new venture of empirical representation of otherness. Yet since Marco Polo could not extricate himself completely from the encyclopaedic archive, he was forced to deploy these names as emblems of the fantastic difference of other places. Marco Polo, as we have seen, treats the space of his travel as if it is a *terra incognita*, as if its difference is so radical that he lacks an adequate language to express it. Yet faced with the task of saying what cannot be said, Marco Polo resorts to the familiar emblems of radical otherness from Christendom itself. How else could Marco Polo have communicated the 'outlandish' nature of the places he had visited to addressees belonging entirely to Christendom, except in the language of Christendom? Hence the displacement of the familiar signs of radical otherness produces the images of exorbitant others. Paradoxically, the emblems of unicorns and gryphons produce an image of otherness that is already too familiar to Marco Polo's addressees. Consequently, the radical otherness collapses into most intimate sameness. And poor Marco Polo, despite so much travelling to foreign places, and so desperate to flee Christendom's regime of signs, falls victim to it. *Same* returns to the *same*: a destiny that befalls all sedentary travellers.

No doubt the assemblage of strange birds and beasts produced through anatomical dislocation, transformation of colour, and hyperbolic extension go a long way to produce an image of natural difference of other places. The displacements of the pure signs of

exorbitance such as unicorns and gryphons add further to the signification of other places as a site of outlandishness. However, in order
to signify the radical otherness of others, Marco Polo needs even
more fantastic emblems. And they do not come any better than
Homo monstrum.

Marco Polo brings the full weight of his authority to bear on the
minds of his addressees to assuage any incredulity that they may
entertain at his claims of the existence of *Homo monstrum*. This is
what Marco Polo tells his readers about certain inhabitants of the
kingdom of Lambi: 'I give you my word that in this kingdom there
are men who have tails fully a palm in length'.[17] And about the island
of Andaman: 'You may take it for a fact that all the men of this island
have heads like dogs, and teeth and eyes like dogs'.[18]

These monstrosities of anatomical disorganisation stretch the
lowest denominator to its extremity for defining humankind as a
species being: they are not merely cases of disfigurement within a
single species (*Homo sapiens*) but represent 'unnatural' mingling of
several species. Yet despite all the monstrosities, they people the
other places: they are equivalent to 'us' as a zoological species living
in the normal nature of Christendom. Hence *Homo monstrum* represents an extreme form of difference within the ambit of relational
differences. Paradoxically, as we shall see, they are closest to 'our'
Christendom than any other image of otherness.

Marco Polo, despite his desire to flee the symbolic space of
pilgrimage, never dithers in his self-conception as a Christian traveller. Yet he betrays the Christian doctrine of onto-genesis by lending
his credence to the existence of *Homo monstrum*. The biblical Genesis,
in its account of the origins of humankind, insists on single parent-
hood for the whole of the species. In the first of these accounts we
have Adam and Eve and their progeny peopling the virgin earth. In
the second account, after the cosmic deluge, Noah and sons – Ham,
Shem and Japheth – begin, from point zero, the task of peopling the
earth all over again. In both these accounts all races, despite any
cultural and geographical variations, belong to a single species. Yet
the Eurocentric retelling of this myth of origin often identified the
blackness of Africans with Noah's cursed son, Ham. It was believed
that the distance from the blessed presence of Christendom put the
African in the realm of moral cursedness, whose signs were borne
by the bodies in their blackness. This notion of bodily degeneration
stretches the notion of mono-genesis to its breaking-point: even if it
is accepted that all humankind originated from a single progeny, the

widening difference of the cursed races through degeneration from the blessed ones, turns them into almost separate species. Although the biblical account does not articulate the notion of bodily degeneration, it allows for servitude on account of cursedness. For instance, the Bible tells us that the Canaans, the progeny of Noah's cursed son Ham, were condemned to servitude on account of their father's wickedness to his father (revealing his nakedness): 'Accursed be Canaan. He shall be his brother's meanest slave'.[19] However, the 'meanest slave', despite belonging to the lowest rung of the human ladder, does not cross the species threshold to become a monster.

Marco Polo derives the true emblems of monstrosities from classical lore, which was recycled in medieval encyclopaedias and bestiaries to form an integral part of Christendom's extended regime of signs. For the classical cosmologists polygenesis did not pose any doctrinal problem: on account of the dialectical logic of opposition and environmental variation they happily invented exotic monstrosities in profusion. It is perhaps in the *Natural History* of the Latin encyclopaedist of the first century AD, Gaius Plinius Secundus, that the accumulated signs of human monstrosities found their most resplendent expression. Throughout the Christian Middle Ages these signs would be repeated in innumerable encyclopaedias.

For Pliny the existence of *Homo monstrum* is a received truth by virtue of its appearance in the pages of the works of classical authorities. Having once appeared as a sign of otherness, it became a 'reality' of strange and distant places, although its referent does not designate anything empirical in the world but only some other signs. Just before letting his readers view the grand assemblage of monstrosities, Pliny invokes classical authorities to assuage the doubts of the incredulous: 'shall preferably ascribe the facts to the authorities who will be quoted for all doubtful points'.[20] Pliny invokes the authority of Homer to lend credence to his presentation of the monstrous 'Cyclops and Laestrygonians', who once made their appearance in *The Odyssey* but now live 'in the central region of the world'.[21] Aristotle and Aristeas confirm the existence of Arimaspi, who are 'remarkable for having one eye in the centre of the forehead'.[22] Beyond the 'Scythian Cannibals', in the valley of the Himalayas, in the region called 'Abrimon' there live a people who 'have their feet turned backward behind their legs, who are extremely fast and range abroad over the country with the wild animals'.[23] Again Aristotle lends his authority to prove the existence of Machlyes 'who are androgyny and perform the function of either sex alternatively'.[24]

Pliny cites the name of Apollonides to present as veritable the strange characteristics of Scythian women, 'whose distinguishing marks ... as being a double pupil in one eye and the likeness of a horse in the other ... they are incapable of drowning'.[25] In India, the land of extremities, 'the inhabitants are more than seven feet six inches high, never spit, do not suffer from headache or toothache or pain in the eyes'.[26] Alexander the Great is given credit for conveying the truth of the existence of the admirable 'Gymnosophists'. However, it is the authority of Megasthenes that Pliny alludes to for the confirmation of Indian monstrosities. Cynocephali, a favourite of the medieval encyclopaedists and travellers, takes its veritable place in Pliny's text on the authority of Megasthenes, who confirms that 'on many mountains there are a tribe of human beings with dogs' heads'.[27] Megasthenes is also invoked to lend credence to the reportings of a strange race of women whose children turn grey immediately after birth, of the race of Monocoli, whose members, despite possessing only one leg, jump with surprising speed, and moreover, they use the same foot for an umbrella, of the race of Troglodytes – the cave dwellers – and so on.

Marco Polo does not cite the authority of Pliny, nor does he invoke the names of other authors of the popular versions of the same monstrous mirabilia, such as Julius Solinus, Pompus Mela and Bishop Isidore of Seville; he takes them as doxological truth, of which he is merely providing an empirical confirmation. Ironically, of course, Marco Polo's repetition of the signs of *Homo monstrum* only returns the empirical traveller to the textual traces – sign referring to sign in a circular movement of 'similitude' – from which he desperately wanted to flee, and see the world for himself. Why then does Marco Polo repeat these monstrous signs? I will come back to this later.

By reporting *Homo monstrum*, Marco Polo, the Christian traveller, squarely betrays the mono-genetic doxa,[28] but then, as Edmund Leach argues, there is hardly an anthropologist in the Western tradition who has not been guilty of that. 'The anthropologists', writes Leach, 'were avowed heretics. They mostly rejected the unity of mankind postulated in the Bible in favour of a theory that these are a man-like species'.[29] Marco Polo, as we shall see in the next section, was one of the trail-blazers of anthropological discourse, long before it was constituted as an academic discipline in the nineteenth century. Since 'modern anthropology', as Stanley Diamond reminds us, has 'germinated ... in a search ... for the primitive'[30] it finds its object of discourse in the otherness that demarcates other cultures from itself. More precisely, modern anthropology, under the imprint of evolutionism, finds its savages in temporal distance.[31]

The othering of the other, enacted through temporal distancing, of course, does not consign the other to the life-form of a separate species, but only to the past of the same species – who are yet to arrive to the present of the species. However, the time-lag between the 'primitive' and the anthropologist's present creates enough distance between them to mark the primitive as the improper member of the species, who is not quite formed to take her/his place as a proper member of the species. Although temporal lag does not presuppose a literal polygenesis, its articulation of an exorbitant time-gap, for all ethical and practical purposes, ends up situating the anthropologist and the 'primitive' as if they belong to different species. In the long Western history of othering, the primitive, marked by the temporal lag, has been the secular, post-Enlightenment way of articulating extreme relational difference, as *Homo monstrum* had been for pre-modern times. Even *Homo monstrum*, for all its anatomical deformities, does not belong to a separate species from 'us' humans of Christendom. If it did there would not have been any scandal or moral disquiet.

Marlow, penetrating the heart of darkness, and facing the 'incomprehensible' frenzy of the 'monstrous' black limbs among the 'motionless foliage' of the river bank, ponders: 'that was the worst of it – this suspicion of their not being inhuman'.[32] It is precisely this suspicion that makes the 'primitive' or *Homo monstrum* a scandal. Like the 'primitive' of anthropology, *Homo monstrum* functions as a mark of extreme relative difference within the parameter of the species *Homo sapiens*, except that it is articulated by differential anatomy rather than by differential time. Ironically, the anatomical distinction, the most archaic marker of difference, would come to provide, albeit in a different form, the basis for the modern 'scientific' discourse of race.

For Marco Polo, as a devoted Christian traveller, the deployment of *Homo monstrum* as a sign of radical otherness should have been more troubling than it appears. The *Homo monstrum* body is not simply a disfigurement of the *Homo sapiens* body, but an 'unnatural' collage of anatomies belonging to different species. Therefore, *Homo monstrum* not only transgresses the bodily boundary proper to the human species, but by doing so, produces an 'unnatural' hybrid, who is 'inhuman' yet human of other places. Unlike the 'primitive',

Homo monstrum is primarily founded on geographical distribution: it is conceived of as being organically tied to the temper of its locale. However, the 'primitive', despite being conceived temporally, is more often than not grounded in space, as if the time of the 'primitive' is equivalent to the organic time of other locals.

Marco Polo's *Homo monstrum* transgresses the bodily boundary – the minimum condition for defining species – to such a radical extent that if it is human then it is a human of an entirely different nature. Consequently, Marco Polo is pushed into a position that betrays the mono-genetic nature of Christian doxa, where God creates mankind through singular progeny and in his own image. Yet the question remains why Marco Polo, who doggedly flies the banner of Christendom, does not see it as a problem? One explanation for this conundrum could be found in the very formation of Christendom as a regime of signs. The figure of the *Homo monstrum*, as we have already indicated, came to Marco Polo's text not from biblical sources but from the doxological lore of classical cosmologies. Christendom's regime of signs, despite many apparent contradictions, was formed as a compromise of these two different traditions. Ironically, it was St Augustine, despite his singular vocation of finding a Christian hermeneutics free of classical (pagan) doxa, who did more than most to mediate them. In *City of God*, using biblical cosmology as his guideline, St Augustine set out not only to evaluate but also to incorporate those elements of classical (pagan) knowledge that 'are not in conflict with the book'.[33] In the process he encountered the signs of the *Homo monstrum* which peopled the *terra incognita* of the classical world. One of these signs was that of the *Antipode* – a dialectical figure of the classical cosmology based on a flat, spherical conception of the earth. Classical cosmologists reasoned that since the earth was a sphere composed of two hemispheres – *Oikoumene* and *terra incognita* – corresponding to them there must operate two mutually opposite laws of nature. So it was believed that in the other hemisphere of *terra incognita* everything, including human anatomy, must be inverted in relation to the hemisphere of the *same*. Since this conception did not accord with the biblical cosmology that conceived of the earth as a flat surface – where, as an expression of God's singular creation, there prevailed a homogenous law of nature across its whole length, where all races descended from a single progeny, and where all inhabitants, despite their differences, are dispersed from a single place of origin – St Augustine rejected the existence of *Antipodes*. Characteristically,

armed with the syllogism of scholastic logic, he argued that even if
the other hemisphere existed, surely the descendent of Noah could
not possibly have reached it:

> it would be too ridiculous to suggest that some men might have sailed
> from our side of the earth to the other, arriving there after crossing the
> vast expanse of ocean, so that the human race should be established
> there also by the descendants of the one first man.[34]

Yet, having refuted the existence of *Antipodes* on cosmological
grounds, St Augustine is not led to dismiss the phenomenon of
Homo monstrum. He takes it so seriously that he devotes an entire
chapter of his *City of God* to it. Having engaged with the classical or
pagan archive of the *Homo monstrum*, he concludes that 'it ought not
to seem incongruous that first as there are some monstrosities
within the various mankind, so within the whole human race there
should be certain monstrous peoples'.[35] For St Augustine, *Homo
monstrum* existed not because of the cosmic division of the earth, but
because of the proliferating variation of nature, which expressed
God's miraculous design on earth. Naturally, therefore, no one 'may
know why the creator so acted'.[36] St Augustine is happy enough to
assert the existence of *Homo monstrum*, but without daring to specu-
late about the exact condition of its emergence. So he says 'how all
this comes about, it is up to these interpreters to decide'.[37]

By dint of the sheer dexterity of his scholastic manoeuvres, St
Augustine imports the 'pagan' signs of *Homo monstrum* within
Christendom's extended regime of signs. Thereafter any Christian
traveller like Marco Polo could litter his text with a grand proliferation of human monstrosities without the risk of being called a
heretic.

For Marco Polo, who set out to represent the exorbitant difference of an unknown world, the emblems of *Homo Monstrum* are the
necessary means for accomplishing this task. Or could it be said that
Marco Polo simply added monstrous human oddities and fabulous
flora and fauna either to entertain his reader or to enact the myster-
ies of romance? After all, in the prologue, Marco Polo himself says
that one of the purposes of the book is 'to afford entertainment to
readers'.[38] Moreover, the scribe of the text, Rustichello, was a profes-
sional romance writer. No doubt Marco Polo wanted to entertain his
readers, but this does not really explain the functions of these exorbitant signs in his representation of otherness. Admittedly, unicorns
and gryphons and the like were common enough figures in medieval

romance, but their presence in Marco Polo's text does not turn it into a book of romance. For Marco Polo's narrative is without a hero, and there is no quest for the self: it is carried along by what he considers to be the veritable description of the world. Moreover, there is no trace of a romance plot structure, no adventure, only the obsession that leads to a monstrous compilation. Marco Polo never poses as a chivalric knight proving himself against supernatural adversaries, nor is he an adventurer like Odysseus, who wanders among the monstrous unknowns so that he can make himself a hero in a series of fantastic encounters. If Marco Polo is a hero, then he is a hero, like an encyclopaedist, of a prodigious compilation. However, unlike the encyclopaedist, he does not simply collect textual signs, but he travels a great distance to gather practical knowledge. Paradoxically, as we have seen, it is to the textual emblems, such as that of the *Homo monstrum*, that he falls back to represent the otherness of the other. Perhaps the most apt description of Marco Polo is a travelling encyclopaedist. The only comparable figure in Western history prior to Marco Polo that I can think of is Herodotus.

Marco Polo, as we have seen, sets out to represent the exorbitant otherness of an 'outlandish' world. How could he do this without mobilising equally 'outlandish' signs? Although the signs of unicorns, gryphons and *Homo monstrum* are pure signs, in so far as their referents are other signs, they are not false: they are characteristics of the semiotics of the originary *logos*. Giambattista Vico, in his description of 'poetic logic', argues that *fabula* and *mythos*, which the classical Greeks treated as synonymous, were the originary logos – the first speech – which, by breaking the mute silence of the world, inaugurated the life of the sign. *Mythos*, as Vico shows, derives from the Latin *mutus* – mute – which is made to resonate by the fabulous discourse to name the world. Vico says, 'for speech was born in a mute time as mental [or sign] language'.[39]

Since *mythos* and *fabula* are the originary signs with which humankind tamed the a-signifying multiplicity of the world, so that each thing would have a name to form an ordered totality of identity and difference, they cannot be regarded as 'false speech'. Rather, as Vico argues, they are 'vera narratio or true speech'.[40] Not surprisingly, it is post-Enlightenment rationalism, for the sake of asserting its authority based on an ostensive mode of discourse, that interprets *mythos* and *fabula* as false speech. If Marco Polo is a fabulist or mythologist it is in the originary sense, for he sets out to map the 'outlandish' difference of a world that struck him as if it were *terra incognita* – and the only way he can do so is by naming it with exorbitant signs.

Lévi-Strauss, despite the rationalist excess of his predilection for reducing all thought to the a priori structure of mind, in his description of *The Logic of Totemic Classification* comes to accord with Vico. Like Vico, Lévi-Strauss argues that mythic and totemic codes are not the signs of a false representation of the world but the basic semiotic tools for the primary ordering of the world through representation. Hence Lévi-Strauss argues that totemic signs are not selected because certain plants and animals are 'good to eat' but because they are 'good to think' with. He writes:

> animals and plants are not known as a result of their usefulness ... The answer to this is that its main purpose is not a practical one. It meets intellectual requirements rather than satisfying needs ... classifying as opposed to not classifying has a value of its own whatever forms the classification may take.[41]

Like the mythologist of the totemic classification, Marco Polo makes use of the fantastic signs of unicorns, gryphons, cynocephali, tailed men, etc. to represent the staggering otherness of another world. Hence for Marco Polo these are signs in an economy of meaning which deliver the truth of their 'outlandish' sense. But the mythologist of the totemic classification, argues Lévi-Strauss, is also a *bricoleur* – a handyman – who 'always has to make do with whatever is at hand'.[42] Similarly Marco Polo, as the traveller of *terra incognita*, is a handyman who scours the doxological archive for signs to represent the staggering otherness of other places. Yet, despite the contingency of his choice of raw materials, argues Lévi-Strauss, a handyman-mythologist's 'heterogeneous repertoire ... even if extensive, is nonetheless limited'.[43] Hence a handyman-mythologist never transcends the boundary that defines the parameter of his own world – he tends to be a conservative – and, as Lévi-Strauss says, 'by inclination or necessity he always remains within them'.[44] Similarly, Marco Polo, as the handyman-traveller of the unknown, gathers the known signs from the doxological archive of his own world to name the 'outlandish' difference of another world. Paradoxically, the signs of exorbitant difference only confine Marco Polo within the boundary of his Christendom. Because, as Vico reminds us, the shattering of *mythos* (silence) with the power of speech does not bear testimony to the other, it inscribes the other through analogy or metaphoric similitude by 'us[ing] the resemblances of things known or near at hand'.[45]

Having inserted a binary frame on the world, the relative difference of the others cannot fail to take on negative values. Hence for Marco Polo the emblems of *Homo monstrum* are not simply a classificatory tool-kit for mapping extreme forms of difference, but also serve as the ultimate indices of savagery. To put it differently: when Marco Polo portrays difference he simultaneously portrays the relative savagery of others. Since the relative difference between 'us' and 'them' is marked by the distance from 'us' – the point of origin, the site of the normal – to 'them', the extent of this distance also speaks the magnitude of others' abnormality, pathology and savagery. The extreme distance, of which *Homo monstrum* is an emblem, also represents the extent to which otherness inverts or defies the decorum of the normal. Polyphemus the Cyclops, the most intractable of Odysseus's barriers before his passage home, in his monstrosity signals the radical extent of his departure from the norm of the Greek world. Homer has Polyphemus retort to Odysseus's invocation of the authority of Zeus: 'we of the Cyclopes race care nothing for Zeus and for his aegis; we care none of the gods in the heaven, being much stronger ourselves than they are'.[46] Similarly, in Marco Polo's representation of otherness, human monstrosities speak the radical departure from the law of the normal: it is the ultimate sign of otherness, and by the same token, of ultimate abnormality, of pathology and savagery. It speaks of a mode of opposition that does away with any semblance of the normal that normal language cannot speak.

We can take the example of cynocephalis, the much vaunted dog-headed hybrids from Andaman. Their savagery is truly astounding: name any criterion of the normal, they happily live oblivious to it. They have 'no kings' (lack of a structured social life and a hierarchic regime of power); they are 'idolaters' (beyond the pale of 'our' cosmology); they obviously 'live like wild beasts' (they ignore all of 'our' civil codes of behaviour); and 'they devour' human flesh (breaks 'our' most despicable taboo). The aggregate of all these infringements push the inhabitants of Andaman beyond the pale: their extreme otherness stretches the minimum condition of 'our' civil and political norm to their limits. How could Marco Polo have spoken this otherness, except through the mediation of monstrous signs? These monstrous signs speak the unspeakable distance between 'us' and 'them' where relational differences cease to be comparable, except through the economy of symbolic allegory (sign referring to sign and comparing with sign).

However, as we have seen, these figures of exorbitant otherness do not announce their presence from other places, but from the doxological archive of Marco Polo's own Christendom: they are Pliny's monsters, Solinus's monsters, Bishop Isidore's monsters. Therefore these monstrous signs of otherness only seal the closed circle of a monologue, where the *same* addresses the *same*; they speak a language so familiar to Marco Polo's addresses that their repetition constructs a mode of radical difference that firmly belongs to the well-worn domestic repertoire. And poor Marco Polo, despite so much travelling and compiling, only returns to the textual signs of the encyclopaedias and bestiaries, whose displacement, dislocation and projection gives him the radical forms of the unknown, which are already too familiar. One result of this circular act of translation is that the strangeness of the other is domesticated by the use of familiar codes. However, between the thwarted passage and the return to the *same*, Marco Polo constructs an image of another world whose very nature is unnatural: a site of cosmic chaos from which only disorder proliferates, the articulation of which I will now trace.

Chaos in the habitude

The marking of relative difference through the displacement of signs of symbolic allegory – signs referring only to other signs – produces such an exorbitant gap between the *same* and the other that they can hardly be comparable with each other. How can one compare gryphons, unicorns, and monsters with 'our' birds and beasts and 'us' the normal humans? Take the case of the anthropomorphic difference: it is only by invoking a double analogy that the monstrous and the normal human types may be compared. The first analogy establishes the domain of comparability by drawing an equivalence between the inhabitants of the world of others and 'us' humans of the world of the *same*. However, since the basic attributes of the other, for instance, regarding the forms of physiognomic composition, differ in kind from 'us', the *same* and the other cannot really be compared. Due to the radical divergence of attributes the first analogy fails to deliver its promise: that of the representation of the humans of other places. For they are monsters, and as such, traverse the minimum boundary that defines 'us' as a species. Consequently, like cannot be compared with like to ascertain their relative divergence. However, in order to sustain the domain of comparability of the first analogy, a second analogy is brought into play. Since the *same* and the other cannot be compared directly, the second analogy functions as the device of an indirect mediation. It keeps up the game of comparison between incompatibles by drawing an equivalence between 'them' and 'our' doxological signs – the *Homo monstrum* of the encyclopaedias – whose referent is another sign. Now 'our' relational difference with others is exactly what obtains between 'us' and the pure but unnatural signs of 'our' own world. This move obviously composes others entirely of signs, and moreover, of the kind of signs with which 'we' cannot share a comparable domain. If he were simply content with the gathering of pure signs, and with using the comparability of symbolic allegory, Marco Polo, like Sir John Mandeville, need not have gone anywhere. But Marco Polo, as we have seen, wanted to be an empirical cartographer of difference. For that he needed to establish a comparable domain between the empirical attributes between the *same* and the other. Whereas *Homo monstrum* and 'us' humans belonged to different signifying economies, rendering them incomparable, now both elements of the bipolar divide must be brought into the same signifying economy. In other words, Marco Polo needs to compare the *same* and the other through the mediation of the singular grid of existence. Or, in order to become an empirical cartographer, which requires 'comparison' and 'measurement', Marco Polo must follow the same protocol as followed by the epistemic assemblage of the classical age, as described by Michel Foucault, and must 'analyse [things] according to a common unit'.[47]

What then is the 'common unit' that enables Marco Polo to establish an empirical domain of comparability between the *same* and the other so that he can represent a measurable distance between them? It can simply be called the habitude: the assemblage of 'manners and customs' distributed in space. Moreover, Marco Polo treats it as a strictly civil domain separated from a political formation. For him the habitude, as an assemblage of 'manners and customs', in the main is composed of three different attributes: religion, sex and diet. Furthermore, as I have argued previously, it is the representation of habitude as a site of relative difference that enables Marco Polo to enact his passage from Christendom to its other. However, just as Marco Polo has constructed the map of the world by only speaking of others, so does he measure the relative distance between habitudes only by speaking of other habitudes. The habitude of the *same* is present through absence because it is the very presence as a point of origin that mediates the difference of other habitudes. The advent of empirical comparability, therefore, does not mark the end of allegory but only a change in its modality. Whereas the monstrous others are constructed through the displacement of signs belonging to the symbolic allegory, the habitudes of other 'manners and customs' are mapped through the allegory of the law of the normal. Moreover, the relative other mapped through the symbolic allegory belongs entirely to the visible surface, to the doxological archives of encyclopaedias and bestiaries, to the familiar storage of otherness. The relative distance of other habitudes, on the other hand, is not mapped with a simple displacement of visible signs, but with the mediation of invisible laws that structure the life of the *same*. Furthermore, when the empirical difference of other habitudes is mapped, a discursive conceit is involved, which grants the act of representation its authority. By a spectacular dissimulation, it pretends that the image of the other is not mediated at all: what is represented is no more than the empirical multiplicity of others, whose locales are entirely the other places. Contrary to this dissimulation, and rising from the ruins of once metaphysical fullness of language, there dawned a realisation that not only questions language's ability to coincide spontaneously with the object of its signification, but provides us with an insight that the other, framed in the binary plane of difference, can only be represented with the mediation of the *same*. Condemned to flex its muscles from the darkness, and burdened by the need to disacknowledge its own operation so that it can pass its representation as contingent and empirical truth, this form of mediation, unlike the symbolic allegory, stays hidden from the discursive surface. It no longer repeats the signs from the glaring surface of the *same*, rather what it repeats is the invisible depth of the *same*. Needless to say, without this invisible allegory the relative difference of others cannot be construed as relative, nor can any judgement be passed on others.

Marco Polo gives the game away not only by passing judgements on other habitudes, but doing so with such dramatic gestures that they never fail to draw attention to themselves. For instance, he never tires of repeating the refrain 'They live like beasts'. Yet even without pronouncing his judgements in such an obvious manner, he would still have judged others, because, given the binary framework of representation, the *same* invariably judges others in the very representational act. For this only produces an othered-other. One significant effect of this move militates to turn other habitudes into transgressive topoi, because it is only by breaking 'our' law of the normal and taboos that others present their otherness to 'us'. Thus constructed, the others easily lend themselves to be tainted with abomination even if they are not subjected to any actual pronouncement of judgement.

Marco Polo, in spite of avoiding the route of pilgrimage and the allegorical pathway coded by Christian hermeneutics, was a Christian traveller from Christendom. Folded in the regime of signs that was Christendom, Marco Polo travelled with a ready-made index to measure and judge the relative distance of other habitudes. When we meet him mapping the otherness of other religions, it does not come as a great surprise. Of these, there are two in particular that claim most of his attention, namely Islam and idolatry. Besides these, there are the Jews, hovering on the margin, and what Marco Polo calls 'imperfect Christians'. The 'imperfect Christians' are presumably the heretic Nestorians, whose imperfection is no doubt accentuated, apart from their distance from the Latin church, by their long exposure to a strange environment that produces peculiar birds, beasts and monsters. It is worth remembering the environmentalist maxim on which Marco Polo's discourse of othering is grounded, which places the other habitude to other nature, whose organic resonance shapes 'manners and customs' as much as it shapes 'outlandish' bodies of men, beasts and birds.

The presence of Islam weighs heavily on Marco Polo's text; his anti-Islamic paranoia reaches the fever-pitch of a Tafur on an apocalyptic crusade. However, Islam is not regarded as the organic expression of other habitudes.[48] For Marco Polo Islam is, as it was for medieval Christendom, a mimetic rival, because it desires the same as 'us' – the truth, heathen souls, and a global empire. Despite his anti-Islamic paranoia Marco Polo accords Islam civility as befits a rival.[49] Since Islam is a rival, it belongs properly to Marco Polo's discourse of the political, and as such, it is not inscribed with the marks of transgression. This leaves us only with idolatry – the other religion par excellence. Although Marco Polo never defines idolatry systematically, two persistent appellations stand out: 'enchantment' and 'diabolic art'. For instance the people of Badakshan 'are idolaters. They are adept at enchantment and diabolic art'.[50] In the ambit of relational difference 'enchantment and diabolic art' signify magical misbelief against the blessed miracle of 'our' true religion. Marco Polo, driven by the logic of symmetry, does not rest content by simply presenting the expression of idolatry, but he traces its origin. Just as the origin of 'our' true religion is traced from the first man

Adam, and through the son of God Jesus, as the working of divine providence, so the origin of idolatry is traced from the personage of Sakyamuni Burkan as the mark of its superstitious passion, which is all too human. According to Marco Polo's narrative, when Sakyamuni Burkan (presumably Gutama Buddah) died his father was so taken by grief that 'he ordered a solemn mourning' and had 'an image made in his likeness, all of gold and precious stones, and he caused it to be honoured by all the people of the country and worshipped as god'. From this excessive display of human passion arose idolatry as an organic religion of other habitudes. Marco Polo writes: 'And you must know that this was the first idol ever made by the idolaters and hence all the idols in the world'.[51] This explanation for the origin of idolatry, is, of course, not unique to Marco Polo.[52] The difference in origin, articulated through the distinction between human passion and divine providence, expresses the cosmology of two cities fashioned by St Augustine in his *City of God*. In the end, Marco Polo, who so laboriously opened a passage through the allegorical pathway of pilgrimage, falls back on the very same allegory to judge the otherness of others.

For Marco Polo civility, at least in the empirico-evolutionist sense, is a secondary category of comparative judgement. Arching over civility stand the basic laws of the habitude, which provide Marco Polo with his primary criteria of comparative judgement. In his scheme of things what matters most is not how civil or uncivil a habitude is but how pure or impure, how near or far it is from the divine light. Of course, in a binary frame, any comparison of others is carried through the mediation of the *same*. In Marco Polo's case the 'manners and customs' of other habitudes are judged against the fundamental laws that define the civil order of Christendom. Consequently, the empirical measurement of the relative difference of others through a 'common unit' is evaluated with criteria which are far from common and far less than empirical: these are the basic civil laws upon which the edifice of Christendom's regime of signs rests.

Although idolatry consigns other habitudes into the cursed city of Babylon, it does not mark the civil/uncivil divide. Nor does it define the moral or immoral practices of everyday life. In fact, those who follow idolatry rigorously tend to live a more moral life. Marco Polo says 'first, you should know that those who live under a religious rule lead more virtuous lives than others. They avoid lechery'.[53] Moreover, some idolaters, like the Brahmans of India, excel in moral virtues: they 'would not tell a lie for anything in the world and do not utter a word that is not true. They take nothing that belongs to another'.[54] However, Marco Polo adds that very few, except the ascetic priests, observe the moral codes of idolatry. Indeed, the laity 'do not observe this rule' and 'live like beasts'.[55]

For Marco Polo civility amounts to no more than living in a city and by trade and industry. The weight of idolatry is not only insignificant regarding the moral state of a habitude, but it has very little bearing on its level of civility. The inhabitants of Somnath, despite being idolaters, live by trade and industry, which guarantee a civilised form of life: 'they are not corsairs but live by trade and industry, as honest folk ought to do'.[56] Similarly, the idolaters from the border zone between Cathay and Manzi live in cities, another mark of civility: 'the people of this district are all quite civilised because of the frequent of cities'.[57] The semblance of civilised life disappears with idolaters who live in mountains or in inaccessible regions and live by hunting and gathering: Marco Polo regards them as savages. For instance, in Belor 'the inhabitants live very high up in the mountains. They are idolaters and utter savages, living entirely by chase and dressed in the skins of beasts. They are out and out bad'.[58] Marco Polo usually names them with harsher epithets, such as 'live like beasts'. Between over-civilised and utter savages, there hardly exists any intermediary category – the other habitudes, for Marco Polo, are places of extremes. Therefore the inhabitants of the open countryside, who live by the cultivation of the land, and who presumably form the majority of the population, rarely get a mention in Marco Polo's narrative. Since Marco Polo set out to map the exorbitant differences of other places, his passion does not get ignited by anything less than spectacular. Thereby Marco Polo refashioned for the 'Occident' of nascent modernity the ancient tropes of exoticism.

Unlike the empirico-evolutionist moment of judgement of post-Enlightenment Eurocentric discourse, of which the notion of civility provided the absolute criterion of evaluation, Marco Polo, as we have seen, regards civility not only as one of many criteria of judgement but secondary compared to the basic laws of social order. One consequence of this non-absolutist notion of civility is that it alone is not sufficient for the deterritorialisation of a habitude. Moreover, Marco Polo's mapping of comparative difference that uses a common unit, such as that of religion, through the symmetrical staging of 'our' practices with 'theirs', does not result in empirical measurement despite being empirical in principle. Therefore it does not produce a rationalist deterritorialisation on which the power of modern European colonial authority comes to rest. To put it another way: for Marco Polo the difference between the *same* and the other is not absolutely marked by the relationship between the civilised and the savage, nor do these categories provide the sole criteria for evaluative judgement, which would be the case for the empirico-evolutionist discourse of modern European colonialism. To see how the latter works we can, from countless examples, take the works of Edward B. Tylor as a case in point.

Edward B. Tylor, one of the early fathers of anthropology, devoted a monumental two volumes, *Primitive Culture*, to the systematic classification of others within the evolutionary scale of civilisation. In his methodological reflection to his study, Tylor sets out to construct a civilisation machine, which through the arrangement of absence/presence would measure the scale of civilisation. Tylor writes:

> the principal criteria of classification are the absence or presence, high or low development of the industrial arts, especially metal-working, manufacture of implements and vessels, agriculture, architecture, etc. The extent of scientific knowledge, the definiteness of principles, the condition of religious beliefs and ceremony, the degree of social and political organisation and so forth. Thus on the definite basis of compared facts, ethnographers are able to set up at least a rough scale of civilisation.[59]

The civilisation machine not only measures the technical arrangements of a society but also evaluates its level of good life; it is the measure of all values and judgement. Tylor writes: 'from an ideal point of view, civilisation may be looked upon as the general improvement of mankind by the higher organisation of the individual and of society, to the end of promoting at once man's goodness, power, and happiness'.[60] Moreover, the civilising machine as the absolute arbiter of all values also judges the moral state of a society. Tylor does not deny the existence of some sort of moral life among the savages, as he acknowledges that the 'savage moral standards are real enough'. However, compared to 'our' own civilised moral standards 'theirs' only show their lag and lack, as 'they are far looser and weaker than ours'.[61]

Tylor's civilising machine thus deterritorialises other habitudes, opening them up for European colonisation. For the savage races can always be improved by a judicious civilisation. This is the classic evolutionist presupposition of the civilising mission: 'but that any known tribe would not be improved by judicious civilisation, is a proposition which no moralist could dare to make'.[62] In order to establish a territorialising logic, it is necessary to show that the civilising mission must come from without. So the traces of civility among the savages, argues Tylor, are 'much more apt to be produced by foreign than by native action'. However, the name of this 'without', invariably, is Europe. For any traces of civility that the civilising machine can detect, Tylor contends, is due to a European presence in the savage habitudes. He writes: 'as regards the lower races, this accords with the result of European intercourse with savage tribes during the last three or four centuries'.[63]

In the post-Enlightenment European discourse of othering, of which Tylor's work is an example, the cognitive genre of discourse colludes with the moral genre to produce a monolithic discursive authority over the destiny of others. It proceeds to measure the truth of other's difference ostensibly so that the otherness of others becomes a luminous fact beyond all reasonable doubt. Yet, this ostensive demonstration of otherness, which aspires to the measurement of quantitative difference, also, by the same token, dramatises the measure of the other's distance from good. Therefore a quantitative demonstration of otherness, which bases its authority on being beyond moral prejudice, effects a moral evaluation of others without appearing to do so. Furthermore, it is the evaluation of values under the shadow of truth, or to phrase it after Lyotard, it is the subsumption of the ethical genre of good or ought by the cognitive genre of ostensive truth, that provides the post-Enlightenment European discourse of otherness with such authority. And civility or civilisation has been the most potent sign of this authority. Consequently, of course, others can never appear as civil – if others are bad they are savages, and if good they are still savages but noble.

For Marco Polo, on the other hand, civility is not such an absolutist sign of cross-cultural judgement. He accords, as we shall see, many habitudes of others with a civility that surpasses his own. Instead of monolithic codes of civility Marco Polo uses the basic laws of the habitude as the ultimate mediator of judgement on others. Therefore, it is not the measurement of others' civility but the impurity or the abomination of others for being dwellers of Babylon that deterritorialise them.

Idolaters could be civilised but they are undone for living in the cosmically damned city of St Augustine's *orbis*. The people of Somnath, owing to the fact that they live by trade and industry, are quite civilised but they are idolaters too, which calls for deterritorialising judgement. 'Yet I must add,' Marco Polo writes of the civil inhabitants of Somnath, 'that the people are harsh and stubborn in their idolatry.'[64] And the Cathayans, the paragon of civility in Marco Polo's text, whose refinements perhaps surpass even that of Christendom, are judged for their religious otherness.[65] 'But they have no regards for the welfare of their souls,' says Marco Polo of the Cathayans, 'caring only for the nurture of their bodies and for their own happiness'.[66] Even the Brahmans, the virtuous Gynosophists of the classical fable, whose asceticism Marco Polo extols in glowing terms, are stamped with the stigmata of disbelief. Of them he says: 'so strict are these idolaters and so stubborn their misbelief'.[67] So in the end, the relative difference of others is not judged so much on account of their civility or for their moral virtues, but for the very fact that they dwell beyond the true spiritual city of 'our' God.

The idolaters, being dwellers of other cities, and being othered in the orbit of a binary difference, are shown to violate the civil order of 'our' city sanctioned by Christendom's regime of signs. However, the otherness of idolatry only frames the cosmic abomination of other topoi. Within this idolatrous frame flourish ever more fundamental violations, which give rise to the images of truly transgressive topoi in their splendid abominations. Since the otherness of other habitudes is founded on laws that transgress the fundamental taboos structuring the basic civil order of 'our' habitude, they incite both the horror and the pleasure of the forbidden. If they incite unrestrained evil and invite chaos in the world, by the same token, they also offer a lure from the law of the normal upon which the order of the *same* rests.

Edmund Leach observes that 'food, sex ... are nearly everywhere the primary focus of taboo'.[68] Leach's universalistic pronouncements of truth may not hold water under close examination, but for Marco Polo these taboos are the primary markers of cross-cultural difference. Moreover, since Marco Polo represents the otherness of others by displacing these primary taboos of his own world, other habitudes suffer the judgement reserved for their infringements. Their practices of eating and having sex are such that 'our' world will crack to its very foundation if they were to be let loose upon it. But luckily they belong to other habitudes and there are uncrossable boundaries between us. Yet it is precisely on the authority of traversing these boundaries that Marco Polo gives himself the right to speak the unspeakable without incurring punishment for defilement upon his own person. The only way by which he can protect himself against contagious defilement in places where taboos are norms is by the protective shield of deterritorialising judgements. Of course, paradoxically, this gesture prevents Marco Polo from encountering the places he claims to have traversed. However, despite the pathology of protective gestures, the very act of naming the unnameable embroils him in the libidinal space that articulates his negative or mimetic desire. Moreover, between the dread and negative desire, it is in this ambivalence that Marco Polo masks the uncanny and daemonic force of the encounter with the outside. However, as we shall see, this mask is hardly ever breached in Marco Polo's narrative, and he stubbornly remains a sedentary traveller.

Let us now see how Marco Polo narrates the comparative otherness of others through the attribution of dietary transgressions. Not only the so-called uncivil or brutish races indulge in dietary transgression, but also the most civilised of other habitudes. Marco Polo names Kinsai as the 'city of heaven' – it is the most civil of all civilised cities.[69] Its splendour is matched by its phenomenal growth of trade and industry and the refinements of its civic virtues. Yet its inhabitants indulge in all sorts of dietary abominations. Marco Polo writes: 'they [Kinsaians] eat all sorts of flesh including that of dogs and other brute beasts and animals of every kind which Christians would not touch for anything in the world'.[70] And they 'do not scruple to eat all sorts of unclean flesh'.[71] The civilised Kinsaians pollute themselves not because of what they eat but because what they eat is unclean to 'us'. In other words, the Kinsaians' dietary habits are unclean not because they violate their own laws but because their habits are equivalent to the dietary taboos of Marco Polo's own world. This displacement of internal taboos onto the Kinsaians, despite their civility, deterritorialises them, because, as Mary Douglas observes, 'a polluting person is always in the wrong'.[72]

Marco Polo's text abounds in dietary transgressions of this sort, which reach their limit in anthropophagy. The nature of this taboo is so fundamental to a civil order that it cannot even be named in a list of dietary prohibitions. Leviticus and Deuteronomy, therefore, despite being meticulous in drawing an exhaustive taxonomy of dietary prohibitions, passed over it in silence. But the otherness of the other as the mark of exorbitant abomination can be named with it. It signals the extreme point of the relative difference between habitudes, where the degree zero of 'our' manners and customs rises up from its absolute silence to become the sonorous norm among 'them'.[73]

Just as dietary pollution is widespread among the uncivil races of other habitudes, so is the habit of man-eating. Moreover, the civil races, following their own dietary abominations, practice cannibalism too. The inhabitants of Fu Chau, owing to the prevalence of trade and industry, are quite civilised, yet that does not prevent them from practising anthropophagy. Marco Polo confides in his readers: 'you must know that the natives eat all sorts of brute beasts. They relish human flesh'.[74] It is not a case of ritual cannibalism but an eating habit pure and simple. Nor is it a case of an occasional or incidental lapse: it is a part of their normal and habitual manners and customs. Marco Polo adds: 'for I assure you that they [Fu Chauans] go about everyday killing men and devour their whole body. This is their daily occupation to go about killing men in order to drink their blood and then devour their flesh'.[75] Similarly, the 'well mannered' Chipanguans are accused of cannibalism. They too eat human flesh simply because they consider it as 'the choicest of all foods'.[76] Since cannibalism represents the basic index of cultural limit, its displacement onto others produces truly monstrous habitudes. This monster of the cultural economy is more horrific than the monster proper of the unnatural economy. Since the naming of cannibalism speaks the unspeakable it serves as the symptom of the libidinal figure of the uncanny (*das Unheimlich*) in its negative dimension. It produces the figure of unhomely dread by the displaced representation of the repressed libidinal forces within. Consequently, the dreaded other, despite being troped through the signs of exorbitant difference, remains the self's own other. Moreover, being a displaced representation of negative desire, the man-eating others, in so far as they violate the basic law of the normal, invite apocalyptic chaos in the world. Hence the violence and aggression in a discourse given to the representation of others with the negative articulation of libidinal drives. Furthermore, it is by subjecting the others so constructed to normative judgement that the *same* masters the threat incited by its contact with the libidinal forces. However, this is not the whole story. Besides the figures of horror, negative desire also conjures up figures of pleasure; the resultant ambivalence serves as the mask of the encounter with the other which eludes the apparatus of representation. However, given his singular pursuit of the representation of otherness, Marco Polo never breaches this mask to risk an encounter with the other.

Sexual manners and customs provide Marco Polo with a perfect *mise-en-scène* for enacting the rapturous play of difference. Indeed, they allow him to construct the images of other habitudes as if they have deliberately reversed themselves in concordance with their antipathy to Christendom. If virginity is exalted as the paragon of virtues in Christendom, others value its diametrical opposite. For instance, in Tibet it is customary 'that no man would even on any account take a virgin to wife. For they say that a woman is worthless unless she has had knowledge of many men'.[77] Sexual jealousy is unknown among them. The women of Pem take lovers as soon as their husbands are away.[78] The men invite travellers to lie with their wives, and moreover, they regard it as a matter of honour. It is indeed a topsy-turvy world, whose extravagant displays of difference incite the pleasure of the erotic and the exotic. In Kamul, for instance, 'the women are beautiful and vivacious and always ready to oblige'.[79] Tibet offers such bounteous erotic pleasures that, in the way of recommending the habitude to the young men of Christendom, he says 'obviously the country is a fine one to visit for a lad from sixteen to twenty-four'.[80]

Other habitudes, in Marco Polo's narrative, seem to bristle with sexual excess. All forms of sexuality are permitted and none prohibited, and the kings are the very libidinal incarnate. The king of Kaugigu has 300 wives, the king of Kayal also has 300, and the king of Malabar 500. The Great Khan Kubilai has the number that befits the lord of such a vast domain. Besides his wives and concubines, he is served by a batch of six virgin damsels for three days, then another batch for another three days, so on throughout the year. King Facfur of Manzi does not do badly either: he has no less than 1,000. Moreover, he takes his pleasure through his eyes, for he is an exorbitant voyeur. His palace is a pleasure dome for the open-air spectacle of frolicking damsels; it is a veritable paradise of voyeurs, where the king's are the only eyes. Marco Polo for his part takes enormous pleasure in narrating the spectacle as if his eyes were taking the place of the king's:

> 1000 damsels, whom the king kept in his service and some of whom used to accompany him ... The other two-thirds of the enclosure were laid out in the lakes filled with fish and groves and exquisite gardens, planted with every conceivable variety of fruit-tree and stocked with all sorts of animals such as roebuck, harts, stags, hares, and rabbits. Here the king would roam at pleasure with his damsels, partly in carriages, partly on horseback, and no man ever intruded. He would have the

damsels hunt with hounds and give chase to the animals. When they were tired, they would withdraw to the groves which rimmed the lakes. Here they would doff their robes and run out naked and plunge into the water and set themselves to swim, some on one side some on the other. And the king would stand and watch them with the utmost delight.[81]

Not only their Kings' palaces, but their cities too offer untold sexual delights. Khanbalik has no less than 20,000 prostitutes adept in administering all sorts of pleasures. But it is Kinsai – the city of heaven – that is the very epitome of libidinal explosion. Here the figure of pleasure passes from the innocent surface of delight to uncanny depths, and assumes the daemonic character proper to the other. In every street of Kinsai, the perfumed, bedecked ladies of pleasure lavish such endearments and caresses that:

> foreigners who have once enjoyed them remain utterly beside themselves and so captivated by their sweetness and charm that they can never forget them. So it comes about that, when they return home, they say they have been in Kinsai; that is to say in the city of heaven, and scarcely wait for the time when they may go back there.[82]

Just as the nymphs of Calypso, the voices of Sirens and the nectarious lotuses deployed their delectable stratagems to prevent Odysseus's home-coming, so does Kinsai entice the traveller from Christendom with its sensual allurements. Yet, as we know, Marco Polo would return to Christendom to tell the fabulous story of his sojourn, and represent the otherness of other habitudes through the mediation of his own. Hence the sexuality of others, like their dietary habits, takes on their transgressive quality. At the extremity of these transgressions lies incest – installed by Lévi-Strauss as the universal focus of prohibitions – where nature finally meets culture. Marco Polo's play with the exotic charm of others' sexual manners and customs comes to an end with the displacement of incest taboos. This move also restores Marco Polo's authority as a soothsayer of relative difference, which the paradoxical figuration of otherness – pleasure and dread all at the same time – threatens to ruin. The paradox, however, remains a mask of a virtual encounter with the other which is rarely actualised in Marco Polo's text. Oblivious to this mask, the incest taboo is made to do what it is supposed to do: it clouds Marco Polo's narrative with a brooding sense of repulsion, and the full weight of normative discourse falls on the other, pronouncing its abominations for all to see and recoil in horror. The Tartars, the Kan-Chauans and the Quilonians are accused of incest.

Marco Polo's characteristic response is typified in his comments on the alleged habits of the Kan-Chauans: 'Many things that we regard as grave sin are not sin at all in their eyes; for they live like beasts'.[83]

The marking of relative difference, through the mediation of the 'common unit' of dietary and sexual manners and customs, not only dramatises the otherness of others but subjects this otherness to an evaluative judgement. In its turn, this all too visible presence of an evaluative judgement makes the true nature of this mediation abundantly clear: the 'common unit', despite structuring the relationship of symmetry ('our' manners and customs against 'their' manners and customs), reveals its uncommon origin; it belongs entirely to Marco Polo's own world. Consequently, Marco Polo gives his reader a panorama of transgressive topoi with their rude chaos and abomination, which deterritorialises other habitudes. Although I have been using the notion of deterritorialisation in a broad Deleuzean-Guattarian sense, my usage of it here is rather restricted. To be more precise, my particular usage of the notion hinges on the different emphasis I want to give to its antonym – territoriality.[84] The notion of territoriality that I have in mind is strictly a politico-geographical one: the legitimacy of the spatial extension of power. Consequently all claims to space, and the power over it, are territorial in so far as, despite whatever means used, they are regarded as legitimate. Deterritorialisation, in this particular sense, therefore, amounts to the denial of rightful claims to a spatial extension, which consequently produces a *terra nulius*, opening it up to a fresh inscription of power. Since Marco Polo's deterritorialisation of other habitudes is mediated by the fundamental codes of civil order, such as the binary difference of purity/impurity, which structures Christendom's regime of signs, an example from Leviticus may illustrate precisely what I mean by it. Upon admonishing the Israelites against sexual transgression Leviticus pronounces:

> Do not make yourself unclean by these practices, for it was by such things that the nations that I have expelled to make way for you made themselves unclean ... the land became unclean; I exacted the penalty for its fault and the land had to vomit out its inhabitants.[85]

Contagious impurities delegitimise claims to territories; they deterritorialise them. Consequently they become empty, ready to be reterritorialised once more. Hence the other topoi, made transgressive by the displacement of dietary and sexual taboos, stand deterritorialised before the judgement of the *same*. The strategy of deterritorialisation has been one of the classic tropes of colonial discourse, albeit not mediated by the fundamental law of the civil order sanctioned by the cosmic frame of purity/impurity. Instead, as we have seen in our reading of Tylor, it is mediated by the absolutist notion of civility founded on empirico-evolutionist logic, where the cognitive and the moral coincide. Marco Polo, on the other hand, does not deploy civility as the absolute category of judgement, yet he does, through the displacement of basic interdictions and taboos, turn other habitudes into sites of impurity and rude chaos. Thus he deterritorialises them. However, unlike colonial deterritorialisation, Marco Polo does not open up the other places for Western colonisation. Instead, his deterritorialisation of other habitudes only serves him as the ground upon which to invent a political technology of order from the very inside of the other place.

5

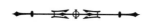

THE POLITICAL

TECHNOLOGY OF ORDER

Marco Polo insists upon a polar opposition between habitude and polity. If habitude is the site for the organic expression of the rooted interior, then polity is the inorganic interloper from the rootless exterior. It is only upon this radical disjunction that Marco Polo can effectively bring polity, now re-fashioned as the technology of order, back into the habitude to tame its immanent chaos. The notions of habitude and polity here, however, must be understood differently from the equivalent Hegelian notions of civil and political society. Hegel's original formulation of these notions in his *Philosophy of Right* and various subsequent Marxist formulations are conceived as relational terms within a totality.[1] In that context, therefore, no matter how oblique the relationship between political and civil society, it can never be conceived as a completely autonomous one. What Marco Polo seeks, however, is no less than their absolute separation; consequently, his habitude and polity do not form a totality, rather they constitute an assemblage of varied parts.

Marco Polo's representation of other habitudes, despite being shaped by the displaced underside of the law of the normal of his own world, is troped as autochthonous, as if their appearance as abominable topoi were entirely due to their own organic resonance. Since the chaos of other places is seen as the spontaneous expression of their immanent nature, instruments of order cannot be found from within. Furthermore, since instruments of order belong to the governing machine, polity must come from without. If the

radical separation between habitude and polity is alien to the
Hegelian conceptualisation of social formation as totality, then it is
very much at home in certain pre-Hegelian discourses of order.

Some three centuries later, in Hobbes's *Leviathan*, we once
more encounter the problematic of order in an uncanny likeness to
the one faced by Marco Polo. The Hobbesian exegesis builds up the
drama of the social contract around a bi-polar difference between
'civil state' or 'natural condition' and 'commonwealth' or 'civitas'.
Apart from *Leviathan*'s mythology of the social contract and the
psycho-anthropological explanation of the origin of disorder, Hobbes's
text enacts the difference between 'civil state' ('natural condition')
and 'commonwealth' ('civitas') in the same way as Marco Polo's own
bi-polar opposition between habitude and polity. Just as Marco Polo
conceives chaos in other habitudes, predicated upon transgressive
manners and customs, so does Hobbes ascribe immanent chaos to
'civil state' or 'natural condition'. It is the originary landscape given
to primal chaos. Hobbes writes:

> Hereby it is manifest, that during the time man live without a common
> power to keep them all in awe, they are in that condition which is called
> warre; and such a warre, as is of every man, against every man. For
> warre, consisteth not in battle onely, or the act of fighting; but in a tract
> of time, wherein the will to contend by battle is sufficiently known: and
> therefore the notion of time, is to be considered in the nature of warre;
> as it is in the nature of weather. For as the nature of foule weather, lyeth
> not in a shower or two of rain; but in the inclination thereto of many
> dyes together: so the nature of warre consisteth not in actual fighting;
> but in the known disposition thereto, during all the time there is no
> assurance to the contrary. All other time is peace. Whatsoever therefore
> is consequent to a time of warre, where every man is enemy to every
> man; the same is consequent to the time, wherein man live without
> other security, than what their own strength, and their own invention
> shall furnish them withall. In such condition, there is no place for
> industry; because the fruit thereof is uncertain: and consequently no
> culture of the earth; no navigation, nor use of the commodities that may
> be imported by sea; no commodious building; no instrument of
> moving, and removing such things as required much force; no knowl-
> edge of the face of the earth; no account of time; no arts; no letters; no
> society; and which is worst of all, continual feare, and danger of violent
> death; and the life of man, solitary, poore, nasty, brutish, and short.[2]

The 'civil state', without the force of polity, is not only plagued by
perpetual war, but represents the degree zero of culture. Given the
immanent disorder in the habitude, polity must come from without

if it is to avoid contagious disorder itself. Hence for Hobbes the covenant between the actors of the 'civil state' and 'civitas' is a contract between two external agents, which gives rise to a giant ordering machine in the form of the colossal body of the Leviathan monarch. Here is the celebrated passage in which Hobbes enacts the drama of the social contact:

> I authorise and give up my rights of governing my selfe, to this man, or to this assembly of men, on this condition that thou give up thay right to him, and authorise all his action in this manner. This done, the multitude so united in one person, is called a commonwealth, in Latin civitas. This is the generation of the great Leviathan, or rather (to speak more reverently) of the mortal God, to which wee owe under the immortal God, our peace and our defence. For by this authoritie, given him by every particular man in the commonwealth, he hath the use of so much power and strength conferred on him, that by terror thereof, he is inabled to forme the wills of them all, to peace at home.[3]

If we take out the mythical covenant and the medieval rationality of 'natural law', the Leviathan monarchy of Hobbes bears an uncanny resemblance to Marco Polo's own construction of the Mongol megamachine of order and its colossal monarch – Kubilai Khan. The Leviathan monarchy, the absolute but benevolent powerhouse of terror, is a functional machine of order, whose legitimacy lies in its production, effects and results. The Hobbesian exegesis, despite glossing its discourse with the mythical covenant and 'natural law', unconsciously recognises this when it rests the legitimacy of the Leviathan monarchy on its capacity to bring 'peace at home'.

The non-totalising discourse of order, founded on the radical disjunction between habitude and polity, paradoxically gives rise to an absolutist vision of governance. For absolutism has been a characteristic response to the anxiety of disorder. It is a magical solution to a world plagued with chaos. The phenomenon, or rather the horror inherent in its less amiable appellation – despotism – might have existed in the 'Orient', but its presence in the 'Occident' is confirmed in its incessant repetition in so many discourses since the seventeenth century. I will explore this in the latter part of this chapter.

For his part Marco Polo constructs his mega-machine of order and its Leviathan-like monarch without the gloss of a covenant or the invocation of the rationality of 'natural law'. The empire of the Mongols came in a whirlwind from without as an impeccable war machine, and established its governance over most of the other habitudes that Marco Polo's narrative journey covers. He never tires

of repeating that 'the Great Khan conquered it by force of arms'.[4] The
first move Marco Polo makes in the way of constructing the Mongol
mega-machine of order is to establish its rigorous xenological character: it is to be a singularly autonomous machine whose condition
of existence demands that it must stay outside of any habitude it
governs. The mega-machine is always foreign to whomever it
governs; it carries the racial sign of the Tartars but it governs such
people as the Cathayans, the Manzians and the Persians. Moreover,
those who man the governing apparatus must also come from without. This radical separation of the governing machine from the
habitudes it governs safeguards it from the contagious disorder
immanent in other habitudes. While narrating the episode of a
Chinese revolt against Mongol domination, Marco Polo writes:

> You must understand that all the Cathayans hated the government of
> the Great Khan, because he set over them Tartar rulers mostly
> Saracens, and they could not endure it since it made them feel that they
> were no more than slaves. Moreover the Great Khan had no legal title to
> rule the province of Cathay, having conquered it by force. So, putting
> no trust on the people he committed the government of the country to
> Tartars, Saracens, and Christians who were attached to his household
> and personally loyal to him and not natives of Cathay.[5]

The Great Khan's imposition of xenological rule over the Cathayans
does not mean that he harbours any special antipathy towards them,
rather it is indicative of the inner logic of the governing machine at
work. Just like any other members of a habitude under Mongol governance, the Cathayans are not excluded from the governing
machine. However, just like everybody else, they form part of the
administrative and army machine on the condition that they are
posted elsewhere than their own habitude. Marco Polo outlines this
general principle in the following passage:

> The men who are recruited from the province of Manzi are not set to
> guard their own cities but are posted to others twenty day's journey
> away, where they stay four or five years. Then they return home and
> others are sent in their place. This arrangement applies both to the
> Cathayans and to the men of Manzi.[6]

No doubt these policies form part of a strategy of security on the part
of an imperial governance from without, and they are symptoms of
paranoia characteristic of an absolutist regime. Yet the overriding
concern of Marco Polo's narrative, by rigorously maintaining the
complete separation of habitude and polity, is to sustain the

xenological character of the latter so that a governing machine can be constructed. But if the governing machine comes from the Mongolian grassland, and it belongs to the Tartar race, then surely it possesses its own habitude? If this were the case Marco Polo's attempt at constructing a governing machine would come to nothing. Here Marco Polo's narrative does something truly audacious: it represents the governing machine as being foreign to itself. In other words, Marco Polo constructs a governing machine out of the Mongol empire by denying it a habitude. The governing machine is designed to function and to produce results; it belongs everywhere and nowhere all at the same time. It is inorganic and forever on the move, seeking chaotic habitudes to tame and territorialise. We learn from Marco Polo that the Tartars of Cathay and Levant, who form the governing dynasty, are not genuine Tartars on account of their adoption of the manners and customs of the Cathayans and Levantians. Here, while describing the manners and customs of 'genuine Tartars', Marco Polo draws the distinction between them and the personnel of the governing machine:

> All that I have told you concerns the usages and customs of the genuine Tartars. But nowadays their stock has degenerated. Those who live in Cathay have adopted the manners and customs of the idolaters and abandoned their own faith, while those who live in the Levant adopted the manners of the Saracens.[7]

The governing machine is truly inorganic and syncretic in its very nature. If the governing machine were organic and belonged to the Tartars, then it would have been contaminated by the Tartar manners and customs, which are just as much, if not more, transgressive than any other of the other habitudes. Of them Marco Polo says:

> They have no objection to eating the flesh of horses and dogs and drinking mares' milk. In fact they eat flesh of any sort ... Their mode of marriage is such that any man may take as many wives as he pleases, even up to hundred ... they marry their cousins, when a father dies the eldest son marries his father's wives.[8]

In so far as the Tartar habitude – the organic locus of manners and customs – transgresses the basic dietary and sexual laws of Marco Polo's own world, it represents chaos. Moreover, being nomadic, and by living by 'grazing and pasturage',[9] autochthonous Tartars belong to the lowest rung of civility. Marco Polo often reserves for them the most violent of his invective: 'they live like beasts'. When Marco Polo describes the organic governance of the 'genuine

Tartars' he shows how a contagious habitude translates its disorder in the polity. Describing the king of Kaunchi, the organic Tartar king of the north, Marco Polo writes, 'He is a Tartar and all his people are Tartars. They observe the Tartar law, which is very brutish ... Altogether they live like brute beasts'.[10] In order to avoid this impeccable logic of organic pollution, the Tartar empire, in so far as it forms the governing machine of order, is made to be foreign to itself. It is a disembodied and a de-localised technology given entirely to functions and results.

If the characteristic marks of Mongol governance are its xenologicity, inorganicity and de-spatiality, they are also preconditions of machine formation. A machine has neither an ontological foundation nor does it belong anywhere. It is without a locus. Its sole existence lies in its monomaniacal workings, and its obsessive preoccupation with techniques of production and results. Although my usage of the notion of machine broadly accords with that of Deleuze and Guattari, its scope is more limited than theirs. For Deleuze and Guattari, the notion of machine is rather complex, with its shifting and multivalent roles that involve both technical and non-technical operations. For them, apart from signifying the functional ensemble of a productive flow without any logocentric depth or without being grounded in a transcendental ego, the machine is also the mode in which the immanent arrangement of desire is articulated. Theirs is a machine given to pure function, or more precisely, it is a co-ordinated assemblage of disparate parts – without forming a totality or expressive relation – which simply works and produces results. In this sense the machine is a factory, a technical apparatus stripped of any hermeneutic gloss. Instead of harbouring signifying codes, its entire being is locked to the questions: 'Given a certain effect, what machine is capable of producing it? And given a certain machine, what can it be used for?'[11] However, a technical machine of function is never purely technical, at least not in the primary sense. It is always a secondary expression of an already existing social machine. Deleuze and Guattari write: 'A technical machine is therefore not a cause but merely an index of a general form of social production'.[12] Since social production is the function of desire, 'desiring-machines are both technical and social'.[13] This is the diagram of the composition of the machine. However, a machine, given the specific function to which it is attached, can take any form, ranging from the schizophrenic to the despotic or paranoiac. For Deleuze and Guattari, the machine is also an expression of desiring production, which produces by constantly breaking down, by making unexpected new connections, by making the blocked flows of stratified assemblages flow again, by recovering its purely aleatory function in the manner of Nietzsche's eternal return, and by foregrounding its 'plane of consistency' or 'body without organs'. For Deleuze and Guattari, a machine formation is constituted by both these two aspects: beneath the diagram of composition lies the virtual force of libidinal intensities, which destroys as much as it creates.

The notion of machine that I am using here is in the restricted sense of Deleuze and Guattari's diagram of the composition alone. It is a techno-functional machine of social production (through inorganic polity); it is a coordinated assemblage geared to produce definitive results and effects. It is an amoral means of power whose legitimacy lies in its productivity. The precise sense in which I want to use the notion of the machine is anticipated by Lewis Mumford in his *Utopia, the City and the Machine*. Mumford writes:

> By royal command the necessary machine was created: a machine that concentrated energy in agreat assemblage of men, each unit shaped, graded, trained, regimented, articulated, to perform each particular function in a unified working whole. With such a machine, work could be conceived and exercised on a scale that otherwise was impossible until the steam engine and the dynamo were invented.[14]

Here Mumford is drawing the diagram of the technology of human organisation under the pre-modern imperium. The condition of articulation of this machine – for a great many dispersed human parts to be assembled, trained, regimented, and put to work as a coordinated whole – is the necessary subjection of all to a singularly monolithic will. Mumford writes: 'the necessary suppression of all human autonomy except that of the king was likewise the imperative condition for operating the giant machine'.[15] Marco Polo invents his giant machine of governance in the process of representing the leviathan imperium of Kubilai Khan. Once he has diagrammed the machine, he meticulously traces the effects of its work towards achieving the monumental task of producing order in the chaotic world of other habitudes.

Mumford points out that the giant machine of human assemblage is composed of two primary machines: the 'labour machine' and the 'military machine'. The military machine is central to the Mongol empire. It is a pyramidically structured machine with a chain of command stretching upwards from the command over 100 to 100,000 men to the Great Khan himself. Apart from being a highly efficient conquering technology, it works as an effective instrument of order. Throughout the vast reaches of the Mongol empire the army not only relays the resonance of the Great Khan's power and displays its terror, but establishes an elaborate network of surveillance to detect the slightest flutter of disorder. Moreover, the army, through its encampment throughout the Mongol empire, provides it with a mobile enclosure. This human rampart of the army imposes a sense of order onto the deterritorialised space of the empire bristling with organic chaos. Marco Polo writes:

> in every province where there are big cities and large populations he [the Great Khan] is obliged to maintain armies. These are stationed in the open country four or five miles from the cities, which are not allowed to have gates or walls so as to bar the ingress of anyone who chooses to enter ... They are stationed at various points, thirty, forty or sixty days journey apart.[16]

The most striking example of a 'labour machine' in Marco Polo's narrative is the postal service. Marco Polo calls it 'horse post'; it is truly a monumental assemblage of men and beasts. It connects the dispersed territories of the Mongol empire to its arch-zone – Khanbalik – and to the person of the Great Khan himself. It is the key administrative technology for the smooth functioning of a highly centralised and absolutist mode of governance. The postal machine deploys 200,000 highly trained horses, distributed between a coordinated network of stations across the empire. After every few miles, at each station, both the horses and couriers are replaced with fresh ones to maximise the speed of communication, which can reach a staggering 250 miles a day. Firmly hinged on the military and postal machines, the governing technology spreads its tentacles over the transcontinental expanse of the Mongol empire, producing order in places plagued with immanent chaos.

Kubilai Khan: the colossal regal body

In order to function, the mega-machine of order requires a constant flow of an enormous amount of energy, which it draws from the colossal body of Kubilai Khan himself. Marco Polo, in order to inflate Kubilai Khan to the proportion of his task, not only attributes traditional signs of power to his body, but also displaces in it the power that once belonged to many fabulous potentates from the vast stretches of other habitudes. Kubilai Khan is so enlarged that 'he is indeed the greatest lord the world has ever known'.[17] Yet, despite being so huge and serving as the generative matrix of the governing machine, or perhaps because of these, Kubilai Khan is without a private body. If he is the first principle of creative energy, this is by virtue of being an engine to the machine, and not by being an all-powerful transcendental subject. An engine body is a machine body too; it is the machine of the machine. Marco Polo, therefore, does not allow Kubilai Khan the luxury of private acts; he transforms even the most trivial of his personal conducts into signs of power.

Marco Polo denies the Great Khan a private body yet he invests it with great singularity. However, the seeming paradox of this position disappears if we discount the anthropomorphic sentimentality that equates the private with singularity. Whereas the private is an attribute of the person of the transcendental subject, singularity simply marks the particularity of a unique function. And what can be more singular than the engine or the matrix of a machine? Yet the singularity of the Great Khan serves a more immediate political logic than simply being at the hub of the machine. For the image of the mega-machine of order that Marco Polo pieces together in his narrative is a prototype of absolutist governance. Destined to function as an engine body to an absolutist technology, Kubilai Khan cannot be anything but singular. So Marco Polo encloses the Great Khan into a Chinese-box-like enclosure of a palace. 'The palace is completely surrounded', writes Marco Polo, 'by a square wall, each side being a mile in length than in breadth ... Within this wall is the Great Khan's palace'.[18] Apart from signalling the presence of an absolutist governance, the resplendent isolation of the Great Khan's regal body safeguards it from the proliferating chaos of the habitude. Even when the Great Khan moves on conquering or hunting expeditions he is walled in by his entourage. Away from the oppressive heat of Khan-balik on summer days, into the green coolness of Shang-tu, where lies the bamboo palace that gave the West its fable of Xanadu, Kubilai Khan still remains enclosed within thick walls. Besides singularity, the enclosing walls vibrate with the dense concentration of power in the regal body, from which the force of order spreads out to the far reaches of Kubilai Khan's vast empire.

When the Great Khan goes out hunting, Marco Polo stalks him with the aim of capturing the grand play of power of his colossal regal body. The Great Khan, who lacks a private body, cannot take pleasure as a matter of personal passion, but in his very pleasure gives expression to the working of a machine body. For Marco Polo this expression only renders visibility to the enormous size of the engine that motors the mega-machine of order. As part of his hunting apparatus, the Great Khan possesses a great many trained leopards, lynxes, lions and eagles, and furthermore, 10,000 hounds manned by 20,000 keepers, and 10,000 gerfalcons and hawks with their 20,000 keepers. When the Great Khan takes to the road with this vast assemblage of men and beasts, the spectacle it stages is truly astounding. Marco Polo confides in his addressees: 'you may rest assured that there never was, and I do not believe there ever will be, any man who can enjoy such sport and recreation in this world as he does, or has such facilities for doing so'.[19] From the innocence of a hunting party we see emerging a grand procession that brings home the prodigious extent of Kubilai Khan's power.

Sexuality, since it is seen as the most private of all private experiences in the West, does not lend itself as easily as hunting to the articulation of the power of a machine body. But for Marco Polo it is precisely in sexual acts that Kubilai Khan gives the definitive sign that he has left his private body behind him to assume the machine function of a colossal governing apparatus. Besides his wives and concubines, the Great Khan, as we have already seen, enjoys six virgins every three days throughout the year, which gives the astounding figure of approximately 730 virgins per year. Surely, this is an extreme case of sexual excess, and in any other situation, it would have aroused Marco Polo's deep sense of repugnance. Whenever he narrates the polygamy of exotic kings, he never fails to raise a condemnatory voice – 'lecherous'. For instance, while describing the king of Kangigu, he writes: 'The king is so lecherous that I assure you that he has fully 300 wives'.[20] Even though Kubilai Khan numerically surpasses the likes of the king of Kangigu, he does not face the wrath of Marco Polo's judgement. Marco Polo is well aware that his readers will raise their eyebrows at this glaring inconsistency. He is not one to shy away from confronting their disquiets, so he gives voice to their objections in his own text, letting them interrogate him, but only to avail himself of the opportunity to answer them effectively. Thus Marco Polo formulates the question: 'You may be inclined to ask: "do not men of this province regard it as a grievance that the Great Khan robs them of their daughters?"'[21] He answers: 'Most certainly not. They esteem it a great favour and distinction; and those who have beautiful daughters are delighted that he should deign to accept them'.[22] Despite appearances, Marco Polo's position here is not driven by a relativist logic: it does not amount to saying

'who are we to judge Kubilai Khan, given that what he does is perfectly legitimate within the manners and customs of his domain?'
For, if you will remember, he judges other potentates and kings
harshly for their sexual excess. Moreover, having divided the world
with the imposition of a binary framework, Marco Polo comes to see
the world as a relational totality composed of Christendom and its
others, with the former serving as the point of origin of the latter.
Consequently, other habitudes are judged, deterritorialised to the
extent they are found to differ from the law of the normal sanctioned
by Christendom's regime of signs. If the structure of Marco Polo's
narrative is given to judging others in its very representation of
otherness, why does he then take such pains to make an exception of
Kubilai Khan? Of course, there are enough credible reasons to suggest that Marco Polo was moved by the Great Khan's generosity
towards him, that he acted in memory of a liege lord whom he
served, to whom he stayed loyal to the ends of his days, but these do
not explain the exception.

It will be remembered that for Marco Polo the Mongol empire is
a governing machine without a habitude. It is an autonomous body
politic without a social body. Furthermore, only a habitude, which
forms the site of civil society, and consequently of moral order, can
be the object of comparative judgement, where the structuring principles of the civil laws of Christendom can be invoked as the allegorical frame for the evaluation of others' relative merits. Hence, only
autochthonous kings and monarchs, who are organically tied to the
habitude, can be subjected to comparative judgement based on civil
and moral laws and, if found wanting, can be called lecherous. For
the nature of their governance is such that they never transcend their
habitudes, let alone remain completely exterior to them, which must
be presupposed for the formation of polity as a governing machine.
Unlike the organic monarchs of other habitudes, Kubilai Khan is an
engine of a governing machine without habitude. Just like the governing machine he is inorganic and lacks the passion natural to a
private body. Since the body of Kubilai Khan is a machine, it cannot,
unlike the private bodies of organic monarchs, be subjected to value
judgements. Hence the Great Khan's sexuality slips through moral,
biological and passional frames of judgements; it can only be measured in a quantitative scale of fluctuating energy and evaluated by its
functional effects – how productive it is and the kind of results it
produces. Following the immaculate logic of machine formation,
Marco Polo narrates the Great Khan's mega-sexual drive as no more

than a sign of an engine function needed to drive the mega-machine of order.

Apart from signifying the power of a machine body, Kubilai's sexuality, glossed with the phallic codes, is made to stand for the military, the vital component of the mega-machine of order. King Facfur the voyeur, as we have seen, does not lag that far behind the Great Khan so far as the possession of damsels is concerned. Whereas the Great Khan is phallic, his innumerable children being a sign of his manliness, King Facfur is a voyeur, and for a very obvious reason, he is unmanly. Since the manly/unmanly bipolar set corresponds to the military/non-military bipolar set, being unmanly signifies the loss of power and the ruin of an empire. Marco Polo describes King Facfur and what has befallen him:

> Amid this perpetual dalliance he idled away his time without once hearing the name of arms. And this at least was his undoing, because through his unmanliness and self indulgence he was deprived by the Great Khan of all his utter shame and disgrace.[23]

The Great Khan's triumph, troped through sexuality, is not a triumph of a sexed body, but a demonstration of the superior functionality of a machine body. Besides, driven to inflate the regal body of Kubilai Khan by numerical addition, Marco Polo adds to Kubilai Khan the power lost by King Facfur. The engine body of a mega-machine, if it were to be up to its tasks, must grow the corpulence of its body. Marco Polo, not content with only the signs of hunting and sexuality, and in the same manner as he displaces the power once possessed by King Facfur, goes on displacing and adding many fabulous potentates from other places into the body of Kubilai Khan. One by one, the legendary princes of power of the 'Orient', such as the Caliph of Baghdad, the Old Man of the Mountain, and Prester John, about whom fantastic tales were told in Christendom, surrender their cities and power so that the Great Khan may keep on growing into a bigger and bigger body and his Khan-balik may become the centre of all centres. Kubilai Khan thus becomes 'the greatest lord the world has ever known' and Khan-balik, like Rome, is the 'centre from which many roads radiate to many provinces'.[24]

Now that Marco Polo has assigned Kubilai Khan a new body with the mega-dimension required for wielding the giant machine, he needs to consecrate the liminal passage that the body has gone through. But here Marco Polo, owing to the fact that Kubilai Khan is not a Christian, faces a serious problem, for he cannot invoke the

science of bodily signatures on a rigorous logical foundation. Aristotle calls the invisible depth or the interior essence 'soul', which is the power that determines the strength, courage, agility, weakness, etc. of a character. Although the body is seen to be a material surface with its own modality of existence, it is organically tied to the inner dynamics of the 'soul'; they are bound by a double articulation – the first principle of physiognomy. Aristotle writes:

> It seems to me that soul and body react on each other; when the character of the soul changes, it changes also the form of the body, and conversely, when the form of the body changes it changes the character of the soul.[26]

Since the 'soul' is not available for direct inspection, its murmurs can be read off from the forms and actions of the body's anatomy; it is the only source of a physiognomist's data. Aristotle writes:

> The physiognomist draws his data from movements, shapes and colours, and from habits as appearing in the face, from the growth of his hair, from the smoothness of his skin, from the voice, from the condition of flesh, from parts of the body, and from the general character of the body.[27]

Medieval Europe took the science of physiognomy to its heart, exalting it as a veritable instrument for divining the truth of man, and Marco Polo dutifully added his number to it. He even offers his own definition of it in the pages of *The Travels*: 'physiognomy, that is, the recognition of the characters of men and women, whether they be good or bad. This is done merely by looking at the man or woman'.[28] Marco Polo, armed with the mastery of the physiognomic art, does not so much read bodily signs to lay bare the mighty 'soul' of the Great Khan, as he constructs a new body for him according to an ideal physiognomic specification. Thus Marco Polo describes the body of the Great Khan:

> Let me tell you next of the personal appearance of the Great Lord whose name is Kubilai Khan. He is a man of good stature, neither short nor tall but of moderate height. His limbs are well fleshed out and modelled in due proportion. His complexion is fair and ruddy like a rose, the eyes black and handsome, the nose shapely and set squarely in place.[29]

Not surprisingly the model from which Marco Polo constructs the body for Kubilai Khan resides firmly in his own Christendom. Historians tell us that the portrait of Kubilai Khan that Marco Polo paints strays far from the marks of his actual physical appearance. Drawing upon extensive Chinese sources, Olschki points out that Marco Polo forgets to mention 'the tuft of the beard at the point of the chin' of the Great Khan, and his 'characteristic Mongol moustache'.[30] Further-more, Olschki points out that Marco Polo's description of Kubilai Khan corresponds to the stylised iconography reserved for the exalta-tion of medieval monarchs in the West. 'In fact', Olschki writes, 'this image [Kubilai's] does not differ in its essentials from those of west-ern rulers and pontiffs to be found in the mosaics of Medieval churches, the artists' intentions having been to exalt rather than offer a realistic picture'.[31]

Here Marco Polo's text is caught in a double axis: the exigency of cross-cultural representation and the ideal figuration of a machine body. First, having taken the task of representing the world of others to his own world, Marco Polo can only convey the ideality of Kubilai Khan in the iconography familiar to his addressees. Second, since Marco Polo is not aiming to represent the private body of the Great Khan, the question of a mimetic copy does not arise. Marco Polo wants to draw attention not to the natural body but to the regal body of the Great Khan, which simply functions as the engine of the gov-erning machine, and which he merely shapes from the prototypes of the ideal essence of regal body. So we have the machine body which is singular and a colossal body which is ideal. Now that Marco Polo has given the mega-machine of order its giant engine, he unleashes it on its monumental task of producing order in the chaotic world of others. More than the hermeneutic gloss of ideality, it is the result of its work that accords legitimacy to the governing machine and its machinic monarch.

The functional logic of legitimation

Marco Polo's legitimation of the Mongol governing machine and its singular monarch Kubilai Khan is effected by a complex set of discursive moves. Among these two distinctive yet interrelated series can be identified: first, there is the functional series proper to the order of the machine, which simply shows how the machine works and the kinds of results it produces; second, there is the displaced series, which, though invisible from the surface of the text except in traces, shapes everything within the relational ambit of the *same* and its others.

Although given entirely to the requisite of work, the Mongol mega-machine of governance is not productive in the usual sense of production of wealth. Rather it is driven by the logic of maximisation of extraction: it collects taxes, gathers tithes, and spends prodigiously the surplus it extracts. Kinsai, the flourishing city of trade and industry, from which the Great Khan extracts an enormous amount of revenue, thus becomes a major point of deployment for both the military and the postal machine. Not only is a garrison of 30,000 armed men posted in Kinsai, but strategic sites, such as the 12,000 bridges, are guarded round the clock. Moreover, the governing machine has constructed an elaborate network of roads to facilitate the efficacy of the postal machine, linking Kinsai with Khan-balik. If there is any doubt as to why the governing machine has so targeted Kinsai, Marco Polo makes it abundantly clear. He writes:

> The reason the Great Khan has such a careful watch kept in this city [Kinsai] and by so many guards is because it is the capital of the whole province of Manzi, a great depository of his treasure and the source of such immense revenue that one who hears of it can scarcely credit it.[32]

However, the governing machine does not extract the immense revenue to the ruination of Kinsai. On the contrary, the enormous productivity of Kinsai under the panopticonic eyes of the Great Khan only flaunts the efficacy of his governance. Although the governing machine is primarily given to the production of order, its productivity secures the necessary condition for the production of wealth. Marco Polo tells his readers: 'for all his thoughts [the Great Khan's] are directed towards helping the people who are subject to him, so that they may all live and labour and increase their wealth'.[33]

The giant machine channels its production of order in two different ways: on the one hand it provides security in the realm, and on the other, it contains the chaos in the habitude. Apart from the elaborate administrative mechanism, extensive postal network and system of surveillance, the order is effected by the imposition of fear. Marco Polo never tires of repeating the phrase 'were it not for the fear of the government' every time he has a safe passage through a habitude that he considers to be chaotic. Furthermore, wherever he sees the laws of the Great Khan being implemented, he comments 'no one dares refuse it on pain of losing his life'.[34] For fear is the immanent mode of operation to a system of governance that is not tied to its habitude by a consenting relationship, and remains radically exterior to it. Moreover, since the habitude is seen as organically disordered, it is not amenable to enlightened pedagogy, and thus can only be ordered by fear and force. Ironically, modern European

colonialism, having conceived of its relationship with other places in
the likeness of the relationship that subsists between Marco Polo's
governing machine and habitude, and despite its civilising mission,
imposed its own rationality of order by means of force. Moreover,
European colonial powers governed the so-called despotic places
with a mode of governance that contained all the elements supposedly belonging to 'Oriental despotism'.

The production of order provides Marco Polo with a crucial
index for measuring the extent of the efficacy of the Mongol governance, and thereby serves as the basis of its legitimation. But why
should the calculation of order serve as the means of legitimation?
How else can a governing machine working in chaotic habitudes be
deemed worthy of its task except through the measurement of its
production of order? There are, however, some other pressing contingent factors that impelled Marco Polo to choose that route of legitimation. When he undertook the task of legitimising the Mongol
governing machine and its machinic monarch, he faced some intractable difficulties. The existing codes of legitimation in Christendom, such as populist consent and resistance and theocentric codes
of divine election, could not be applied: the former because it could
only be related to an organic polity, and not to a machine which remained a perennial outsider; and the latter because it could only be
attached to a Christian monarchy. Ullman calls the former the
'ascending' and the latter the 'descending' theses of government
prevailing in the Middle Ages. The 'ascending' thesis of government
belonged, argues Ullman, to the pre-Christian communal form of
tribal organisation, which under Christendom's regime of signs was
'driven underground'.[35] Hence it is doubtful whether this code of
legitimation was available to Marco Polo, who carried with him
Christendom's regime of signs everywhere he went. Perhaps it was
only the 'descending' thesis that was available to Marco Polo as the
code of legitimation of governance. But, as we have seen, he could
not possibly have applied this thesis to the Mongol governance or to
Kubilai Khan, because the idea of divine election could not be
applied to someone who did not reside in the city of God. Nonetheless, following a logic similar to that which made him substitute
coronation for the birthday ceremony, Marco Polo brings into play a
number of other signs, selected for their easily discernible equivalence with the signs from Christendom, for the legitimation of the
Mongol governance. I will shortly explore some of these. However,
their function remains purely semiotic, they are driven by the exi-

gency of cross-cultural hermeneutics, that is to say, they are impelled by the problematics of having to translate the goodness of a governance from the other side of the binary divide, and translating it in the language of the *same*.

Unable to deploy the available codes for the legitimation of governance from Christendom to the service of the Mongol megamachine of order, Marco Polo invents one of his own: the functional code of legitimation which Machiavelli was to theorise some two hundred years later. When the great Florentine treatist Niccolò Machiavelli expressly theorised the functional logic of exercising power, and in the process invented what Foucault calls the 'art of government'[36] – the precursor to modern political science – his work caused a scandal. Machiavelli not only dragged political discourse out of the scholastic orbit and reconstituted it in terms of a 'principle of rationality', but exiled the morals of theologians from the arena of politics. It was no longer a question of deciphering the signs of divine providence with the help of sacramental hermeneutics in order to evaluate the legitimacy of a system of governance, nor was it even a question of just power, but power as such in its pure functionality: how does power work? what must one do to stay in and exercise power effectively?

Machiavelli is as uninterested in the speculative question of power as he is in its moral dimension; his orientation is pragmatic, guided by the actuality of things. In the infamous section of *The Prince* entitled 'The things for which men, and specially princes, are blamed' he writes:

> The gulf between how one should live and how one does live is so wide that a man who neglects what is actually done for what should be done learns the way to self-destruction rather than self-preservation.[37]

On the pragmatic plane of power the categories of 'praised and blamed' – on which the legitimation of governance rests – are loosened from their moral moorings to be offered to the strategic armoury, where power justifies itself by the sheer efficiency with which it manages to remain in power and by the result it produces. Here are some of the crucial moments from *The Prince*, which are worth quoting at length, because they offer us a diagram of the anatomy of the functional legitimacy of power which Marco Polo assumes and uses, without, however, articulating them in so many words:

> So a prince has of necessity to be prudent that he knows how to escape the evil reputation attached to those vices which could loose his estate,

and how to avoid those vices which are not dangerous if he possibly can: but if he cannot, he needs not worry so much about the latter. And then, he must not flinch from being blamed for vices which are necessary for safeguarding the state. This is because, taking everything into account, he will find that some of the things that appeared to be virtuous will, if he practices them, ruin him, and some of the things that appear to be vices will bring him security and prosperity.[38]

So the prince must not worry if he incurs reproach for his cruelty so long as he keeps his subjects united and loyal.[39]

Contemporary experience shows that princes who have achieved the great things have been those who have given their word lightly, who have known how to trick men with their cunning, and who, in the end, have overcome those abiding by honest principles.[40]

And:

A prince, therefore, needs not necessarily have all the good qualities I mentioned above, but he should certainly appear to have them.[41]

These passages hardly need any exposition as the functional logic of power is all too visible for everybody to see. When we return to Marco Polo's narrative it will be worth remembering that the functional legitimation that Machiavelli outlines here hinges on the productivity of 'security' 'prosperity' 'unit[y]' 'loyal[ty]', etc. Marco Polo, as we shall see, owing to some very particular contingent factors gripping Christendom, adopts these very same criteria for the legitimation of the Mongol governance. More generally though, unable to use the codes of legitimation available to Christendom in relation to Kubilai Khan, and still faced with the urgent need to legitimise his rule, Marco Polo invents a functional logic long before Machiavelli diagrammed its anatomy.

Having been driven to adopt the functional logic of legitimation, Marco Polo goes into numerical overdrive, obsessively collecting instances of good effects and good deeds as if their accumulation would bring home the ideal nature of the Mongol mega-machine of order. The catalogue of good effects and good deeds are too numerous to recount. However, a few will suffice to illustrate Marco Polo's basic strategy. His text, as we have noted earlier, narrates the effecting of order on two accounts: the establishment of security in an otherwise lawless domain and the containment of organic excesses of the habitude. In the province of Persia, for instance, the inhabitants are 'brutally blood thirsty, they are forever slaughtering one another', but were it not for the Tartar lordship, Marco Polo tells his readers 'they would do great mischief to travelling merchant'.[42] The imposition of security guarantees both the circulation of men and wares – the basic requirement of mercantile proliferation – which in turn guarantees production and accumulation of wealth. Marco Polo never tires of recounting the opulence of the cities in the domain of the Great Khan, which he attributes to his judicious policies intended, as he says, 'so that they [subjects of the Great Khan] may all live and increase their wealth'. We will soon see how the mercantilist drive of a burgeoning city like Venice, which required security to circulate freely and be productive, impelled Marco Polo to overcode the Mongol governance with a utopian desire.

In so far as the containment of the excesses of the habitude is concerned, Marco Polo's text recounts, for instance, how the Great Khan's decrees corrected the gambling habits of the civilised but transgressive Cathayans, and how the Great Khan put a stop to the practice of ritual killings among the inhabitants of Kara-jung. On recounting this event, Marco Polo draws his readers' attention to the fact that 'they [the inhabitants of Kara-jung] have abandoned this evil practise for fear of the Great Khan who has strictly forbidden it'.[43]

Yet the giant machine of order is incapable of reforming completely the transgression of habitudes. For instance, the Mongol governance tried and failed to correct the transgressive sexual habits of the inhabitants of Kamul. There are a number of reasons that can be adduced for this failure: first, for Marco Polo the transgressions of other habitudes are organic, and as such, no amount of effort can eliminate them; secondly, the failure of the governing machine, like Foucault's modern prison system, keeps the governing machine in the business of ordering. If all the transgressions of habitudes are corrected, then without a sense of looming chaos, and in the midst of utter normality, the governing machine will lose the basic condition of its existence. Hence the failure does not make the governing machine redundant but only highlights the need for its continuing existence.

The machine of order not only takes on the task of producing security and taming the transgression of habitude, it also undertakes the duties of public good, which range from systematic famine control to astute environmental management. In Marco Polo's narrative their function is partly semiotic, for they serve as signs of benevolence with which to address his readers in Christendom, and communicate the wonder of that governing machine from the other side. But Marco Polo has machinised the Mongol governance too well to leave it to the mercy of hermeneutic glossing, for results and numerical calculations are its immanent and ultimate index of legitimacy. For instance, on recounting the Great Khan's environmental policies, Marco Polo draws attention to their numerical goals – the proliferation of wild animals so that they can be hunted in perfect economy and in profusion. Marco Polo writes: 'So that they [wild animals] increase and multiply'.[44]

Before we untangle the complex loops of Marco Polo's narrative, which serves as a conduit for displacing the imperatives of political drama from the theatre of the *same* to the other, one more question must be asked about his machinisation of polity. If the Mongol governance is a hereditary monarchy, how can its machinisation be sustained? There is one code of legitimation of authority, which both the biblical and monarchical traditions share, namely, the code of filial lineage, which sanctions the power to govern on the basis of inherited rights of blood. But this kind of inherited legitimation militates against the functional legitimacy proper to the machine formation. Faced with this problem Marco Polo introduces machinisation in the very genealogical chain of filial descent. It is true that Kubilai Khan is of impeccable imperial lineage, for he is a direct descendant of Chinghiz Khan, the founder of the Mongol dynastic empire. But Chinghiz Khan as the source of this transmission of legitimacy is neither divinely ordained nor installed in his position by birth right. Marco Polo tells his readers that Chinghiz Khan found himself at the head of that emerging empire because he was 'a man of great ability and wisdom, a gifted orator and a brilliant soldier'.[45] And when people followed him, it was solely on account of his 'good government'.[46] This meritocratic legitimation reintroduces a functional logic into the genealogy, and thereby machinises it. Consequently, the very idea of genealogical legitimacy becomes redundant, for the machinic legitimation cannot be transmitted from one machine to another as each one must prove itself in its efficacious functioning and the production of results. Hence Kubilai Khan, the machine of the machine, cannot inherit his legitimation by filial descent but must prove his worth by his own functionality and production. Thus the apparatus of order is reassembled as a true machine formation: a technical apparatus of governance, wielded by a huge machine-bodied monarch, linked to a dynasty whose destiny had already inscribed the logic of machine in the very transmission of its blood.

Displacement of the same and the shadow of the despot

Since Marco Polo's narrative is founded upon a binary division, the representation of others, who are subject to remain instances of relative difference, is structured by the projection and displacement of his own Christendom. Just as the other habitudes are mapped in relation to 'our' basic laws of manners and customs, so is the other polity in relation to conflicting political exigencies at home. Yet the projection and dislocation of the latter assumes the opposite role to the former: whereas the other habitudes represent chaos as they are measured against Christendom's regime of signs, the polity at home represents chaos, and the other polity, in the form of the Mongol mega-machine, represents order. Although the imperatives that inform these reverse projections and dislocations of polity are numerous and unrecountable, there are at least three we can hardly avoid, because they leap up concurrently from Marco Polo's text and its intertextual orbit: the anxiety over fragmentation in Christendom, the exigency of mercantilism, and the longing for a secular unified absolutist imperium.

The chaos that gripped Christendom in the thirteenth and fourteenth centuries is well known. Exhausted by a long-drawn-out battle, the Hohenstaufen dream of a unified imperium was virtually over with the death of Frederick II in 1250. Yet the demise of the Hohenstaufens did not lead to the ascendancy of papacy, which claimed the unified imperium for itself in mortal combat against the Hohenstaufens, but plunged Christendom, especially the Italian peninsula, into proliferating fragmentation and internecine warfare. Karl Federn has sharply mapped the dominant events and their effects on the Italian peninsula at a time when Marco Polo was telling the tales of his travels:

> Every territory was continually splitting up and developing smaller administrative units, every one of which tried to become as independent as possible and to enlarge its estate at its neighbour's expense.[47]
>
> Nor was there any common established law to smooth all this confusion.[48]
>
> Every few miles the traveller found a new government and new laws; if he went a little further, coinage, customs, dress and even the language of the people were different, for the many dialects of Italy were practically so many tongues ... every hour almost the traveller was barred, and a toll, lawful or unlawful, was extracted.[49]

Nobody lamented more lyrically than Dante, a contemporary of

Marco Polo, over the malaise brought upon Italy by fragmentation and internecine warfare. In the cantos of *Purgatorio* he gave expression to his grief:

> O enslaved Italy, a place of grief, a ship
> without a master in a greater storm. Not a
> mistress of provinces but a brothel.[50]

> And now your living children are always at war;
> People thrown together within the same wall and
> ditch cannot live without biting one another.[51]

Notwithstanding the growth of autonomous cities such as Dante's native Florence or Marco Polo's Venice, which gave impetus to the proliferation of mercantilism, and the blossoming of Renaissance humanism, of which Dante's own work stands as a crowning monument, the Italian peninsula appeared bereft of a legitimate governance – a wretched 'brothel' without a semblance of order. Burdened by anxiety over this disorder and called to the task of finding a solution to it, the poet was led to break off from his exalted labour on *The Divine Comedy* and to delve into the prosaic genre of political pamphleteering. And what kind of solution does he advocate? As if bound by a secret complicity with Marco Polo, he places solicitously before the bewildered Italy a mode of governance that bears an uncanny likeness to the Venetian traveller's own megamachine of order, whose formal features are characterised by the secular, universal absolute monarchy. Given the anxiety over fragmentation, perhaps one can understand why unified absolutism should be so appealing, but how do we explain this predilection for a non-clerical monarchy?

However unique the idea of a non-clerical monarchy appeared in Marco Polo and Dante's discourse, this was not exclusive to them; it had in fact a wide currency in the thirteenth and the fourteenth century. Driven by a sense of historical mission, the anti-papal monarchists, who gathered around the party of the Ghibellines, to which Dante subscribed, fought a running battle with the papists (Guelf) for much of the thirteenth and early fourteenth century for the unified throne of Western Christendom. Strange though it might sound, but not surprisingly, given the scholastic temper of the time, an important part of the battle was fought out in the hermeneutic arena, where contestants produced mutually opposite readings of the metaphor of the two swords. According to the ecclesiastical tradition, the metaphor of the two swords representing the spiritual and the earthly domains was divinely bestowed, through the mediation of Christ, upon St Peter, who received it on behalf of Christendom. Since the tradition did not clearly spell out which of the domains had precedence, it became a focus for the hermeneutic drive of both parties for the assertion of their own supremacy. The Guelfs, who championed the cause of papal monarchy, inferred from the reading of the metaphor a claim that subordinated the earthly domain to the spiritual authority. The following passage attributed to Pope Bonifice, who supposedly wrote it in 1302, is a good example of the Guelfian interpretation of the metaphor:

> We are told by the word of the Gospel that in His fold there are two swords – a spiritual, namely, and a temporal. For when the apostle said 'behold here are two swords' – when, namely, the apostles were speaking in the church – the lord did not reply that this was too much, but enough. Surely he who denies that the temporal sword is in the power of Peter wrongly interprets the word of the Lord when he says 'put up thy sword in the scabbard'. Both swords, the spiritual and material, therefore, are in the power of the church; the one, indeed, to be wielded for the hands of the priests, the other by the hands of kings and knights, but at the will and sufferance of the priest. One sword, moreover, ought to be under the other, and temporal authority to be subjected to the spiritual.[52]

Not to be outdone, the claimants of temporal supremacy interpreted the metaphor with equal virtuosity for their own advantage. A typical example of this is the *Manifesto of the Emperor*, a work attributed to Frederick Barbarossa, the architect of the Hohenstaufen imperial claim against the papacy:

> And, in as much as the kingdom, together with the empire, is ours by the election of the princes alone, who, by the passion of His son Christ subjected the world to the rule of the two necessary swords; and since the apostle Peter informed the world with his teaching, 'fear God, honor the king': whoever shall say that received the imperial crown as a benefice from the lord Pope contradicts the divine institutions and the teachings of Peter, and shall be guilty of lie.[53]

Even philosophically the above claims began to find support, and none more unexpected and influential than the works of St Thomas Aquinas, who, in the process of composing *Summa Theologica* under the influence of Arab Aristotelians, not only took the rational theology of scholasticism to its highest point of development but also laid the rational grounds for the separation of worldly from divine concerns. St Thomas's meditation on the interrelationship between 'nature' and 'grace' led him to assert the autonomy of the former from the latter. Since he attributed polity to 'nature' and 'grace' to the divine, his position cleared the grounds for the assertion of autonomy by the secular political authority. To the discomfort of medieval theocentric certainty, this position signalled a break with the hermeneutics of the two cities of St Augustine, on which much of Christendom's regime of signs was built. Consequently, this position, argues D'Entreves, 'implies that even a non-Christian or pagan state is endowed with a positive value, as against Saint Augustine's conception of the pagan state as the embodiment of the civitas terra and the works of sin'.[54] Among many others, this line of argument was vigorously reinforced by anti-papal theorists such as John of Paris and Marsiglio of Padua.

When Dante came to ponder on the origin of chaos in Christendom he was in no doubt that it lay in papal meddling in worldly affairs. In *Purgatorio* he writes:

> One has put out the other; and the sword is
> combined with the pastoral crooks, the two held
> together, it must of necessity be that things go
> badly.[55]

And:

> You may now put it that the church in Rome, by
> confounding two powers within itself, falls in the
> muck and dirties itself with its load.[56]

Furthermore, in order to validate his critique of papal intrusion in worldly affairs in terms of scholastic language, in *De Monarchia* Dante conducts his own interpretation of the allegory of 'two swords' or 'two luminaries'. According to ecclesiastical tradition, the 'two luminaries' consisted of the power of the sun and the moon: the former being the symbol of spiritual and the latter of temporal authority. From this the papal supremacists argued that since the sun possessed greater luminosity than the moon, and moreover, the sun being the source of the moon's luminosity, temporal authority should be subordinated to papal authority. Dante does not question the nature of this allegory. Instead he produces his own interpretation, validating the arguments for the separation between spiritual and temporal authority. He concedes that the moon indeed receives its luminosity from the sun, but the scope of this luminosity is rather limited; it only serves spiritual needs. Besides drawing light from the sun, argues Dante, the moon exudes luminosity from the depth of its own being which accords it with an autonomy with which to decide the destiny of the temporal domain. Once this argument is resolved, establishing the mutual autonomy and difference of temporal and spiritual authority, it provides Dante with the basis upon which to fashion the model for an ideal order. Dante writes:

> Wherefore man had need of a two-fold power according to his two-fold end, to wit, the supreme pontiff, to lead the human race, in accordance with the things revealed, to eternal life and the emperor, to direct the human race to temporal felicity in accordance with the teachings of philosophy.[57]

By philosophy Dante means practical reason orientated to results produced rather than revealed articles of faith subject to hermeneutic illumination; it is a system of operational logic attuned to functions. Dante writes:

> Again, in the case of anything that is done it is the ultimate end which constitutes the first principle and causes the whole things, for it is that end which, in the first instance, set the ascent in motion; so it follows that the whole theory of the means which make for the end must be derived from the end itself.[58]

Once Dante has armed himself with a logic eminently suitable for his analysis and has established the autonomy of temporal authority, he sets about devising a mode of governance with the aim of delivering Italy from chaos. In order to facilitate the achievement of this end Dante becomes a practitioner of practical philosophy. He writes: 'and that is why there ring out to the shepherds from the high, not riches, not pleasures, not honours, not length of life, not health, not strength, not beauty, but peace'.[59] Not surprisingly, the kind of government to which Dante assigns the task of rescuing Italy from chaos and of establishing peace is absolutist in nature. He writes: 'There must be one king to rule and govern, else not only do they in the kingdom fail to reach the goal, but kingdom itself lapses into ruin.'[60] Not only is this form of governance absolutist but it is also unitary. By deploying the metonymic causality of part/whole relations he establishes the necessity of a territorially unitary monarchy under the command of an absolutist monarch. Dante writes:

> Now the part is related to the whole as to its end and supreme good; wherefore the order in the whole as to its end and supreme good ... And thus all the parts enumerated above as subordinated to kingdoms, together with the kingdoms themselves, should be ordered with reference to a single prince or princedom, that is the monarch or monarchy.[61]

Finally we have before us all the elements contributing to Dante's model of order. The impetus that began the process was the sense of chaos that struck him with ominous gloom as he contemplated the proliferating fragmentation that gripped the Italian peninsula. To the disorientating fragmentation which split Italy into ever smaller administrative units was added the machinations of the ambitious warlords, which had thrown the entire peninsula into internecine conflicts. As a result, the free circulation of goods, commercial dealings and the movement of men were blocked every few miles by the presence of competing boundaries and barriers, different currencies, and excessive toll charges. Paradoxically, the growth of autonomous towns, which originally gave rise to mercantilism in the Italian cities, became an obstacle to its further growth. We shall see how the exigency of mercantilism, which impelled Marco Polo to legitimise the governance of the Great Khan, punctuated the repetition of absolutism in the West. Apart from the anxiety over fragmentation, as we have also seen, Dante not only held a strong anti-papal position, but in concurrence with a growing philosophical and political current argued for the separation of secular power from the religious. In order to form his ideal governance of order Dante adds unitary absolutism to the secular conception of temporal authority. Now it should be obvious that Dante's ideal governance bears more than a passing resemblance to Marco Polo's representation of Mongol governance, which he held up as the ideal machine of order. However, by this fact of resemblance I am not suggesting that Marco Polo was influenced by Dante or vice versa, and even less that they came under the influence of St Thomas's philosophy. What I am merely suggesting is that the contingent congruence of their positions indicates a very particular type of response to the sense of disorder in the West. Consequently, Marco Polo's legitimation of Kubilai Khan on the grounds that he brought order in chaotic habitudes by the means of a non-religious, unitary and absolutist governing machine suggests a certain projection and dislocation of the imperatives at home. Let us now return to Marco Polo's narrative to see how this process is dramatised.

Throughout his text Marco Polo habitually debunks organic potentates belonging to other habitudes in relation to the universal empire of the Mongol Khans. However, it is the delegitimation of the Christian powers that proves most interesting. During the late Middle Ages Prester John, the fabulous Christian monarch of the

East, inspired a literary genre and an intense millennial fantasy. Christian travellers went East to seek him out; even a papal mission was sent to make contact with him. It was rumoured that he had established the New Jerusalem somewhere in the East. But Marco Polo, an avowed Christian, surprisingly relegates him to the position of a petty lord of the Mongolian plains who schemed against Chinghiz Khan – the founder of the Mongol empire. One of the crimes of Prester John, Marco Polo relates, is his attempt to fragment the Mongol confederacy. Marco Polo writes:

> Now it happened that their [Mongol] population increased greatly. When Prester John saw their numbers had grown, he realised that they might be a danger to him; so he resolved to divide them into several countries.[62]

Apart from attempting fragmentation, Prester John, who 'through arrogance and presumption rebelled against the suzerain', is guilty of 'treachery and disloyalty'.[63] Here in the debunked figure of Prester John we see a resemblance to the petty seigniorial princes, among whose ranks were included a number of popes, who engendered the fragmentation of the Italian peninsula for their own self-aggrandisement. Incidentally, Machiavelli, who wrote *The Prince* nearly two centuries after Dante and Marco Polo, found himself in the grip of the same anxiety caused by the same lingering fragmentation of the Italian body politic. He, like Dante, singled out the papacy as the catalyst for fragmentation. Machiavelli writes: 'You must realise that as soon as in more recent times Italy started to repudiate the empire, and the stand of the Papacy became higher in the temporal sphere, the country split into several states'.[64]

In Marco Polo's delegitimation of Prester John, a Christian religious icon, on the grounds of promoting fragmentation and disloyalty, we see the drama of another polity being underwritten through the displacement of the anxiety over fragmentation and the ideals of non-theocentric absolute monarchy which Dante and others were advocating at home. Like Prester John, Nayan, one of the Mongol chieftains, was a 'baptised Christian'. He rebelled against Kubilai Khan and was rightly vanquished by him. Yet the defeat of a Christian protagonist by a heathen power is, paradoxically, turned by Marco Polo into a victory for Christianity. In the event of Nayan's defeat, when 'Saracens, idolaters and Jews' mock the Christian cross for its failure to protect him, Marco Polo invokes the voice of the Great Khan himself addressing his Christian subjects:

> If the cross of your God has not helped Nayan, he said, 'it was for a good reason. Because it is good, it ought not to lend its aid except in a good and righteous cause. Nayan was a traitor who broke faith with his liege lord. Hence the fate that has befallen him was a vindication of the right. And the cross of your God did well in not helping against the right.[65]

To this Marco Polo has the Christian subjects reply:

> Most mighty lord, what you say is quite true. The cross would not lend itself to wrong doing and disloyalty like that of Nayan, who was a traitor to his liege lord. He has received what he well deserved.[66]

This paradox can only be understood if we see Nayan as equivalent to a seigniorial lord from Christendom who, like Prester John, militates against the ideal of universal imperium. Therefore, the defeat of Nayan is a victory for the principle of a universal imperium, which was upheld by the anti-papal monarchists as the best solution for the ills of Christendom. If the figures of Prester John and Nayan are the mirror images of the so-called Christian protagonists of fragmentation in the Italian peninsula, then the Mongol absolutist rule is the very image of the ideal imperium of the *same* refracted elsewhere.

We have already seen how Marco Polo's narrative legitimises the Mongol governing machine, which produces unity and security and thereby guarantees unhindered circulation and production of wealth. The mega-machine of order in the end helps to secure astounding mercantile proliferation. Marco Polo tells his readers that in the domain of the Great Khan: 'the merchants, they are so many and so rich and handle such quantities of merchandise that no one could give a true account of the matter; it is so utterly beyond reckoning'.[67] This scenario bears an uncanny resemblance to the second phase of mercantile growth in Europe between the sixteenth and the eighteenth centuries, when the mercantile classes depended on absolutist states for their security, circulation, legal guarantees and overseas expansion. It is a well-known fact that under the absolutist states, the mercantile classes did not form the governing class despite being the dominant economic force. The formation of absolutist governance was constituted by the realigned feudal aristocratic classes modelled on resurgent Roman laws. Yet, despite not being linked organically with mercantilism, the absolutist states became the support for mercantilism to spread its wings. Perry Anderson aptly describes this paradox:

> For the apparent paradox of absolutism in Western Europe was that it fundamentally represented an apparatus for the protection of the

aristocratic property and privileges, yet at the same time the means whereby this protection was promoted could simultaneously ensure the basic interests of the nascent mercantile and manufacturing classes.[68]

Yet, as we have seen, it was fragmentation that allowed medieval cities their autonomy, and which in turn provided mercantilism with its initial condition of growth. Perry Anderson again: 'The Medieval town had been able to develop because the dispersal of sovereignties in the feudal mode of production for the first time freed urban economies from direct domination by a rural class'.[69] Once mercantilism had established itself, its inner drive for growth came up against the narrow territoriality of small autonomous towns. For it to grow further it required the suppression of particularist barriers and the unification of domestic markets so that a larger territory would be available to it from which to trade and profit. Moreover, it required a generalised security to circulate freely beyond a localised point, which was made impossible due to lawlessness in the countryside and constant internecine warfare. Even more damaging for mercantilism was the lack of a unified system of law. Since the absolutist state assumes the functional necessities of mercantilism as its own mode of existence, the growth of mercantilism could not do without the absolutist state. B. Hindess and P. Hirst sum up the functional reliance of mercantilism on the absolutist state:

> On the one hand regular and systematic commodity circulation on an extensive scale presupposes some degree of legal guarantee of contracts and a legally guaranteed equality of buyer and seller in respect of certain contracts. There must therefore be a legal and political apparatus capable, at least at a minimal level, of enforcing such guarantees. On the other hand, regular commerce presupposes the pacification of the countryside (i.e. it should be relatively free of robber bands and irregular warfare between feudal lords) and it requires that commerce be free from arbitrary interference. In these respects the extensive development of trade and commodity production is dependent on the centralised state political and legal apparatus capable of enforcing its decision against the wishes of individual feudal lords. It presupposes, in other words, the 'absolutist' form of feudal state.[70]

Faced with the chaos of fragmentation, and driven by the exigency of mercantilism, Marco Polo displaces the dream of an absolutist solution at home onto other places. Consequently, the Mongol mega-machine of order, which parallels the absolutist desire at home, is installed as the ideal mode of governance. However, from the seventeenth century onwards a new tendency began to emerge. European travellers to the 'Orient', such as Jean Chardin, François Bernier, Jean Baptist Travernier, Sir Thomas Roe, Edward Terry and John Ovington, among others, were developing a systematic discourse on the despot, who not only represented all the ills of governance but whose locale was always in other places. This sudden change, which was to restructure the 'Occidental' relationship with the 'Orient' in terms of an oppositional relationship between modes of governance, i.e. between democracy and despotism, requires the tracing of a genealogy. Unfortunately, given the complexity of the task, I cannot give it the kind of attention it deserves. However, I cannot leave it without showing, even if only tentatively, how that discourse on despotism was emerging, because it not only played a major role in European colonialism in the 'Orient' but continues to inform an important strand of Western foreign policy.

John M. Steadman has located the veritable locus of the 'Oriental despot':

> The Oriental despot is, in fact, a tyrant of imagination. He reigns with foremost authority in the realms of fiction. The secrets of the seraglio, the intrigues of the eunuchs, the avarice of corrupt bureaucrats, the extravagance of court ceremonials that barely fall short of idolatry, the arbitrary cruelty of over civilised princes and barbaric conquerors, palace revolutions achieved by patricide – all these have loomed large in the imagination of the West.[71]

From the seventeenth century onwards the ascending bourgeoisie, who no longer needed the absolutist state, would displace their nightmarish images of governance to the 'Orient'. Moreover, this governance of nightmare, despite its origin in 'Occidental' imagination, began to be given a topological permanence in the 'Orient', which not only served the exigency of colonialism, but also contributed to the refashioning of Western history as an uninterrupted continuum of democracy. 'Oriental despotism' thus both marks an internal difference in the West and its new relationship with the so-called civilised East.

When a seventeenth-century traveller ventured beyond the confines of Europe, he carried with him two very different conceptions of otherness. On the one hand, there were the 'primitive others' whose uncivility and transgressive manners echoed the earlier *Homo monstrum*. On the other hand, there were the 'civilised others', whose formal civility made them an uncomfortable mirror image of 'our' sameness. Yet the so-called 'civilised others' needed to be othered so that upon their deterritorialisation the West could establish an asymmetric relationship with them, hence the notion of 'Oriental despotism'. Instead of civility, body politics became the marker of difference, but with the same deterritorialising effects. Lothrop Stoddard, an archetypal colonialist, reinvoked in the 1930s what had become a received notion since the seventeenth century: 'the contrast between East and West appears most strikingly in the field of government'.[72] Of course it is a contrast marked by the difference between the democracy of the West and the despotism of the East.

When Jean Chardin – a jewel merchant with a predilection for Hippocratic environmentalism, to whom Montesquieu turned for insights towards shaping the reportage of a strange mode of governance from the East into the concept of 'Oriental despotism' – arrived at the Safavid court, he found his worst fears confirmed:

> This was the day before, the king getting drunk, as it had been his daily custom for some years, fell into a raze against a player on the lute, who did not play well to his taste, and commanded Nesaralibec, his favourite, son to the governor of Irvin, to cut his hands off. The prince in pronouncing the sentence threw himself on a pile of cushions to sleep. The favourite, who was not so drunk, and knowing no crime in the condemned person, thought that the king had found none either, and that this cruel order was only a transport of drunkenness, he therefore contented himself with reprimanding the player very severely, in that he did not study to please his master better; the king wak'd in an hours time, and seeing the musician touch the lute as before, he call'd to mind the orders he had given to his favourite against the musicians, and flying into great passion with the young lord, he commanded the lord high steward to cut off the hands and feet of them both; the lord steward threw himself at the king's feet, to implore mercy for the favourite; the king, in the extreme violence of his indignation and fury, cryed out to his eunuchs and his guards, to execute the sentence upon all three; Cheic-Ali-Can, the Grand Vizier who was out of the post, happen'd to be there, as good luck would have it, he flung himself at the king's feet and embracing them, he beseech'd him to show mercy; the king making a little pause upon it, said I who can't obtain of thee to resume the charge of prime minister, Sir, replied the supplicant, I am your slave, I will ever do what your Majesty shall command me. The king being thereupon appeas'ed pardoned all the condemn'd person.[73]

On another occasion the king had the Grand Vizier's beard shaved off on yet another drunken frolic. It is a governance of absolute insecurity, arbitrariness, and passion. Yet Chardin did not fail to admire the civility of the Persians: 'The Persians are the most civilised people of the East, and the greatest complimenters in the world. The polite men amongst them, are upon a level with the politest men of Europe.'[74] However, Chardin also observed that a certain degeneration had crept into the Persians, which he attributed to their 'being subject to a despotic power'.[75]

If Chardin remains largely anecdotal, François Bernier, steeped in the rationalism of his master René Descartes, brought the apparatus of systematic analysis to the travelling representation of other modes of governance. In fact, from the writings of Bernier 'Oriental despotism' appears more than a system of government. Indeed, it represents a social formation with a structured social and economic relationship, and a corresponding psychopathology. Appropriately, these two men met in Surat in India to partake in the spectacle of suttee – the self-immolation of Hindu widows. It was Bernier, more than Chardin, who gave Montesquieu the decisive material for the formation of the concept of 'Oriental despotism'. When Karl Marx, exiled in London, took some time off from his monumental labour on *Das Kapital*, and pondered on the role of British colonialism, which was to form the basis of his concept of the Asiatic mode of production, he turned to Bernier. On 2 June 1893, in a letter to Engels, Marx wrote:

> Bernier correctly discovers the basic form of all phenomena in the East – he refers to Turkey, Persia, Hindostan, to be the absence of private property in land. This is the real key even to oriental haven.[76]

Bernier, who served as a physician at the Mogul court of India, claimed to have observed the pathos of despotism at close quarters. The following passage, prompted by Bernier's reflection on emperor Aurung-zebe's worries about the pedagogy of his son, Prince Akbar, is worth quoting at length. For it provides the lineaments upon which the concept of 'Oriental despotism' would come to rest. Bernier writes:

> He is very sensible that the cause of the misery which afflicts the empires of Asia, of their misrule, and consequent decay, should be sought, and will be found, in the deficient and the pernicious mode of instructing the children of their kings. Instructed from infancy to the care of women and eunuchs, slaves from Russia, Circassia, Mignrelia, Gurgistan, or Ethopia, whose minds are debased by the very nature of their occupation; servile and mean to superiors, proud and oppressive to the dependants – these princes, when called to the throne, leave the walls of the seraglio quite ignorant of the duties imposed upon them by their new situation. They appear on the stage of life, as if come from another world, or emerged, for the first time, from a subterraneous

cavern, astonished, like simpletons at all around them. Either, like children, they are credulous in everything, in dread of everything; or, with obstinacy and heedlessness of folly, they are deaf to every sage councillor, and rash in every stupid enterprise. According to their natural temperament, or the first ideas impressed upon their minds, such princes, on succeeding to a crown, affect to be dignified and grave, though it be easy to discern that gravity and dignity form no part of their character, that the appearance of those qualities is the effect of some ill-studied lesson, and that they are in fact only other names for savageness and vanity; or else they affect a childish politeness in their demeanour, childish because unnatural and constrained. Who that is conversant with the history of Asia can deny the faithfulness of this delineation? Have not her sovereigns been blindly and brutally cruel, cruel without judgement or mercy? Have they not been addicted to the gross and mean vice of drunkenness, and abandoned to an excessive and shameless luxury; ruining their bodily health; and impairing their understanding, in the society of concubines? Or, instead of attending to the concerns of the kingdom, have not their days been consumed in the pleasure of the chase? A pack of dogs will engage their thought and affection, although indifferent to the suffering of so many poor people who, compelled to follow the unfeeling monarchs in the pursuits of game, and left to die of hunger, heat and cold, and fatigue. In a word, the kings of Asia are constantly living in the indulgence of monstrous vices, those vices varying, indeed as I said before, according to their natural propensities, or to the ideas early installed in their minds. It is indeed a rare exception when the sovereign is not profoundly ignorant of the domestic and the political condition of his empire. The reins of government are often committed to the hands of some vizier, who, that he may reign absolute, with security and without contradiction, considers it an essential part of his plan to encourage his master in all his low pursuits, and diverts him from every avenue of knowledge. If the sceptre be not firmly grasped by the first minister, then the country is governed by the king's mother, originally a wretched slave, and by a set of eunuchs, persons who possess no enlarged and liberal view of policy, and who employ their time in barbarous intrigues; banishing, imprisoning, and strangling each other, and frequently the grandees and the vizier himself. Indeed, under their disgraceful domination, no man of any property is sure of his life for a single day.[77]

For Bernier, the pathology of the seraglio dramatises in microcosm the ills of the entire social formation under despotism. The princes of the seraglio, instructed by the meanest of the slaves – women and eunuchs – are so deformed that they are only fit for the asylum. Yet they become rulers with absolute power. Indeed, it is a nightmarish scenario. As a true rationalist, Bernier is not content with merely drawing a *mise-en-scène* of the grotesque drama of the despotic household, he seeks causes, traces effects, and formulates a structural logic to explain the phenomenon. Among the structural principles of 'Oriental despotism' as presented by Bernier, the most enduring, the one that most impressed both Montesquieu and Marx, was the assertion that in the 'Orient' the despot is the 'sole possessor of the lands, and the right of the private property'.[78] Consequently, between the despot and the destitutes, there does not exist an intermediary class or an aristocracy. Bernier compares this structural principle with that of France: 'It must not be imagined that the omrahs as lords of the Mogul's courts are members of ancient families, as our nobility in France'.[79] Without a nobility and intermediary classes, the society lacks Montesquieu's notion of 'honour' to restrain the arbitrary passion of the despot. Moreover, not only does the effective governance of the household lie in the hands of depraved slaves, but the courtiers and governors of provinces are also wretched slaves. Total absence of security and the lack of a legal framework, argues Bernier, 'obstructs the progress of trade ... [and] commercial pursuit'.[80] Consequently, the onerous presence of despotism, as Bernier shows, transforms the entire social space of the 'Orient' into a landscape of 'ruins' and 'decay' where the pathological monarchs 'reign over solitude and deserts'.[81]

By subjecting the anecdotes of eastern eccentricities of govern- ance to a systematic analytics of reason, by alluding to structural factors behind these phenomena, and by showing these to be an expression of a social formation, Bernier almost shaped the concept of 'Oriental despotism'. After Bernier all Montesquieu had to do was to arrange the data of what Althusser called 'political exoticism'[82] into a rational order of comparative taxonomy to give the notion of 'Oriental despotism' a final push towards its emergence as a concept in its modern form. Like a good Baconian inductivist, or in the 'spirit of new Physics' as Althusser describes it, Montesquieu gathered the raw materials from the 'political exoticism' of the travelogues, from their description of climates, property laws, habits and customs, pedagogy, passion, the legal system (the lack of it) and produced their 'fundamental law'. The metalanguage in which this 'funda- mental law' is expressed gives us the concept of 'Oriental despot- ism'. In *The Spirit of the Laws*[83] Montesquieu distributed his typologies of government topographically; if republicanism and monarchy belong to the West, then despotism is the natural destiny of the East. Montesquieu writes:

> Power in Asia ought, then, to be always despotic: for if their slavery was not severe they would make a division inconsistent with the nature of the country ... there reigns in Asia a servile spirit, which they have never been able to shake off, and it is impossible to find in all the histories of that country a single passage which discovers a freedom of spirit; we shall never see anything there but the excess of slavery.[84]

It seems that despite all the analytical innovations, at the heart of Montesquieu's typologies of government lies the old environmentalist doxa of Hippocrates, albeit mediated through Aristotle, Chardin and Bernier among others. It is worth remembering here that although Aristotle originally conceived despotism (from the Greek 'dems-pata' and 'despotes' signifying 'lord of the house' and 'master' respectively) to be a natural and legitimate condition for the constitution of the Hellenic household, he also showed how it took on a completely different disposition in the Asiatic world. 'The primary or simplest element of a household [Hellenic]', writes Aristotle in *Politics and the Athenian Constitution*, 'are a master and slave, husband and wife, father and children, given rise to three relationships – despotic, marital and paternal'.[85] Since all Greeks are natural masters, slaves, who are naturally slaves, must come from outside the Greek world. Aristotle even advises the Greeks to procure their slaves by raiding barbarian lands. A similar constitution is also obtained in the organisation of the state, where the despotic father assumes the role of kingship. Moreover, since all Greeks are naturally and legitimately masters and despots and all barbarians are naturally slaves, a similar relationship is obtained between the Greek world and the barbarian beyond. Aristotle approvingly quotes Euripides: 'Wherefore the poet declares: right it is that Hellenes rule barbarians; as if recognising that a barbarian and a slave are one in nature'.[86] So Aristotle does not see anything wrong with despotism, he even endorses, as we have seen, Hellenic despotism over its others. For Aristotle, instead of despotism, it is 'tyranny' that represents the evil of a political system; it is the unnatural blurring of the confines of rightful governments. Aristotle writes: 'for despotic, kingly, and constitutional governments are all three just and advantageous according to circumstances; but the role of a tyrant is never so – nor any of the deviation forms, because they are of unnatural origin'.[87] A king becomes a tyrant by exceeding his authority, a democracy by infringing the rights of the aristocracy, and a bureaucracy such as the Spartan ephoralty by misusing its position. However, there is something peculiar about the rule of Asiatic barbarians which

makes it congenitally tyrannous. In order to facilitate this argument
Aristotle makes an analytical distinction between absolute and relative nobility. Since all barbarians are naturally slaves, their governing caste can only be a relative nobility, which is no more than a
mark of internal stratification among slaves. Only the Greek ruling
class is absolutely noble. Moreover, since only an absolute noble has
the right to govern, the barbarian monarch, who is also a natural
slave, infringes the natural law by assuming the role of governor.
Hence all barbarian kingships, of which the Asiatic rulers are the
prime example, are naturally and congenitally tyrannous. In his
classification of the second order of kingship, Aristotle writes:

> There is another type, which is not uncommon among barbarian
> people. It closely resembles tyranny, except that it is constitutional and
> hereditary. The barbarians are more servile in character than Greeks,
> and are therefore prepared to tolerate despotic government. Thus such
> kingships bear the mark of tyranny because the people are by nature
> slave.[88]

For Aristotle the Asiatic monarchy is tyrannical simply because it is
barbarian on account of its natural difference. Hence the very fact of
the otherness of the Asiatic people or their ontological difference
from the Hellenic people makes them prone to tyranny.

Now we can see how Montesquieu's concept of 'Oriental despotism', despite being processed through the apparatus of new rationalism, and despite being defined as a social formation in its social and
psychic deep structure, is dependent upon the Aristotelian doxa of
the natural and ontological difference between the West and its
others. Before Montesquieu brought to bear the 'spirit of new
Physics' on the data of 'political exoticism' in The Spirit of the Law, he
undertook to write a piece of 'political exoticism' of his own in
Persian Letters, written as a form of reverse travelogue in which a
Persian despot, Usbek, and his companion, Rica, visit France and
observe with critical eyes French manners and customs and politics.
While travelling in France they also receive letters from home, which
allows Montesquieu to dramatise the despotic scene in the imaginary Persian seraglio. Montesquieu mobilises all the tropes of
'Oriental despotism' from Aristotle to Bernier in the epistolary
narrative which allows him both to critique absolutism at home, and
to displace it into far-away Persia.

The structure of Persian Letters repeats the trope of despotism as
a governance in absence by placing the despot far away from the

seraglio. In his absence, it is the eunuchs, the most wretched of the wretched slaves, who effectively govern the seraglio. In the strange world of the seraglio eunuchs assume the role of nobility but at the price of being castrated. This fact never fails to signal on the symbolic plane their structural role as parodic nobles who, unlike the proper nobility of Montesquieu's world, lack both property rights and aristocratic lineage. Watched over by the eunuchs, women are the real inmates of the dark confines of the seraglio. Ever since Aristotle pronounced that barbarians make no distinction between women and slaves, and that this unnatural practice contributed to the tyrannical propensities of Asiatic monarchies, it is made into a distinctive feature of exotic governance. Never raised beyond the status of slaves, women are kept in the seraglio for the sole purpose of serving the master with the voluptuous cornucopia of their bodies. Yet even this function they cannot deliver because they are too many for one master, and moreover, he is always absent. There reigns generalised paranoia, intrigue, and insecurity from which even Usbek the master is not immune. In this turmoil only Roxana, the most loyal of Usbek's wives, seems to be serenely upholding the laws of the seraglio. But Montesquieu brings the narrative to a climax by revealing that it is none other than Roxana who is the real betrayer of the law of the seraglio. Her betrayal suddenly brings the seraglio crumbling down, with the message that despite its formidable appearance a despotic regime is as fragile as a house of cards.

What is often commented about *Persian Letters* is not its dramatisation of the tropes of despotism, but Montesquieu's critique of Louis XIV's absolutism. However, the critique is hinged on the logic of equivalence; that is, the Persian travellers perceive an uncanny resemblance between the rule of Louis XIV and their own mode of governance. Usbek writes to his friend Ibben:

> The king of France is old. There is no case, anywhere in our history, of a king having reigned for such a long time. They say he possesses in a very high degree the talent of making himself obeyed: he governs his family, his court, and his country with equal ability. It has often been heard to say that of all types of government in the world he would most favour either that of the Turk, or that of our own august sultan, such is his esteem for oriental policies.[89]

If this amounts to a critique of Louis XIV's absolutism, it draws its rhetorical cogency from the indubitable and immanent corruption of the despotism of the 'Orient'. Hence, the critique of Louis XIV's absolutism appears as mere accident in an otherwise noble and democratic France. Despotism, therefore, is seen as a temporary disease in the body of France, its real locale being the 'Orient', where it is immanently and eternally present.

Henceforward, the ascending bourgeoisie, who no longer needed the absolutist state, would displace their nightmarish images of governance onto the 'Orient'. The consequence was a rewriting of Western history as an uninterrupted continuum of democracy. Moreover, upon these displaced images a new code of difference between 'Occident' and 'Orient' was formulated – underwritten by two different methods of governance: despotism and democracy. Far from being an innocent trope for the mapping of the world, it played a crucial part in deterritorialising the so-called civilised others, who could not be deterritorialised in the name of a civilising mission, and thereby opening them up for colonial territorialisation. When the so-called 'Orientals' were clamouring for self-rule and almost on the verge of it, Stoddard once more invoked 'Oriental despotism' to prop up the millennial fantasy of colonial rule:

> We have seen that the political tradition of the East is the cycle of despotism – a cycle barren in itself and rendering sustained progress impossible ... Do not let us for one moment imagine that the fatally simple idea of despotic rule will give away to the far more complex conception of an ordered liberty. The transformation, if it ever takes place at all will probably be the work, not of generations, but of centuries ... good government, however, has the merit of presenting a more or less attainable idea. Before Orientals can attain anything approaching the British ideal of self-government, they will have to undergo very numerous transformations of political thought.[90]

Marco Polo, in contrast, travelled back from other topoi with the message that the absolutist dream at home had found its resplendent embodiment elsewhere. He travelled, as we have seen, under the imperatives of a world plagued by anxieties over fragmentation, to which was added the contingent exigency of nascent mercantilism, allied with a vision of a governance founded on a secular unified absolutist imperium. He also travelled to other topoi shrouded in Christendom's regime of signs, whose displacements unfolded before him a world of chaotic habitudes. Upon this deterritorialised ruin he founded an empire that embodied the very principle of order. In the process he almost silently effected the redundancy of the papal empire in whose name he travelled to the empire of the Mongols, and invented a functional logic of political legitimation, which was to be theorised by Machiavelli nearly two hundred years later. The empire of order and its colossal monarch that his narrative weaves, which despite lacking a habitude and a private body, amount to no more than a machine and a machine of a machine respectively – and perhaps because of this – Marco Polo holds them up to Christendom as the ideal images of governance.

Although Marco Polo's text is the beginning of a flux of sedentary voyages, and their corresponding proliferation of machines of representation, whose function has been to map the world in relation to itself, it does not harbour the narcissism and the extreme paranoia of the fully formed discourse of the other found in the texts of the European voyages of discovery and colonialism. Marco Polo can still come back from other places to tell the story of peoples whose civilisation (Cathay) exceeds his own. Not to forget, of course, the fact that he does return from other places with a model of ideal governance. This model of governance, as we have seen, despite being grounded in the displaced image of utopian desire at home, comes back to Marco Polo's world as the glorious technology of the other. Marco Polo's unreserved and reverential avowal of its other-origin in his narrative, signals a certain openness and humility to a world which is very different from his own. Consequently, despite deterritorialising other places, and despite putting into general circulation many of the representational devices of sedentary travel, Marco Polo's world is not yet quite Eurocentric. He does not, as a sedentary traveller, quite become other, but carries the trace of the other when he comes back to his own world.

POSTSCRIPT

In the course of this book I have followed the trajectories of two very different kinds of traveller: one sedentary and the other nomadic. The former inhabit a striated space, moving only from point to point, folded in the inside, dragging their 'moved body' along a rigid line, failing to encounter difference, and returning the *same*. Since they fail to encounter difference, and fail to cross boundaries while moving in space, they cannot really be called travellers. If we are to call them travellers then we must reserve for them the oxymoronic designation 'sedentary traveller'. A 'sedentary traveller', frigid with the morbid fear of encounter, moves in space either to seek confirmation of her/his egocentric self in the mirror of the other, or to capture the other in representation in the paranoiac gesture of othering, thus never becoming-other. Moreover, sedentary travel has been an important technology in the armoury of the West in its pursuit of mastery over the rest of the world. Marco Polo's narrative, as we have seen, marks the tentative beginning of a long course of sedentary voyaging by modern Europe. However, his text, despite othering and deterritorialising the other habitudes, had not yet fixated upon a supremacist narcissism, which would be the hallmark of the Eurocentric discourse of the Enlightenment and of the colonial period. Marco Polo's text could still show humility before the other.

Nomadic travellers, on the other hand, dwell in a smooth space (*Gegend*-region, or *Heterotopia*), letting their 'moving body' slide along the supple line, crossing boundaries with speed and experiencing the intensities of encounter, never returning the *same*, and becoming-other.

Now if I were to be asked whether, despite all of my attempts to overcome binary distinction, by structuring this book around the division between sedentary and nomadic traveller, I hadn't confirmed that very binary mode of thought, how would I answer? Of course, I cannot claim that binary division does not play a part in the presentation of my positions. However, without some kind of binary division, not only do the evaluation of values and critical discrimination become impossible, but to a large extent, so too does thought itself. Moreover, like the paradox involved in opposing dialectics, which involves dialectical moves in the very gesture of opposition, any attempt at overcoming binary thought, unless one accepts silence, involves a certain amount of binary thought. There is no absolute way out of this paradox. But the very struggle with this paradoxical mode of thought constitutes the ethical project itself. Even Nietzsche could not avoid this paradox. The very process of transvaluation of all values and the affirmation of affirmative thought involves saying *No* to what is negative and to what is seized by *Ressentiment*. Furthermore, Nietzsche simply did not say *No* to negative values, but proposed the tracing of their genealogy so that they could be effectively overcome. I have tried to follow a similar course in this book. In our case, the affirmative ethics of nomadic travel, which involve saying *Yes* to the other, require overcoming the rigid boundary and the paranoia of othering, which are the characteristics of sedentary travel. Hence, it was necessary not only to distinguish the nomadic from the sedentary traveller, but also to trace the genealogy of the latter. However, it is worth remembering that nomadic travel is always the virtual possibility of all travel. In practice, one becomes a nomadic or a sedentary traveller on one's performative actualisation or repression of this virtual possibility.

Another objection to this book, not unrelated to the above, might also be made by arguing that my ethical exploration betrays ethical language. Again, if one is not willing to accept the quietism of silence, rational and critical language is unavoidable. I have shown this in my discussion of Levinas's work, where Levinas came to realise that a wholly ethical language of *saying* (*Le dire*) is not possible. No matter how far one tries to bear an authentic testimony to the language of *saying*, it will always be compromised or expressed unfaithfully in the rational, critical language of *said* (*Le dit*). The ethical task, as Levinas sees it, is not to do away with the language of *said*, but to bear testimony to the *saying* in the *said*. This paradox, or double-bind, is unavoidable in any ethical project. And my own ethical exploration is no exception.

Finally, there is a paradox in the very parameters of cross-cultural ethics that I have proposed. On the one hand, there is the moral sense of justice and obligation towards the other; on the other, there is the joyful affirmation of encounter and becoming-other. I have argued that the active ethical moment of becoming-other in encounter, which involves the process of 'a parallel involution',

NOTES

Part I Travel and the ethics of the other

1 Marking boundaries/crossing lines

1 Daniel Defoe, *Robinson Crusoe*, Penguin, Harmondsworth 1965, p. 77.
2 Michel Tournier, *Friday or the Other Island*, trans. Norman Denny, Penguin, Harmondsworth 1974.
3 Joseph Conrad, *Heart of Darkness*, in Tod K. Bender *et al.* (eds.), *Modernism in Literature*, Holt, Rinehart and Winston, New York 1977, p. 508.
4 Echo, the figure of refrain, is difference herself. If Narcissus immobilises himself within a rigid boundary, Echo's entire existence is given to crossing boundaries. She doesn't speak the tales of her self-same being; she only repeats others. She is always there for others, responding to their summons. The three rare occasions on which Echo speaks without repeating, she says, 'Here!', 'Come!', 'Come here, and let us meet', Ovid, The *Metamorphosis*, trans. Mary M. Innes, Penguin, Harmondsworth 1955, p. 91. These phrases do not locate a self presence; they are simply variations of repetition and refrain, the going towards others.
5 *Ibid.*, p. 93.
6 *Ibid.*, p. 92.
7 Gabriel García Márquez, *One Hundred Years of Solitude*, trans. Gregory Rabassa, Picador, London 1978, p. 27 and p. 336.
8 The image of the mirror as a labyrinth or Infinite appears in many of Jorge Luis Borges' tales. For instance, in 'The Library of Babel', he writes: 'In the hallway there is a mirror which faithfully duplicates all appearances. ... I prefer to dream that its polished surfaces represent and promise the infinite', in *Labyrinths*, Penguin, Harmondsworth 1970, p. 78.
9 Lewis Carroll, *The Annotated Alice*, ed. Martin Gardner, Penguin, Harmondsworth 1965, p. 181.
10 Gilles Deleuze, *The Logic of Sense*, trans. Mark Lester and Charles Stivale, Columbia University Press, New York 1990, p. 236.
11 Salman Rushdie, *Midnight's Children*, Picador, London 1981, p. 167.
12 Hippocrates, 'Airs, Waters, Places', in *Hippocratic Writings*, trans. J. Chadwick and W. N. Mann, Penguin, Harmondsworth 1950.
13 Herodotus, *The History*, Penguin, Harmondsworth 1954, p. 624.
14 Aristotle, *Politics and the Athenian Constitution*, trans. John Warrington, Everyman Library, London, 1959.
15 Georg Wilhelm Friedrich Hegel, *The Philosophy of History*, trans. J. Sibree, Dover Publications, New York 1956, p. 80.
16 *Ibid.*
17 *Ibid.*, p. 91.
18 'What we properly understand by Africa, is the Unhistorical, Undeveloped

Spirit, still involved in the condition of mere nature', *ibid.*, p. 99.

19 *Ibid.*, p. 93.

20 *Ibid.*, p. 81.

21 Baron de Montesquieu, *The Spirit of the Laws*, vol. One, chs. XIV-XX, trans. Thomas Nugent, Hafner Press, New York 1949, pp. 221-316.

22 If 'We' the people of the land provide the legitimacy for the sovereignty of the nation-state, then the possession of 'their' land by a nation-state loses all legitimation.

23 My understanding of Kant owes a great deal to Gilles Deleuze's *Kant's Critical Philosophy*, trans. Hugh Tomlinson and Barbara Habberjam, The Athlone Press, London 1984.

24 *Ibid.*, p. 14.

25 Immanuel Kant, *Critique of Pure Reason*, Everyman's Library, London 1934, p. 46.

26 *Ibid.*, p. 44.

27 Robert E. Dickenson, *The Makers of Modern Geography*, Routledge & Kegan Paul, London 1969.

28 Kant's confirmation of the empirical through the legislation of faculties contains the aleatoric multiplicity of the empirical. It simply confirms the normal and the given. Gilles Deleuze puts it like this, 'The legislators and the priest practise the ministry, the legislation and the representation of established values; all they do is internalise current values. Kant's "proper usage of the faculties" mysteriously coincides with these established values: true knowledge, true morality, true religion'. *Nietzsche and Philosophy*, trans. Hugh Tomlinson, Columbia University Press, New York 1983, p. 93.

29 Gilles Deleuze and Félix Guattari, *A Thousand Plateaus*, trans. Brian Massumi, The Athlone Press, London 1988, p. 489.

30 Henri Lefebvre, *The Production of Space*, trans. Donald Nicholson-Smith, Blackwell, Oxford 1991, p. 17.

31 Michel Tournier, *Friday or the Other Island*, trans. Norman Denny, Penguin, Harmondsworth 1969, p. 175.

32 Giles Deleuze and Fèlix Guattari write in *A Thousand Plateaus* 'We can say of the nomads, following Toynbee's suggestion; *they do not move*. They are nomads by dint of not moving', p. 482.

33 M. Merleau-Ponty, *Phenomenology of Perception*, trans. Colin Smith, Routledge, London 1962, p. 286.

34 George Jackson, *Soledad Brothers*, Penguin, Harmondsworth 1971, p. 28.

35 Michel de Certeau, *Practice of Everyday Life*, trans. Steven Rendall, University of California Press, Berkeley 1984, p. 111.

36 Paul Auster, *City of Glass*, in *The New York Trilogy*, Faber and Faber, London 1987, p. 111.

37 *Ibid.*, pp. 3-4.

38 Emmanuel Levinas, *Totality and Infinity*, trans. Alphonso Lingis, Duquesne University Press, Pittsburgh 1969, p. 153.

39 Martin Heidegger, *Being and Time*, trans. John Macquarrie and Edward Robinson, Basil Blackwell, Oxford 1962, p. 138.

40 *Ibid.*, p. 135.

41 *Ibid.*

42 *Ibid.*, p. 143.

43 *Ibid.*

44 *Ibid.*, p. 136.

45 *Ibid.*, p. 140.
46 *Ibid.*, p. 137.
47 *Ibid.*, p. 136.
48 *Ibid.*
49 Merleau-Ponty, *Phenomenology of Perception*, p. 291.
50 *Ibid.* p. 287.
51 *Ibid.*, p. 264.
52 *Ibid.*, p. 279.
53 *Ibid.*, p. 250.
54 Tournier, *Friday or the Other Island*, p. 82.
55 Martin Heidegger, 'Building Dwelling Thinking', in *Poetry, Language, Thought*, trans. Albert Hofstadter, Harper and Row, New York 1975, p. 151.
56 *Ibid.*, p. 152.
57 *Ibid.*
58 Jacques Derrida, *Différance*, in *Margins of Philosophy*, trans. Alan Bass, The Harvester Press, Brighton 1982, p. 22.
59 Despite the importance of Heidegger's work, which is invaluable for opening up the rigid spaces of geometry and geography, I feel a profound unease in my engagement. Heidegger's brief affiliation to the National Socialist party in the early 30s is well-known. However, the question is: does this tendency appear in his work as a thinker? Heidegger's infamous rectoral address (University of Freiburg 1933) and its resonance carried throughout the dark pages of *An Introduction to Metaphysics* leave one in no doubt about a disturbing aspect of Heidegger's thinking. Heidegger's drift back to answer the originary question of being, on the one hand, reveals the thrownness of existence; and on the other, leads to a nostalgic quest for the lost Beings in the pre-Socratic Greek language, whose true heir, he believed, to be German. This second route of Heidegger's drift back and return, coupled with his preoccupation with the 'spirit' in the late 20s and early 30s, colluded to produce a *volkish* valorisation of the German language, and through it, to the spiritual renewal and destiny of the fatherland, which the National Socialist party represented. In *An Introduction to Metaphysics* (trans. Ralph Manheim, Yale University Press, New Haven 1959), we find Heidegger still speaking of the 'inner truth' and 'greatness' of 'National Socialism' (p. 199). What do these 'inner truth' and 'greatness', against what Heidegger considered to be the false philosophies of National Socialism, refer to? It seems that his valorisation of the German language, via the rightful descent from Greek, as the carrier of originary presence, is now accorded the burden of 'spirit'. 'For along with German and Greek is ... at once the most powerful and most spiritual of all languages' (p. 57). And the spirituality of the language gets entwined with the destiny of the nation 'because the destiny of language is grounded in a nation's *relation to being*' (p. 51). That in turn leads to the 'historical mission' of 'our nation' (p. 50) to rescue the 'darkening world' with its 'emasculation of the spirit' (p. 45). By 'the world', incidentally, Heidegger means only 'Europe' (p. 45). In his rectoral address, he clearly adds 'forces of earth and blood' to the domain of the spirit (quoted from Jacques Derrida, *Of Spirit*, trans. Geoff Bennington and Rachel Bowlbey, *Critical Inquiry*, Winter 1989, p. 467). Heidegger's invocation of the 'spirit', then, and his linking of it with the earth and blood, which led to the preoccupation with the destiny of Germany and Europe, has a decidedly nationalistic orientation. There is no doubt that this line of

thought accords well with the philosophy of National Socialism. However, it is contingent to his main philosophy. The same cannot be said of his valorisation of the German language, which, for Heidegger, is the real house of Being. This is a major strand of Heidegger's philosophy. To move from here to the blood and soil *volk*ism of the national destiny is not a great distance to jump. This strand, however, does not invalidate the Heideggerian insight into *Dasein*'s 'thrownness', and the contingent nature of its dwelling. In fact, to reiterate, this strand of Heidegger's thought remains invaluable for opening up the rigidity of geographical and geometric space for an alternative vision of habitation and boundary. Before we end this rather long footnote, however, a few comments on Derrida's essay *Of Spirit* are in order. Derrida begins well by showing the return of spirit (*Geist*) in Heidegger's rectoral address, which was exiled in his early work. He also notes that by bringing spiritual preoccupation to 'earth and blood', Heidegger 'spiritualizes National Socialism' (p. 468). However, after that, Derrida makes certain moves which reveal deconstructionist reading at its worst. They produce a liberalism in the manner of the 'balanced' both-sides-of-the-argument approach of the BBC. Let us see how the other side of Derrida's argument proceeds: 'But on the other hand, by taking the risk of spiritualizing Nazism he might have been trying to absolve or save it with this affirmation (spirituality, science, questioning, and so on). By the same token, this sets apart (*démarque*) Heidegger's commitment and breaks an affiliation. This address *seems* no longer to belong simply to the "ideological" camp, but natural, biological, racial, according to an anything but spiritual interpretation of "earth and blood" ... Because one cannot demarcate oneself off from biologism, from naturalism, from racism in its genetic form; one cannot be *opposed* to them except by re-inscribing spirit in an oppositional determination ... The constraint of this program remains very strong, it reigns over the majority of discourses that, today and for a long time to come, state their opposition to racism, to totalitarianism, to Nazism' (p. 469). By a miraculous act of reading, Heidegger's spiritualisation of National Socialism is made to stand as its opposition. Here the double reading does not deconstruct but exonerates Heidegger's Nazism. Now we have Heidegger the opponent of Nazism. Has Derrida forgotten Hegel's history of the *Geist*? Hasn't Hegel marked the essential difference between 'Orient' and 'Occident' on the basis of the stages of the *Geist*, where Africa – the *Geist*-less – disappears from history altogether? *Geist* can just as much be invoked to mark an essentiality as nature and biology. The spiritualisation of 'earth and blood' remains precisely that: a marker of essentiality, of 'We' people.

60 Heidegger, 'Building Dwelling Thinking', in *Poetry, Language, Thought*, p. 154.
61 *Ibid.*
62 Gaston Bachelard, *The Poetics of Space*, trans. Maria Jolas, Beacon Press, Boston 1969, p. xi.
63 *Ibid.*, p. xxxii.
64 *Ibid.*, p. 13.
65 *Ibid.*, p. 8.
66 *Ibid.*, p. 17.
67 *Ibid.*, p. 215.
68 *Ibid.*, p. 40.

69 *Ibid.*, pp. 40-1.
70 *Ibid.*, p. 212.
71 Martin Heidegger, 'Language', in *Poetry, Language, Thought*, p. 204.
72 Mark C. Taylor, *Alterity*, The University of Chicago Press, Chicago 1987, p. 51.
73 Obviously, I am here using the notion of the supplement in the Derridean sense. 'But the supplement supplements. It adds to replace. It intervenes or insinuates itself *in-the-place-of*; if it fills, it is as if one fills a void', Jacques Derrida, *Of Grammatology*, trans. Gayatri Chakravorty Spivak, The Johns Hopkins University Press, Baltimore 1976, p. 145.
74 Existential geographer Marwyn S. Samuel confirms this view when he writes, 'At root, existential space (meaning any spatial projection) is nothing more than the assignments of place', 'Existentialism and Human Geography', in D. Hay and M. S. Samuel (eds.) *Human Geography*, London 1978, p. 30.
75 Derrida, *Différance*, in *Margins of Philosophy*, p. 6.
76 *Ibid.*, p. 27.
77 Heidegger, *Being and Time*, p. 155.
78 *Ibid.*, p. 158.
79 *Ibid.*, p. 165.
80 *Ibid.*, p. 166.
81 *Ibid.*, p. 165.
82 Thomas De Quincey, *Confession of an English Opium Eater*, Penguin, Harmondsworth 1971, p. 81.
83 *Ibid.*, p. 108.
84 Franz Kafka, 'At the Door of the Law', in *Stories 1904-1924*, trans. J. A. Underwood, Futura, London 1981, p. 194.
85 Edmund Leach, *Culture and Communication*, Cambridge University Press, Cambridge 1976, p. 33.
86 Jacques Derrida, *The Law of Genre*, in Derek Attridge (ed.), *Acts of Literature*, Routledge, London 1992, p. 230.
87 I am indebted to Robert E. Dickenson's work for this analysis of the history of geography as an academic discipline. See *The Makers of Modern Geography*, Routledge & Kegan Paul, London 1969.
88 Quoted from Lucien Febvre, *A New Kind of History*, ed. Peter Burke, Routledge & Kegan Paul, London 1973, p. 215.
89 *Ibid.*
90 *Ibid.*
91 Gilles Deleuze, *Difference and Repetition*, trans. Paul Patton, The Athlone Press, London 1994, p. 10.
92 Lucien Febvre, *A Geographical Introduction to History*, London 1925, p. 309.
93 Lewis Mumford, *The City in History*, Secker and Warburg, London 1961, p. 39.
94 *Ibid.*, p. 51.
95 *Ibid.*, p. 47.
96 Michel Foucault, 'Questions on Geography', in *Power/Knowledge*, ed. Colin Gordon, The Harvester Press, Brighton 1980, p. 73.
97 Michel Foucault, *Discipline and Punish*, trans. Alan Sheridan, Penguin, Harmondsworth 1977, p. 236.
98 Michel Foucault, *Madness and Civilisation*, trans. Richard Howard, Tavistock Publications, London 1967, p. 46.

99   Foucault, *Discipline and Punish*, p. 200.
100 Gilles Deleuze, *Foucault*, trans. Seán Hand, University of Minnesota Press, Minneapolis 1988, p. 32.
101 *Ibid.*
102 Foucault, 'Questions on Geography', p. 73.
103 Foucault, *Discipline and Punish*, p. 200.
104 Foucault, *Madness and Civilisation*, p. 11.
105 *Ibid.*
106 *Ibid.*
107 Deleuze, *Foucault*, p. 97.
108 Michel Foucault, *The Order of Things*, Tavistock, London 1970, p. xviii.
109 *Ibid.*, p. xv.
110 Friedrich Nietzsche, *Thus Spoke Zarathustra*, trans. R. J. Hollingdale, Penguin, Harmondsworth 1961, p. 173.
111 *Ibid.*, p. 174.
112 *Ibid.*, p. 108.
113 *Ibid.*, p. 176.
114 *Ibid.*, p. 173.
115 Franz Kafka, *The Great Wall of China*, in *Description of a Struggle and The Great Wall of China*, trans. Willa and Edwin Muir and Tania and James Stern, Secker & Warburg, London 1960, pp. 77-8.
116 *Ibid.*, p. 76.
117 *Ibid.*, p. 80.
118 de Certeau, *The Practice of Everyday Life*, p. 107.
119 Henri Lefebvre, *The Production of Space*, trans. Donald Nicholson-Smith, Blackwell, Oxford 1991, p. 244.
120 Mumford, *The City in History*, p. 367.
121 Lefebvre, *The Production of Space*, p. 279.
122 Nuruddin Farah, *Maps*, Picador, London 1986.
123 *Ibid.*, p. 11.
124 *Ibid.*, p. 18.
125 Ernest Renan, *What is a Nation*, trans. Martin Thom, in Homi K. Bhabha (ed.), *Nation and Narration*, Routledge, London 1990, p. 11.
126 *Ibid.*, p. 18.
127 *Ibid.*, p. 19.
128 Friedrich Nietzsche, *On the Genealogy of Morals and Ecce Homo*, trans. Walter Kaufmann, Vintage Books, New York 1967, p. 61.
129 *Ibid.*, pp. 61-2.
130 Mumford, *The City in History*, p. 66.
131 Lefebvre, *The Production of Space*, p. 245.
132 Amos Oz, *Where the Jackals Howl*, trans. Nicholas de Lange and Philip Simpson, Flamingo, London, 1983.
133 *Ibid.*, pp. 10-11.
134 Derrida, *The Law of the Genre*, p. 224.
135 *Ibid.*, pp. 224-5.
136 *Ibid.*, p. 227.
137 *Ibid.*, p. 230.
138 Oz, 'Nomad and Viper', in *Where the Jackals Howl*, p. 30.
139 *Ibid.*, p. 34.
140 *Ibid.*, p. 35.
141 *Ibid.*, p. 38.

142 *Ibid.*, p. 36.
143 Gilles Deleuze and Félix Guattari, *Kafka: Towards a Minor Literature*, trans. Dana Polan, University of Minnesota Press, Minneapolis 1986, p. 35.
144 Benedict de Spinoza, *Ethics*, Hafner Press, New York 1946. My understanding of Spinoza's work owes a great deal to Deleuze's fascinating readings, which, it must be admitted, are just as much his as they are Spinoza's. Spinoza, in the first chapter of *Ethics*, makes this astonishing proposition: 'Let no one then be astonished that before proving the existence of body, and other necessary things, I speak of imagination of body, and of its composition', *Ethics* (p. 29). He distinguishes bodies from one another 'in respect of motion and rest, quickness and slowness, and not in respect of substance' (p. 91).
145 *Ibid.*
146 Gilles Deleuze, *Spinoza: Practical Philosophy*, trans. Robert Hurley, City Lights Books, San Francisco 1988, p. 54.
147 Deleuze and Guattari, *Kafka: Towards a Minor Literature*, p. 35.
148 Deleuze and Guattari, *A Thousand Plateaus*, p. 510.
149 Franz Kafka, 'The Metamorphosis', in *Stories 1904-1924*, trans. J. A. Underwood, Futura, London 1981, p. 91.
150 *Ibid.*
151 *Ibid.*, p. 92
152 *Ibid.*
153 Kafka, 'The Spur-of-the-moment Stroll', in *Stories 1904-1924*, p. 22.
154 Kafka, 'The Way Home', in *Stories 1904-1924*, p. 29.
155 Kafka, 'Home-Coming', in *Description of a Struggle and The Great Wall of China*, p. 144.
156 Wilson Harris, *The Four Banks of the River of Space*, in *The Carnival Trilogy*, Faber & Faber, London 1993, p. 352.
157 Kafka, 'The Bridge', in *Description of a Struggle and the Great Wall of China*, p. 116.
158 Kafka, "The Fat Man; an address to the landscape (No 3 Description of a Struggle)', in *Description of a Struggle and The Great Wall of China*, pp. 38-9.
159 Kafka, 'Wanting to be a Red Indian', in *Stories 1904-1924*, p. 36.
160 Franz Kafka, *The Departure*, in *Description of a Struggle and The Great Wall of China*, p. 119.
161 E. M. Forster, *A Passage to India*, Penguin, Harmondsworth 1936, p. 31.
162 *Ibid.*, p. 32.
163 Frantz Fanon, *The Wretched of the Earth*, trans. Constance Farrington, Penguin, Harmondsworth 1967, p. 31.
164 *Ibid.* p. 29.
165 *Ibid.*, p. 30.
166 Forster, *A Passage to India*, p. 40.
167 *Ibid.*, p. 68.
168 *Ibid.*, p. 130.
169 *Ibid.*, p. 79.
170 *Ibid.*, p. 94.
171 *Ibid.*, p. 176.
172 *Ibid.*, p. 278.
173 *Ibid.*, pp. 277-8.
174 *Ibid.*, p. 316.
175 *Ibid.*, p. 46.

176 *Ibid.*, p. 48.
177 *Ibid.*, p. 154.
178 *Ibid.*, p. 149.
179 *Ibid.*
180 *Ibid.*, p. 212.
181 *Ibid.*, p. 137.
182 *Ibid.*, p. 138.
183 It is interesting that Forster both alludes to India's geological formation and to the temporality of the aeon (eternity, infinity). Gilles Deleuze argues that behind the mask of representation lies the metastable substance that implicates the forces of being: it is a groundless ground of becoming. Its temporality is *aion* which animates 'unlimited past-future ... in an empty present', *The Logic of Sense*, p. 150. It is a time of 'counter-actualisation' (*ibid.*, p. 151). It both unforms molar identities and unleashes the forces of becoming. Hence Deleuze equates *aion* with Nietzsche's eternal return.
184 *Ibid.*, p. 164.
185 *Ibid.*, p. 203.
186 *Ibid.*, p. 263.
187 *Ibid.*
188 *Ibid.*, p. 43.
189 *Ibid.*, p. 45.
190 *Ibid.*, p. 161.
191 *Ibid.*, p. 255.
192 John Kirkland Wright, '*Terrae Incognitae*: the place of imagination in Geography', in *Human Nature in Geography*, Harvard University Press, Cambridge, Massachusetts 1966, p. 69.
193 Deleuze and Guattari, *A Thousand Plateaus*, p. 482.
194 *Ibid.*, p. 479.
195 *Ibid.*, p. 478.
196 Gilles Deleuze, *Bergsonism*, trans. Hugh Tomlinson and Barbara Habberjam, Zone Books, New York 1988, p. 23.
197 *Ibid.*, p. 28.
198 Deleuze and Guattari, *A Thousand Plateaus*, p. 474.
199 Gilles Deleuze interprets *thanatos* as the groundless ground of libidinal force in *Masochism: Coldness and Cruelty*, trans. Jean McNeil, Zone Books, New York 1989. See 'The Death Instinct', pp. 111-21. Deleuze sees in Freud's philosophical reflections in *Beyond the Pleasure Principle* an attempt to develop a positive ontology of self-difference, which is not unlike that of Bergson, Spinoza and Nietzsche. In *Difference and Repetition* (trans. Paul Patton, The Athlone Press, London 1994) Gilles Deleuze writes 'the death instinct is discovered, not in connection with the destructive tendencies, not in connection with aggressivity, but as a result of a direct consideration of repetition phenomena. Strangely, the death instinct serves as positive, originary principle of repetition' (p. 16). Moreover, Deleuze and Guattari's use of desire and the unconscious in *Anti-Oedipus*, against the hermeneutic negativity of the Lacanian school, as a productive, affirmative force of becoming, also attests to their evaluation of Freud as the ontologist of self-difference.
200 Deleuze and Guattari, *A Thousand Plateaus*, p. 486.
201 *Ibid.*, p. 482.
202 *Ibid.*, p. 122.
203 *Ibid.*, p. 320.

204 *Ibid.*, p. 293.
205 Deleuze and Guattari make a distinction between the map of geography, which is the map of tracing and representation, and the map of intensity, which is the performative map of becoming. See *A Thousand Plateaus*, p. 164. They also call the map of intensity, diagram. In order to avoid confusion I will call the map of representation 'map' and the map of intensity 'diagram'.
206 Harris, *The Four Banks of the River of Space*, p. 395.
207 Deleuze and Guattari distinguish chess from Go. Chess, they argue, is a game on a striated space. It is territorial, and belongs to the polis and the state and semiology. Its pieces are coded; its conduct of war is institutionalised and regulated. Go is the game of the smooth space; it belongs to nomos and the desert. Its war is without battle lines; strategic encirclement in open space. It conducts itself like a nomadic war machine. Deleuze and Guattari distinguish between two types of refrain. The expressive refrain of territorialisation and the intensive musicality (rhythm) which exist between chaos and the ever-changing milieux. The former is dimensional (fixity), the latter is directional (virtual). The latter is very similar to Nietzsche's eternal return.
208 Deleuze and Guattari, *A Thousand Plateaus*, p. 54.
209 Wilson Harris, *The Infinite Rehearsal*, in *The Carnival Trilogy*, p. 258.
210 Deleuze and Guattari, *A Thousand Plateaus*, p. 25.
211 Harris, *The Infinite Rehearsal*, p. 257.
212 Most historians of space attest to the zonal and the discontinuous nature of pre-modern or pre-nation-state territorial formation. Lucien Febvre writes of pre-modern territoriality as 'composed of isolating zones, separating thresholds', *A New Kind of History*, p. 211.
213 Deleuze, *Bergsonism*, p. 38.
214 Henri Bergson, *Creative Evolution*, trans. Arthur Mitchell, Macmillan, London 1913, p. 3.
215 *Ibid.*, pp. 4-5.
216 Deleuze, *The Logic of Sense*, p. 150.
217 Deleuze, *Nietzsche and Philosophy*, p. 24.
218 Dante Alighieri, *The Divine Comedy*, Canto 1, Inferno 1, trans. C. H. Sisson, Pan Books, London, 1981, p. 47.
219 de Certeau, *The Practice of Everyday Life*, p. 101.
220 Claude Lévi-Strauss, *Tristes Tropiques*, trans. John and Doreen Weightman, Penguin, Harmondsworth 1976, p. 169.
221 *Ibid.*
222 Michel de Certeau, *Heterologies: Discourse on the Other*, trans. Brian Massumi, Manchester University Press, Manchester 1986, p. 68.
223 Roland Barthes, *Empire of Signs*, trans. Richard Howard, The Noonday Press, New York 1989.
224 Joseph Conrad, 'Landfalls and Departures', in *The Mirror of the Sea*, Methuen, London 1906, p. 1.
225 *Ibid.*
226 Joseph Conrad, 'The Nigger of the "Narcissus"', in *The Nigger of the 'Narcissus'/Typhoon and Other Stories*, Penguin, Harmondsworth 1963, p. 35.
227 de Certeau, *Heterologies*, p. 71.
228 Giambattista Vico, *The New Science of Giambattista Vico*, trans. T. G. Bergin and M. H. Fish, London 1970, p. 234.

229 The spelling of the name of the Mongol emperor varies widely. Italo
    Calvino, for instance, uses 'Kublai Khan'; Coleridge uses 'Kubla Khan', and
    in the standard translation of Marco Polo's travel text it appears as 'Kubilai
    Khan'.
230 Italo Calvino, *Invisible Cities*, trans. William Weaver, Picador 1979, p. 36.
231 *Ibid.*, p. 69.
232 Samuel Taylor Coleridge, *Kubla Khan*, in *The Rime of the Ancient Mariner
    and Other Poems*, Dover Publications, New York 1992, p. 58.
233 K. Burke, 'Kubla Khan, Proto Surrealist Poem', in *Language as Symbolic
    Action*, Berkeley 1966, p. 201.
234 Deleuze and Guattari, *A Thousand Plateaus*, p. 270.
235 The notion of simulacrum used here owes its origin to Gilles Deleuze's
    appendix to *The Logic of Sense*, 'The Simulacrum and Ancient Philosophy'.
    In one sense, Deleuze's appendix is a classic deconstructionist exercise,
    which proceeds to reverse Platonism from within Plato's own vast *oeuvre*.
    As such, it shares a great deal with Jacques Derrida's own deconstructionist
    reading of Plato: see 'Plato's Pharmacy,' in *Dissemination*, trans. Barbara
    Johnson, Chicago University Press, Chicago 1981. Within the circuit of
    representation, as ground rules for arriving at legitimate knowledge, Plato
    devises the binary mechanics of the model and the copy. However, Plato's
    purpose in staging this binary division is not simply to distinguish different
    orders or stages of knowledge but to sort out the adequacy of representa-
    tion. In other words, since all representations are copies, the task of the
    philosopher is to discriminate the good from the bad copies. Plato's
    'purpose of division', as Deleuze, in subtle readings of *Sophist* and
    Phaedrus, shows, 'is not at all to divide a genus into species, but, more
    profoundly, to select lineages: to distinguish pretenders; to distinguish the
    pure from the impure, the authentic from the inauthentic' (p. 254). Plato
    then goes down the rungs of the ladder, tracing progressively the less and
    less authentic forms of copies. When he hits the bottom, he finds the least
    authentic, and the most degraded copy of all: the simulacrum. It is a pure
    mirage and a phantasm. However, Deleuze finds in *Sophist* 'the most
    extraordinary adventure of Platonism', when 'Plato discovers, in the flash of
    an instant, that the simulacrum is not simply a false copy, but that it places
    in question the very notions of copy and model' (p. 256). The copy works by
    means of establishing resemblance with the model; it represents the model
    in discourse, and aspires to stay true to its inner essence. But a simulacrum
    is not a copy of the copy because it leaves any pretence of resemblance far
    behind its savage ghost dance. It launches a violent assault on resemblance
    and any sober pursuit of representation. Although it might insinuate an
    effect of resemblance, it is animated by the creative force of difference. It
    harbours the 'Other' and 'flows an internalised dissemblance' (p. 258).
    Hence, if the simulacrum resembles the model at all, it is simply to stage a
    cunning *coup* against representation; and it signals the presence of the
    other. It shows the yawning gap, 'depths and distance', which the epistemo-
    logical subject cannot master. Here, at the end of demonstrating the undo-
    ing of the representational authority from within Plato's text and rescuing
    the simulacrum from its degradation, Deleuze parts company with the
    Deconstructionists. He lets the simulacrum emerge as the joyful *élan* of a
    positive ontology of becoming. Deleuze sees the simulacrum as the bearer
    of the libidinal as Freud had conceived it, and makes it converge with

Nietzsche's eternal return. The simulacrum, thus, not only undermines representation, but unleashes the elemental force of becoming, which is always a question of difference, to be otherwise than the *same*, and becoming-other.

236 Deleuze and Guattari derive the notion of haecceity from Duns Scotus, who coined it from *hace*, 'this thing'. In fact, haecceity neither stands for a thing nor a subject. It has been suggested that the mistranslation of haecceity as ecceity, which is derived from *ecce*, 'here is', captures the sense of non-personalised individuation that Deleuze and Guattari want to convey. Like simulacrum, haecceity belongs to a state outside the subjective circuit of enunciation, which validates representation. It articulates the simmering passion of the body, as defined by Spinoza. It is the ontological site of becoming, which Deleuze, in his discussion of simulacrum in *The Logic of Sense*, does not state clearly. In *A Thousand Plateaus*, in defining the nature of haecceity, Deleuze and Guattari reveal its locus, which is the home of all becomings. Here is their definition: 'They are haecceities in the sense that they consist entirely of relations of movement and rest between molecules or particles, capacities to affect and be affected' (p. 261). However, despite its existence in molecular intensities, haecceity has its own semiotic: its plane of content and expression. Deleuze and Guattari identify three elements as the basic chain of expression of haecceity. They are: indefinite article, proper name and the infinitive verb. The time of the infinitive, Deleuze and Guattari argue, belongs to the molecular time of *Aeon*, as against the molar time of *Chronos*. It is the nomadic time of pure event and becoming. It cannot be fixed in a frozen moment of time like other verbal categories; it always carries indeterminacy and fluidity with it. The proper name, having long been identified as the signature of personal identity, surprisingly appears as belonging to the semiotic of haecceity. It is due to a very particular usage of the proper name that Deleuze and Guattari have in mind. For them, 'the proper name is not a subject of a tense but the agent of an infinitive' (p. 264). Their proper names belong to the subterranean field of intensities where the names do not invoke subjects but provide energy for becoming, which is always becoming-other. So the proper name they have in mind belongs to the men of war and animals, where individuation does not mark individuality but affirms the collective anonymity of the pack. 'If Tick, Wolf, Horse, etc., are true proper names, they are so not by virtue of the specific and generic denominators that characterise them but of the speed that compose them and the affects that fill them; it is by virtue of the event they are in themselves and in the assemblages' (p. 264). Finally, the third marker of the semiotic of the haecceity is the indefinite article and the indefinite pronoun. Like the proper name, the individuation marked by the indefinite article and the indefinite pronoun are indeterminable, and undermine a determinable subject who is deemed to be the necessary condition for all enunciation. It is 'an individuating function within a collectivity' (p. 264). One, He, They, are not the subjects of enunciation, but part of a collective assemblage of statements. They mark the individuation beyond representation, and signal the moments of becoming, becoming-other.

237 Wilson Harris, *Palace of the Peacock*, in *The Guyana Quartet*, Faber & Faber, London 1985, p. 116.

2 Othering and the other

1 William Shakespeare, *The Tempest*, Act 1, Scene 2, Methuen, London 1964, p. 21.
2 Frantz Fanon, *Black Skin, White Masks*, trans. Charles Lam Markmann, Pluto Press, London 1986, p. 176.
3 G. W. F. Hegel, *The Phenomenology of Mind*, trans. J. B. Ballie, George Allen & Unwin, London 1910, pp. 236-7.
4 Gilles Deleuze, 'Michel Tournier and the World without Others', trans. Graham Burchell, *Economy and Society*, 13(1), 1984-5, p. 57.
5 Gilles Deleuze and Félix Guattari, *A Thousand Plateaus*, trans. Brian Massumi, The Athlone Press, London 1987, p. 23.
6 *Ibid.*, p. 229.
7 *Ibid.*, p. 231.
8 Emmanuel Levinas, *Totality and Infinity*, trans. Alphonso Lingis, Duquesne University Press, Pittsburgh 1969, p. 38.
9 Levinas defines totality in the following way: 'The negator and the negated are posited together, form a system, that is, a totality', *ibid.* p. 41.
10 *Ibid.*, p. 39.
11 Levinas writes: 'Both ontology and the theory of the subject-object relation have in common a notion of the truth as an expressible content, regardless of the particular structure of being revealed by that content. Hence the truth is expressible in words but the original function of truth on which such expression depends, is to signify an inner meaning, of a solitary mind, which appeals to no interlocutor. The monumental solidity of being hinges on this possibility of expressing the truth and of conceiving it as an achieved result although being has in fact been interpreted from the time of the Permenides and Sophist of Plato, as a relation, or since Descartes, as thought', 'Martin Buber and the Theory of Knowledge', in Seán Hand (ed.), *Levinas Reader*, Basil Blackwell, Oxford 1989, p. 61.
12 Emmanuel Levinas, *Ethics as First Philosophy*, p. 76 *ibid.*
13 Gilles Deleuze, *Difference and Repetition*, trans. Paul Patton, The Athlone Press, London 1994, p. 29.
14 Fanon, *Black Skin, White Masks*, p. 112.
15 Deleuze and Guattari, *A Thousand Plateaus*, p. 178.
16 *Ibid.*, p. 135.
17 *Ibid.*, p. 222.
18 Sigmund Freud, 'Taboo and Emotional Ambivalence', in *Totem and Taboo*, Ark Paperbacks, London 1983.
19 *Ibid.*, pp. 34-5.
20 *Ibid.*, p. 30.
21 Deleuze, *Difference and Repetition*, p. 18.
22 Sigmund Freud, 'The Uncanny', in *Art and Literature*, The Pelican Freud Library vol. 14, Harmondsworth 1985.
23 *Ibid.*, pp. 363-4.
24 *Ibid.*, pp. 360-1.
25 Homer, *The Odyssey*, trans. Walter Shewring, Oxford University Press, Oxford 1980.
26 *Ibid.*, pp. 105.
27 *Ibid.*, p. 1.
28 *Ibid.*, p. 101.
29 *Ibid.*, p. 144.

30   Levinas, *Totality and Infinity*, pp. 45-6.
31   *Ibid.*, p. 46.
32   Levinas, *Ethics as First Philosophy*, p. 82.
33   Levinas, *Totality and Infinity*, p. 84.
34   *Ibid.*, p. 25.
35   Levinas, *Ethics and Infinity: Conversations with Philippe Nemo*, trans. Richard
     A. Cohen, Duquesne University Press, Pittsburgh 1985, p. 48.
36   Emmanuel Levinas, *Otherwise than Being and Beyond Essence*, trans.
     Alphonso Lingis, Martinus Nijhoff, The Hague 1981, p. 100.
37   Levinas, *Ethics and Infinity*, p. 95.
38   Levinas, *Otherwise than Being and Beyond Essence*, p. 14.
39   *Ibid.*, p. 89.
40   Levinas, *Totality and Infinity*, p. 213.
41   Levinas, *Otherwise than Being and Beyond Essence*, p. 12.
42   *Ibid.*, p. 15.
43   *Ibid.*, p. 55.
44   Levinas, *Ethics as First Philosophy*, p. 83.
45   Levinas, *Ethics and Infinity*, p. 101.
46   Levinas, *Otherwise than Being and Beyond Essence*, p. 7.
47   *Ibid.*, p. 146.
48   Jean-François Lyotard in his essay, 'Levinas's Logic', trans. Ian McLeod (in
     Andrew Benjamin (ed.), *The Lyotard Reader*, Basil Blackwell, Oxford 1989),
     strongly emphasises the prescriptive nature of Levinas's writing, which is
     not open to scrutiny in the proposition language of statement (*énoncés*) but
     must be received as a case of perlocutionary address which foregrounds the
     act of ennunciation (*énonciation*).
49   Jacques Derrida, *Violence and Metaphysics: An Essay on the Thought of
     Emmanuel Levinas*, in *Writing and Difference*, trans. Alan Bass, Routledge
     and Kegan Paul, London 1978.
50   *Ibid.*, p. 112.
51   Levinas, *Otherwise than Being and Beyond Essence*, p. 7.
52   *Ibid.*
53   *Ibid.*, p. 159.
54   *Ibid.*, p. 157.
55   *Ibid.*
56   *Ibid.*
57   *Ibid.*, p. 159.
58   *Ibid.*, p. 160-1.
59   Jean-François Lyotard, *The Differend: Phases in Dispute*, trans. Georges Van
     Den Abbeele, Manchester University Press, Manchester 1988.
60   For Lyotard a generalised scepticism is untenable: there is always some-
     thing or something happens. 'The only one that is indubitable, the phrase,
     because it is immediately presupposed. (To doubt one phrase is still to
     phrase, one's silence makes a phrase)', *ibid.*, p. xi.
61   *Ibid.*, p. 13.
62   *Ibid.*, p. 80.
63   *Ibid.*, p. xii.
64   *Ibid.*, p. xi.
65   *Ibid.*, p. 8.
66   *Ibid.*, p. 48.
67   *Ibid.*, p. 108.

68 *Ibid.*, p. 115.
69 *Ibid.*, p. 116.
70 *Ibid.*, p. 134.
71 *Ibid.*
72 Jean-François Lyotard, 'Judiciousness in Dispute, or Kant after Marx', trans. Cecile Lindsay, in Andrew Benjamin (ed.), *The Lyotard Reader*, Basil Blackwell, Oxford 1989, p. 346.
73 Lyotard, *Differend*, p. 168.
74 *Ibid.*, p. 170.
75 Michel Foucault, Preface to Gilles Deleuze and Félix Guattari's *Anti-Oedipus*, trans. Robert Hurley, Mark Seem, and Helen R. Lane, The Athlone Press, London 1984, p. xiii.
76 Gilles Deleuze, *Nietzche and Philosophy*, trans. Hugh Tomlinson, Columbia University Press, New York 1983, pp. 8-9.
77 Gilles Deleuze and Félix Guattari, *What is Philosophy*, trans. Graham Burchell and Hugh Tomlinson, Verso, London 1984, p. 112.
78 Deleuze, *Michel Tournier and the World without Others.*
79 Gilles Deleuze writes: 'the Other is neither an object in the field of my perception, nor a subject who perceives me: the Other is first of all a structure of the perceptual field without which this field, in its totality, could not function as it does ... *The Other-a Priori* as an absolute structure is the foundation of the relativity of other people as terms effectuating the structure in the field', *ibid.*, p. 58.
80 *Ibid.*, p. 57.
81 Michel Tournier, *Friday or The Other Island*, trans. Norman Denny, Penguin, Harmondsworth 1969, pp. 57-8.
82 Gilles Deleuze and Claire Parnet, *Dialogues*, trans. Hugh Tomlinson and Barbara Habberjam, The Athlone Press, London 1987, p. 7.
83 Deleuze and Guattari, *A Thousand Plateaus*, p. 11.
84 *Ibid.*, p. 238.
85 Gilles Deleuze, *Spinoza: Practical Philosophy*, trans. Robert Hurley, City Lights Books, San Francisco 1988, p. 127.
86 *Ibid.*, pp. 127-8.
87 *Ibid.*, p. 27.
88 Gilles Deleuze, *Foucault*, trans. Seán Hand, University of Minnesota Press, Minneapolis 1988, p. 101.
89 Deleuze, *Spinoza*, pp. 27-8.
90 *Ibid.*, p. 58.
91 Deleuze and Guattari, *A Thousand Plateaus*, p. 275.
92 *Ibid.*, p. 293.
93 *Ibid.*, p. 106.
94 *Ibid.*, p. 291.
95 Frantz Fanon, *The Wretched of the Earth*, trans. Constance Farrington, Penguin, Harmondsworth 1967, pp. 252-3.
96 Quoted from Rosi Braidotti, *Patterns of Dissonance*, trans. Elizabeth Guild, Polity Press, Cambridge 1991, p. 120.
97 *Ibid.*, p. 122.
98 Deleuze and Guattari, *A Thousand Plateaus*, p. 276.
99 Aimé Césaire, *Return to My Native Land*, trans. John Berger and Anna Bostock, Penguin, Harmondsworth 1969, p. 49.
100 Juan Goytisolo, *Count Julian*, trans. Helen Lane, Serpent's Tail, London, 1989, p. 112.

101 Césaire, *Return to My Native Land*, p. 48.
102 Wilson Harris, *The Four Banks of the River of Space*, in *The Carnival Trilogy*, Faber and Faber, London 1993, p. 423.
103 *Ibid.*, p. 313.

Part II Marco Polo: travelogue as a machine of othering

3 Marco Polo and his travels

1 Samuel Taylor Coleridge, *The Rime of the Ancient Mariner and Other Poems*, Dover Publications, New York 1992, pp. 58-9.
2 John Milton, *Paradise Lost and Paradise Regained*, Airmont, New York 1968, p. 262.
3 Bruce Chatwin, *The Songlines*, Picador, London 1987, p. 8.
4 *Ibid.*, p. 11.
5 Eduardo Galeano, *Genesis*, trans. Cedric Belfrage, Methuen, London 1986, p. 46.
6 William Dalrymple, *In Xanadu: A Quest*, Flamingo, London 1990; Paul Griffiths, *Myself and Marco Polo*, Pan Books, London 1989.
7 Italo Calvino, *Invisible Cities*, trans. William Weaver, Picador, London 1979. In Calvino's text Kubili is spelt as Kubli.
8 Marco Polo, *Le Devisement de Monde*, trans. Louis Hambis, La Découverte, Paris 1991. This French translation is based on A. C. Moule and P. Pelliot's compilation of all the known Marco Polo manuscripts into a single text, entitled *The Description of the World* (1938).
9 François Hartog, 'Herodotus and the Historical Operation', *Diacritics*, vol. 22, no. 2, Summer 1992.
10 Leonard Olschki, *Marco Polo's Asia*, trans. John A. Scott, Berkeley and Los Angeles 1960.
11 Marco Polo, *The Travels*, Penguin, Harmondsworth 1958, p. 41.
12 *Ibid.*, p. 33.
13 *Ibid.*, p. 41.
14 *Ibid.*, p. 33.
15 Edward Said, *Orientalism*, Routledge & Kegan Paul, London 1978.
16 Marco Polo, *The Travels*, p. 33.
17 Michel Foucault, *The Order of Things*, Tavistock Publications, London 1970, p. 40.
18 Marco Polo, *The Travels*, p. 33.
19 *Ibid.*
20 *Ibid.*, p. 226.
21 *Ibid.*, pp. 261, 273.
22 J. A. Boon, *Other Tribes, Other Scribes*, Cambridge 1982, p. 31.
23 Marco Polo, *The Travels*, p. 37.
24 *Ibid.*, p. 46.
25 *Ibid.*, p. 52.
26 Denys Hay, *Europe in the Fourteenth and Fifteenth Centuries*, Longman, London 1966, p. 24.
27 Marco Polo, *The Travels*, p. 46.
28 *Ibid.*, p. 344.
29 L. D. Kristof, 'The Nature of Frontiers and Boundaries', in W. A. D. Jackson and S. M. Samuel (eds.), *Politics and Geographical Relations*, Prentice Hall, New Jersey 1971, p. 137.

30 Marco Polo, *The Travels*, p. 74.
31 Here the notion of 'habitude' is preferred over comparable notions such as 'manners and customs' and 'civil society', because, with its etymological origins in the Latin words 'habitus' and 'habitare', it indicates the spatial locale of cultural practice. Since travel accounts cross space through the representational play of cultural difference, 'habitude', with its duel connotations of habit and habitation, seems immanent to these accounts.
32 Marco Polo, *The Travels*, p. 46.

4 Exorbitant others and transgressive topoi

 1 Margaret T. Hodgen, *Early Anthropology in the Sixteenth and Seventeenth Century*, University of Pennsylvania Press, Philadelphia 1964, p. 59.
 2 *Ibid.*, p. 57.
 3 Fredric Jameson, *The Political Unconscious*, Methuen, London 1981, p. 114.
 4 Marco Polo, *The Travels*, pp. 287-8.
 5 *Ibid.*, p. 265.
 6 *Ibid.*, p. 288.
 7 Hippocrates, 'Airs, Waters, Places', in *Hippocratic Writings*, trans. J. Chadwick and W. N. Mann, Penguin, Harmondsworth 1978. Hippocrates of Cos (460-360 BC) is not only reputed to be the father of orthodox medicine but also the founder of the environmentalist explanation of difference. For Hippocrates the otherness of Asia issues from its peculiar climatic condition, which shapes everything differently in that continent in comparison to Europe. Hippocrates writes

> Asia differs very much from Europe in everything that grows there, vegetable or human. Everything grows much bigger and finer in Asia, and the nature of the land is tamer, while the character of the inhabitants is milder and less passionate. The reason for this is the equable blending of climate' (p. 159).

The influence of Hippocratic environmentalism was so widespread that even the great North African philosopher of history, Ibn Khaldun, in his *Muqaddimah* made use of it. In the European tradition, notably through the writings of Montesquieu, the idea of Oriental despotism was constructed on the authority of Hippocratic environmentalism.
 8 Marco Polo, *The Travels*, p. 63.
 9 *Ibid.*
10 St Augustine, *City of God*, trans. Henry Bettenson, Penguin, Harmondsworth 1972, p. 478.
11 Marco Polo, *The Travels*, p. 104.
12 *Ibid.*, p. 232.
13 *Ibid.*, p. 228.
14 *Ibid.*, p. 178.
15 *Ibid.*, p. 253.
16 *Ibid.*, p. 300.
17 *Ibid.*, p. 256.
18 *Ibid.*, p. 258.
19 Genesis 9:25, *The Jerusalem Bible*, London 1966, p. 25.
20 Gaius Plinius Secundus, *Natural History*, vol. II, Book VII, The Loeb Classical Library, London 1936, p. 513.
21 *Ibid.*
22 *Ibid.*

23   *Ibid.*, pp. 513-14.
24   *Ibid.*, p. 517.
25   *Ibid.*
26   *Ibid.*, p. 521.
27   *Ibid.*
28   Marco Polo is not alone in reporting human monsters. Marco Polo's near-contemporaries also reported the existence of human monsters. Friar Caprini, the emissary of Pope Innocent IV to the Mongol Court, despite the matter-of-fact narrative of his travels, reported the existence of cynocephali (Friar John Caprini, *The Journal of Friar John de Caprini to the Court of Kayuk Khan as Narrated by Himself,* in M. Komroff (ed.), *Contemporaries of Marco Polo,* New York 1928). Even Friar William of Rubruck, the most sceptical of thirteenth-century travellers, who dismissed the myth of Prester John and much of the monstrous mirabilia compiled by Solinus and Bishop Isidore, ended up reporting the existence of Troglodytes in Cathay (Friar William of Rubruck, *The Journal of Friar William of Rubruck,* in M. Komroff (ed.), *Contemporaries of Marco Polo,* New York 1928). And the travel accounts of Sir John Mandeville (*The Travels of Sir John Mandeville,* trans. C. W. R. D. Moseley, Penguin, Harmondsworth 1983), despite devoting the first half to the devotional journey of pilgrimage to the Holy Land, devotes the second half to recording a grand proliferation of monstrous races.
29   Edmund Leach, *Social Anthropology,* Oxford 1982, p. 15.
30   Stanley Diamond, *In Search of the Primitive,* Transaction Books, New Brunswick 1974, p. 120.
31   Johannes Fabian has argued that the object of anthropological discourse the 'primitive' has been constituted by the evolutionary schema of temporal distance between the subject of anthropological enunciation (anthropologist's presence or present as the master of discourse) and the referent of his statement. To put it another way: the primitive other is othered as belonging to other times than the anthropologist. Fabian puts it this way: 'As an indication of relationship between the subject and the object of anthropological discourse, it clearly expresses temporal distancing: *Savagery* is a marker of the past, and if ethnographic evidence compels the anthropologist to state that savagery exists in contemporary societies then it will be located, by dint of some sort of horizontal stratigraphy, in *their* Time, not ours' (*Time and the Other,* Columbia University Press, New York 1983, p. 75).
32   Joseph Conrad, *Heart of Darkness,* in Todd K. Bender *et al.* (eds.), *Modernism in Literature,* Holt, Rinehart and Winston, New York 1977, p. 530.
33   St Augustine, *City of God,* p. 974.
34   *Ibid.*, p. 664.
35   *Ibid.*
36   *Ibid.*, p. 669.
37   *Ibid.*, p. 983.
38   Marco Polo, *The Travels,* p. 33.
39   Giambattista Vico, *The New Science of Gianbattista Vico,* trans. T. G. Bergin and M. H. Fisch, Cornell University Press, Ithaca 1970, p. 85.
40   *Ibid.*
41   Claude Lévi-Strauss, 'The Logic of Totemic Classification', in *The Savage Mind,* Weidenfeld and Nicolson, London 1966, p. 9.
42   *Ibid.*, p. 17.
43   *Ibid.*

44   *Ibid.*, p. 19.
45   Giambattista Vico, *The New Science of Giambatista Vico*, p. 234.
46   Homer, *Odyssey*, trans. Walter Shewring, Oxford University Press, Oxford 1980, p. 105.
47   Michel Foucault, *The Order of Things*, Tavistock Publications, London 1970, p. 53.
48   Marco Polo clearly separates Islam from the idolaters, the organic religion of other habitudes. For instance, he describes the religio-ethnic composition of Tangut as follows: 'Tanguit, whose inhabitants are all idolaters, except that there are some Turks who are Nestorian Christians and also some Saracens', *The Travels*, p. 85.
49   In the description of the people of Ferlec Marco Polo clearly identifies the civilising influence of Islam: 'You must know that the people of Ferlec used all to be idolaters, but owing to contact with Saracen merchants, who continually resort here in their ships, they have all been converted to the law of Mahomet. This applies only to the inhabitants of the city. The people of the mountains live like beasts', *ibid.*, p. 253.
50   *Ibid.*, p. 78.
51   *Ibid.*, p. 283.
52   In fact, this type of explanation for the origin of idolatory forms part of orthodox Judaeo-Christian tradition. The only difference is that in the orthodox explanation it is linked with the figure of Nimrod, the mighty hunter who dared to build the audacious Tower of Babel, and not with Buddah. For instance, Sir John Mandeville, who was a near-contemporary of Marco Polo, explains that once Nimrod's father was dead 'he had also an image made in memory of his father, and commanded all his subjects to worship that image. Other great lords did the same; and thus began idolatry first', Sir John Mandeville, *The Travels of Sir John Mandeville*, trans. C. W. R. D. Mosely, Penguin, Harmondsworth 1983, p. 61.
53   Marco Polo, *The Travels*, p. 91.
54   *Ibid.*, p. 227.
55   *Ibid.*, p. 91.
56   *Ibid.*, p. 293.
57   *Ibid.*, p. 164.
58   *Ibid.*, p. 80.
59   Edward B. Tylor, *Primitive Culture*, vol. 1, John Murray, London 1903, pp. 26-7.
60   *Ibid.*, p. 27.
61   *Ibid.*, p. 31.
62   *Ibid.*
63   *Ibid.*, p. 53.
64   Marco Polo, *The Travels*, p. 293.
65   Of Cathayans Marco Polo says, 'they surpass other nations in the excellence of their manners and the knowledge of many subjects', *ibid.*, p. 160.
66   *Ibid.*
67   *Ibid.*, p. 281.
68   Edmund Leach, *Social Anthropology*, Fontana, Glasgow 1982, p. 118.
69   Of Kinsai Marco Polo writes: 'It well merits a description, because it is without doubt the finest and the most splendid city in the world', *The Travels*, p. 231.
70   *Ibid.*, p. 220.
71   *Ibid.*, p. 215.

72 Mary Douglas, *Purity and Danger*, Ark, London 1984, p. 113.

73 W. Arens, after exhaustively scrutinising innumerable reportings of supposed cannibalism, observes: 'we assume cannibals exist, but not because the act has been physically observed, since the evidence is lacking. The assumption therefore rests primarily on the accusation made by one group or individual against it', *The Man-eating Myths*, Oxford University Press, Oxford and New York 1979, p. 154.

74 Marco Polo, *The Travels*, p. 231.

75 *Ibid.*, p. 232.

76 *Ibid.*, p. 248.

77 *Ibid.*, p. 172.

78 Marco Polo writes of the sexual custom of the inhabitants of Pem: 'when a woman's husband leaves her to go on a journey of more than twenty days, then, as soon as he left, she takes another husband, and this she is fully entitled to do so by local usage. And the men, whereever they go, take wives in the same way', *ibid.*, pp. 82-3.

79 *Ibid.*, p. 88.

80 *Ibid.*, p. 172.

81 *Ibid.*, p. 226.

82 *Ibid.*, p. 216.

83 *Ibid.*, p. 91-2.

84 In so far as Deleuze and Guattari's notion of deterritorialisation is conceived as a process of decoding – which amounts to the de-legitimation or the displacement of existing codes – my usage is similar to theirs. However, since I want to restrict its usage to a strictly politico-geographical process of decodation, it diverges from their usage, at least the sense they give to it in their tracing of the history of 'social machines' in *Anti-Oedipus* (trans. Robert Herley *et al.*, The Athlone Press, London 1977). For Deleuze and Guattari in *Anti-Oedipus*, only primitive societies, rooted in the immanent body of the earth before the coming of the abstract principle of property and state, exist under territorial imperatives. The representational mode of this notion of territoriality is governed by geo-graphism, the literal figuration of sign. The societal system belonging to this territoriality is governed by the immobile codes of filiation and alliance. Deleuze and Guattari only consider subsequent history, in a surprisingly linear mode, as a process of deterritorialisation which decodes the primitive geo-graphic signs and re-codes it with various transcendental principles which effect re-territorialisation.

85 *The Jerusalem Bible*, Darton, Longman and Todd, London, 1966, p. 156.

5 *The political technology of order*

1 G. W. F. Hegel, *Philosophy of Right*, Oxford 1967, pp. 76, 126, 160. The Hegelian idea of political and civil society culminated in Gramsci's work where they represent the articulated totality of a social formation through their dialectical linkage, even though each maintain its relative autonomy. See A. Gramsci, 'State and Civil Society', in Q. Hoare and G. N. Smith (eds.), *Prison Notebook*, London 1971, pp. 206-72.

2 T. Hobbes, *Leviathan*, Penguin, Harmondsworth 1968, pp. 185-6.

3 *Ibid.*, p. 227.

4 Marco Polo, *The Travels*, Penguin, Harmondsworth 1958, p. 195.

5 *Ibid.*, p. 133.

6   *Ibid.*, p. 223.
7   *Ibid.*, p. 101.
8   *Ibid.*, p. 98.
9   *Ibid.*, p. 97.
10 *Ibid.*, p. 329.
11 Gilles Deleuze and Félix Guattari, *Anti-Oedipus*, trans. Robert Hurley *et al.*, The Athlone Press, London 1984, p. 3.
12 *Ibid.*, p. 32.
13 *Ibid.*
14 L. Mumford, 'Utopia, the City and the Machine', in F. E. Manuel (ed.), *Utopia and the Utopian Thought*, Boston 1965, p. 16.
15 *Ibid.*, p. 17.
16 Marco Polo, *The Travels*, p. 115.
17 *Ibid.*, p. 113.
18 *Ibid.*, pp. 124-5.
19 *Ibid.*, p. 144.
20 *Ibid.*, p. 190.
21 *Ibid.*, p. 123.
22 *Ibid.*
23 *Ibid.*, p. 226.
24 *Ibid.*, p. 150.
25 *Ibid.*, pp. 139-40.
26 Aristotle, 'Physiognomica', p. 105, in *Minor Works*, trans. W. S. Hett, The Loeb Classical Library, Cambridge and Massachusetts 1963, p. 105.
27 *Ibid.*, p. 73.
28 Marco Polo, *The Travels*, p. 267.
29 *Ibid.*, pp. 121-2.
30 Leonardo Olschki, *Marco Polo's Asia*, trans. John Scott, University of California Press, Berkeley 1960, pp. 400-1.
31 *Ibid.*, p. 399.
32 Marco Polo, *The Travels*, p. 221.
33 *Ibid.*, p. 155.
34 *Ibid.*, p. 148.
35 W. Ullman, *A History of Political Thought: The Middle Ages*, Penguin, Harmondsworth 1965, p. 77.
36 Michel Foucault, 'On Governmentality', in *Ideology and Consciousness*, no. 6, Autumn 1979.
37 Niccolò Machiavelli, *The Prince*, trans. George Bull, Penguin, Harmondsworth 1961, p. 91.
38 *Ibid.*, p. 92 .
39 *Ibid.*, p. 95.
40 *Ibid.*, p. 99.
41 *Ibid.*, p. 100.
42 Marco Polo, *The Travels*, p. 61.
43 *Ibid.*, p. 181.
44 *Ibid.*, p. 147.
45 *Ibid.*, p. 93.
46 *Ibid.*, p. 94.
47 Karl Federn, *Dante and his Time*, William Heinemann, London 1902, p. 62.
48 *Ibid.*, p. 63.
49 *Ibid.*, p. 64.

50 Dante Alighieri, *The Divine Comedy*, trans. C. H. Sisson, Pan Books, London 1980, p. 222.
51 *Ibid.*, p. 223.
52 Pope Bonifice VIII, 'The Superiority of the Spiritual Authority', in J. B. Ross and M. McLaughlin (eds.), *The Portable Medieval Reader*, Penguin, Harmondsworth 1949, p. 234.
53 Frederick Barbarossa, 'The Independence of the Temporal Authority', in Ross and McLaughlin (eds.), *The Portable Medieval Reader*, p. 261.
54 A. P. D'Entreves, *The Medieval Contribution to Political Thought*, London 1939, p. 24.
55 Dante Alighieri, *The Divine Comedy*, p. 269.
56 *Ibid.*
57 Dante Alighieri, *De Monarchia*, trans. P. H. Wicksteed, Temple Classics, London 1904, p. 278.
58 *Ibid.*, p. 130.
59 *Ibid.*, p. 138.
60 *Ibid.*, p. 141.
61 *Ibid.*, pp. 142-3.
62 Marco Polo, *The Travels*, p. 93.
63 *Ibid.*, p. 166.
64 Machiavelli, *The Prince*, p. 81.
65 Marco Polo, *The Travels*, p. 118.
66 *Ibid.*
67 *Ibid.*, p. 217.
68 Perry Anderson, *Lineages of the Absolutist State*, Verso, London 1974, p. 40.
69 *Ibid.*, p. 21.
70 B. Hindess and P. Q. Hirst, *Pre-Capitalist Modes of Production*, Routledge and Kegan Paul, London 1975, p. 289.
71 John M. Steadman, *The Myth of Asia*, Macmillan, London 1969, pp. 159-60.
72 Lothrop Stoddard, *Clashing Tides of Colour*, Charles Scribner, New York and London 1935.
73 Sir Jean Chardin, *Sir John Chardin's Travels in Persia*, The Argonaut Press, London 1927, pp. 7-8.
74 *Ibid.*, p. 189.
75 *Ibid.*, p. 192.
76 Karl Marx, *Karl Marx on Colonialism and Modernisation*, ed. S. Avineri, New York 1968, p. 427.
77 François Bernier, *Travels in the Mogul Empire*, trans. Irving Brock, Archibald Constable, Westminster 1891, pp. 144-6.
78 *Ibid.*, p. 226.
79 *Ibid.*, p. 211.
80 *Ibid.*, p. 225.
81 *Ibid.*, p. 232.
82 Louis Althusser, 'Montesquieu: Politics and History', in *Politics and History*, trans. Ben Brewster, NLB, London 1972, pp. 13-110.
83 Baron de Montesquieu, *The Spirit of the Laws*, trans. Thomas Nugent, Hafner Press, New York 1949.
84 *Ibid.*, p. 269.
85 Aristotle, *Aristotle's Politics and the Athenian Constitution*, trans. John Warrington, Everyman's Library, London 1959, p. 9.
86 *Ibid.*, p. 8.

87 *Ibid.*, p. 99.
88 *Ibid.*, pp. 92-3.
89 Baron de Montesquieu, *Persian Letters*, letter 37, trans. C. J. Betts, Penguin, Harmondsworth 1973, p. 91.
90 Stoddard, *Clashing Tides of Colour*, pp. 202-3.

INDEX

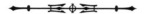

absolute deterritorialisation 40,
    42-3
Acre 129, 130, 131
Akbar, Prince 200
Alexander the Great 145
Althusser 202
Andaman, island of 143
Anderson, Perry 196, 197
Antipodes 147, 148
Apollonides 145
Aquinas, St Thomas 194
    Summa Theologica 191
Aristeas 144
Aristotelian logic 44, 45
Aristotle 144, 203, 204
    *Politics and the Athenian
    Constitution* 6, 203
Asia Minor 133-4
asylum 27, 28
Augustine, St 141, 147, 148, 192
    City of God 126, 147, 148, 156
Aurung-zebe, emperor 200
Auster, Paul: *City of Glass* 10-11
axiomatic of geometry 12

Bachelard, Gaston 19, 24, 56
    Poetics of Space, The 18
Baghdad 128
Barbarossa, Frederick: *Manifesto of
    the Emperor* 191
Barthes, Roland: *Empire of Signs* 69
Belor 157
Bentham, Jeremy 27
Bergson 57, 58, 65, 101, 105
    Creative Evolution 65
Berlin wall 32
Bernier, François 198, 200-4
binarism 58

black/white divide 82-4
bodies 39-40
Bonifice, Pope 191
Boon, James A. 126
Borges, J.L. 4
Brahmans 160
Braidotti, Rosi 109
Burke, Kenneth 72

Caliph of Baghdad 178
Calvino, Italo: *Invisible Cities* 71, 120
cannibalism 162
Caprini, Friar 127
carceral 27
Carroll, Lewis: *Alice in Wonderland* 4
Cathayans 160, 170
Certeau, Michel de 10, 32, 40, 67,
    69, 70
    Heterologies 69
Césaire, Aimé 109
    Return to My Native Land 114
Chardin, Jean 198, 199, 200, 203
Charlemagne 130
Chatwin, Bruce: *Songliner, The* 119
Chauvin, Rémy 105
Cheic-Ali-Can 199
Chinghiz Khan 188, 195
Christendom 129, 130-2, 139
    arch zone 131
    language of 142
Citizen Kane 118-19
civil state 168, 169
civilisation machine 158-9
civility 156-60, 166
Coleridge, Samuel Taylor 74, 75,
    76-7, 119, 127
    Kubla Khan 72, 73
colonialism 47

Columbus, Christopher 120
Conrad, Joseph 28, 69
    Heart of Darkness 3
    Landfalls and Departure 69
    Nigger of the 'Narcissus', The 70
Constantine 130
cultural space 24
culture of Enlightenment 27
cynocephalis 151

Dante 66-7, 189, 195
    model of order 192-4
    Divine Comedy, The 66, 190
    Purgatorio 190, 192
    De Monarchia 192
Danton 26
Dasein, Heidegger's 13-14, 17, 22-3
Defoe, Daniel 103
    Robinson Crusoe 2-3
Deleuze, Gilles 10, 39, 56-60, 64,
        74, 79, 80, 83, 88, 101-15
    on a-parallel evolution 104-5,
        107, 108, 110
    on Bergson 65
    on deterritorialisation 40-1, 58
    on dwelling 57
    on geometry 9
    haecceity and 76
    on the madman 29
    on mask of the unconscious 85
    on the mirror 4
    nomads 10, 45
    notion of machine 172, 173
    on Panopticism 28
    on racism 83
    on transcendental idealism 7
    Anti-Oedipus 101
    Difference and Repetition 82,
        101
    Logic of Sense, The 65
    Nietzsche and Philosophy 101
    Thousand Plateaus, A 57, 105
    What is Philosophy 102
D'Entreves 192
De Quincey, Thomas 23, 24
Derrida, Jacques 17, 22, 37
    Law of Genre, The 36

    Violence and Metaphysics 92
Descartes, René 200
    Meditation 88
deterritorialisation 40, 42-3, 79,
        165-6
diabolic art 155
Diamond, Stanley 145
dietary transgressions 161-2
Différance 21, 22
Divisement du Monde, Le 138
Don Quixote 3
Douglas, Mary 161
dwelling 2, 11, 57

empirical reality 8
enchantment 155
Engels, F. 200
epistemological tradition 11
Euclidean geometry 8, 9
Euripides 203
Existenzialien 13

fabula 149
Facfur, King of Manzi 125, 163, 178
Fanon, Frantz 45, 78, 109
    Black Skin, White Mask 82, 83,
        84
Farah, Nuruddin: Maps 33
Febvre, Lucien 26
Federn, Karl 189
Forster , E.M.: Passage to India, A
        43, 47-55
Foucault, Michel 37, 102, 124, 153,
        185
    on the madman 27, 30
    on nation-state 28
    on prison 27, 187
    Madness and Civilisation 27
    Order of Things, The 30
Frederick II 189
Freud, Sigmund 3, 58
    Taboo and Emotional Ambiva-
        lence 84
    Thanatos 102
    Uncanny, The 85
Fu Chau 162

Gaius Plinius Secundus: *Natural History* 144
gaze 29
Geist 6
genealogies of divisions 27
geographical space 16, 22
Ghibellines 190
governing machine 171
Goytisolo, Juan 113
Great Wall of China 31, 32, 39
Gregory X 129
Guattari, Félix 56-60, 64, 74, 80, 88, 101-15
  on a-parallel evolution 104-5, 107, 108, 110
  on deterritorialisation 40-1, 58
  on dwelling 57
  on geometry 9
  haecceity and 76
  on the madman 29
  nomads 10, 45
  notion of machine 172, 173
  on racism 83
  Anti-Oedipus 101
  Thousand Plateaus, A 57, 105
  What is Philosophy 102
Guelfs 190, 191

habitudes 153-4
haecceity 76
Harris, Wilson 41, 61, 77
  Four Banks of the River of Space, The 59, 114
  Infinite Rehearsal, The 60
Hartog, François 122
Hay, Denys 130
Hegel, G.W.F. 6, 101, 111
  Phenomenology of Mind, The 79, 80
  Philosophy of History 6
  Philosophy of Right 167
Hegelian logic 44, 45
Heidegger, Martin 3, 20, 22, 56, 57, 89, 98
  Being and Time 11, 13
  on bridge 16-17, 20
  bridging 16-18

Das Sein des Seienden 12, 57
  on dwelling 12-17
  on epistemological tradition 11-12
Herodotus 6, 149
  Histories, The 122, 139
heterotopia 30, 31, 57
Hindess, B. 197
Hippocrates 6, 141, 203
Hirst, P. 197
Hobbes, Thomas 169
  Leviathan 168
Hodgen, Margaret T. 139
Hohenstaufen 189, 191
Holy Land 132-3
Homer: *Odyssey, The* 86, 120, 121, 144, 149, 151
Homo monstrum 143, 144, 145-9, 151, 198
Husserl, Edmund 13

idolatry 155, 156, 157
illieity 91
Image du Monde, L' 138
immobile traveller 10
imperfect Christians 155
incest taboos 164-5
Innocent IV, Pope 127
Irigaray, Luce 109
Isadore, Bishop of Seville 145, 152
  Etymologiiae 138, 139
Islam 155

Jackson, George 10
Jakobson, Roman 94
Jerusalem 133
Jews 155
John of Paris 192

Kafka, Franz 39-43, 52, 110
  on the Great Wall 31-3, 39
  Great Wall of China, The 31
  parable of the law 25
Kamul 187
Kanggigu, king of 176
Kant, Immanuel 7, 12, 91, 99
  Critique of Judgement 100
  Critique of Pure Reason 9

on geometry 8-9
'Transcendental Exposition of
    the Conception' 8
Kara-jung 187
Kaugigu, king of 163
Kaunchi, king of 172
Kayal, king of 163
Kerman, kingdom of 141
Khanbalik 131, 164
Kien-ning-fu 142
Kinsai 161, 164, 183
Kristof, Ladis 134
Kubilai Khan 71, 128, 129, 163
    birthday ritual 179-80
    as colossal regal body 174-82
    hunting 176
    physiognomy 180-2
    sexuality 176-8
    see also Coleridge: Kubla Khan

labour machine 173, 174
Lacan, Jacques 3, 23
Lambi, kingdom of 143
landscape space 16
law of the law of genre 36
Leach, Edmund 25, 145, 160
Lebenswelt 13
Lefebvre, Henri 32, 34
Lesser Armenia 131
Lévi-Strauss, Claude 68, 164
    Logic of Totemic Classification,
        The 150
Leviathan monarch 169
Levinas, Emmanuel 14, 81, 88-94,
        97, 98, 101, 111-12, 210
    Otherwise than Being and Beyond
        Essence 90, 92
    Totality and Infinity 12
linguistic boundaries 5
Louis IX, King 127
Louis XIV, absolutism of 205-6
Lyotard, Jean-François 88, 111-12, 159
    on the Differend 94-101

Machiavelli 185, 207
    Prince, The 185-6, 195
machinisation of polity 188

madman 29-30
Malabar, king of 163
Mandeville, Sir John 153
Manichaean boundary of colonial
        space 43-55
Manzians 170
map-making 33-4
Márquez, Gabriel García: One
        Hundred Years of Solitude 4
Marsiglio of Padua 192
Marx, Karl 202
    Kapital, Das 200
Megasthenes 145
Mela, Pomponius 139, 145
    De Situ Orbis 138
mercantilism 196-7
Merleau-Ponty, M. 10, 18, 22, 56
    Phenomenology of Perception 16
military machine 173
Milton, John: Paradise Lost 119
mirror 3-4
Mongol empire 169-74
    legitimation of governing
        machine 182-8
Montaigne, Michel 70
Montesquieu, Baron de (Charles de
        Secondat) 6, 199, 200, 202-4
    Persian Letters 204, 205
    Spirit of the Law, The 202, 204
Mumford, Lewis 26, 27, 32
    Utopia, the City and the Machine
        173
mythos 149

Narcissus 3, 4
nation-state 28, 32, 33
national border 33
national boundary 37
national frontier 32
natural boundaries 26
natural law 169
Nayan 195, 196
Nietzsche, Friedrich 21, 22, 26, 37,
        58, 79, 84, 105, 210
    Deleuze on 101-2
    eternal return 61, 65, 173
    Genealogy of Morals 34

Noah's Ark 133

Occident/Orient boundary 47-55, 134
Oikoumene 147
Old Man of the Mountain 178
Olschki, Leonard 122, 182
ontology of space 4-5
Orient 47, 55
Oriental despotism 198-206
Ovington, John 198
Oz, Amos 35, 37
    'Nomad and Viper' 37

Panopticism 28-9
Panopticon 27, 28, 30, 31, 32
Papacy 195
Persians 170
phenomenology 18
physiognomy 180-2
Plato 89
Pliny 139, 144, 145, 152
    Natural History 138
Poetic Geography 70-1
political technology of order 167-207
Polo, Marco 72, 73, 74
    Mappa Mundi 139, 140
    Travels 118-207 *passim*
Polo, Niccolò 128, 129
Polo, Maffeo 128, 129
power 31, 32
pragmatic rules of movement 61-77
Prester John 178, 194, 195, 196
principle of encounter 211
principle of opposition 44, 45
principle of rationality 185
principle of sovereignty 33, 63, 130
principle of subjectivity 44
principle of telos 44
principle of territoriality 131
projected space 21
Purchas, Samuel: *Pilgrimes* 119

Quilon, India 140-1

racism 83

Ramusio 121
Ratzel, Fredric 25
re-marking 36-7
relative deterritorialisation 40, 42
Renan, Ernest 34
res cogitans 7, 9
res extensa 7, 9
Ressentiment 38, 53, 76, 79, 80, 84, 101, 104, 109, 112, 210, 211
rigid boundary 4
rigid lines 55-61
Rimbaud: *Déserts de l'amour, Les* 19
Ritter, Carl 25
Roe, Sir Thomas 198
Rushdie, Salman: *Midnight's Children* 5
Rustichello the Pisan 121, 129, 148

Said, Edward 124
Sakyamuni Burkan (Gutama Buddah) 156
schizophrenic experience 16
sexual manners and customs 163-5
Shakespeare: *Tempest, The* 78-80
smooth space 57
Solinus, Julius 139, 145, 152
    De Mirabilibus Mundi 138
Somnath 157, 159-60
space 6, 7, 8
    of affects 56
    cultural 24
    of geography 16, 22
    of geometricism 22, 56
    landscape 16
    ontology of 4-5
    projected 21
    smooth 57
    striated 57
    and time 33, 65
Spinoza 39, 53, 58, 101, 105, 106, 107, 108
Steadman, John M. 198
Stoddard, Lothrop 199, 206
striated space 57
Stultifera Navis 29, 30
sublating movement 44
supple boundary 4

supple lines 55-61
symbolic allegory 152, 154

taboos 160
Tangut 142
Tartars 171-2
terra incognita 55, 147, 149-50
Terry, Edward 198
Thomas the Baptist, St 133
Tibet 163
topoanalysis 18
Torres, Luis de 120
Tournier, Michel 103
    Other Island, The 2, 10, 16, 103,
        104
Toynbee, Arnold 10, 45
Trakl, Georg: 'Winter Evening, A'
    19
transcendental idealism 7, 8, 9
transgression of habitudes 187

travel of speed 41
Travernier, Jean Baptist 198
Tylor, Edward B. 166
    Primitive Culture 158

Ullman, W. 184
Unheimlich, Das 85-6, 162

Venice 129
Vico, Giambattista 70, 149, 150
Visconti, Tedaldo 129

walled city 26, 32-3, 34, 35, 37, 45
Welles, Orson 118-19
William of Rubruck 127
Wittgenstein's language game 94-5
Wright, John Kirkland 55

Xanadu computer program 120